SCHOLARS PRESS
GENERAL SERIES

Number 4

SHORT HISTORY OF SYRIAC CHRISTIANITY
TO THE RISE OF ISLAM

W. Stewart McCullough

A SHORT HISTORY OF SYRIA
TO THE RISE OF

A SHORT HISTORY OF SYRIAC CHRISTIANITY TO THE RISE OF ISLAM

W. Stewart McCullough

SCHOLARS PRESS

Published by
Scholars Press
101 Salem Street
P.O. Box 2268
Chico, CA 95927

A SHORT HISTORY OF SYRIAC CHRISTIANITY TO THE RISE OF ISLAM

W. Stewart McCullough

© 1982
Scholars Press

Map of the Sassanian Empire reprinted from the *Cambridge Ancient History*, Vol. XII, with permission of Cambridge University Press.

Library of Congress Cataloging in Publication Data

McCullough, William Stewart, 1902–
    A short history of Syriac Christianity to the rise of Islam.

    (SP General Series ; no. 4)
    Bibliography: p.
    Includes index.
    1. Syrian Church—History. 2. Church history—Primitive and early church, ca. 30–600. I. Title. II. Series.
BX173.2.M3   270.2'0935   80-29297
ISBN 0-89130-454-1

Manufactured in the United States of America

Contents

Abbreviations   vii–viii
Preface   ix
Map   x

SYRIAC CHRISTIANITY TO 643 A.D.
Part One
In the Roman (Byzantine) World
I. In Parthian Times (to 224 A.D.)

Chapter 1. The Milieu of Early Syriac Christianity   3
    1. Parthia and Rome in Western Asia. 2. Trade between the Roman empire and the Orient. 3. The Languages of Syria. 4. The Religions of Syria, excluding Christianity. 5. Early Christianity in Syria. 6. Christians vis-à-vis the Roman Government.

Chapter 2. The Beginnings of the Syriac Church   21
    1. Abercius Marcellus. 2. The Flood in Edessa. 3. The Easter Controversy and Osrhoene. 4. The Story of Addai. 5. The Scriptures. 6. Marcionism. 7. Bardaisan. 8. Tatian and the Diatessaron. 9. Julius Africanus. 10. *The Chronicle of Edessa*. 11. *The Odes of Solomon*.

II. In Sasanian Times (224-651 A.D.)

Chapter 3. The Milieu of the West Syriac Church.   37
    1. The Roman East to the Reign of Diocletian (284–305). 2. Persia: the Founding of the Sasanian Dynasty. 3. The Era of Constantine. 4. Rome and the Barbarian Invasions. 5. Persia's Confrontation with the Roman World from Varahran I (273–76) to Khusro I (531-79). 6. The Arabs of Northern Arabia. 7. The Final Struggle between Persia and Byzantium. 8. The Early Expansion of the Muslim Arabs. 9. Troublesome Theological Movements in the Greek Church. 10. The Monophysites as a Dissident Sect within the Church.

Chapter 4. Syriac Christians in the Third and Fourth Centuries.   53
    1. The Dearth of Information. 2. Dura Europus. 3. The Last of the Roman Persecutions of Christianity. 4. The Persistence of Paganism down to the Sixth Century. 5. Arianism. 6. Ephraim of Nisibis and Edessa. 7. The School of Edessa.

Chapter 5. The Heyday of the West Syriac Church: The Fifth to Seventh Centuries.   63
    1. Marutha of Maiperqaṭ. 2. Acacius, Bishop of Amid. 3. Rabbula of Edessa. 4. Ibas of Edessa. 5. Isaac of Antioch. 6. Theodoret of Cyrrhus. 7. The Closing of the Edessan School. 8. The Chronicle of Joshua the Stylite. 9. The Early History of Asceticism and Monasticism. 10. Monophysitism in Syria and the Orthodox Reaction. 11. The Scriptures. 12. Canon Law in the Western Syrian Church.

Part Two
In the Parthian and Persian Worlds
I. In Parthian Times (to 224 A.D.)

Chapter 6. The Beginnings of Eastern Christianity. 93
    1. Cultural Background: Religion, with special reference to Zoroastrianism and Judaism. 2. The Early Church in Parthia.

II. In Sasanian Times

Chapter 7. The Cultural Surroundings of the Church. 101
    1. Zoroastrianism. 2. Manichaeism. 3. Judaism. 4. Mazdakism.

Chapter 8. The Church in the Third and Fourth Centuries. 111
    1. In the Third Century: Toleration and Persecution. 2. In the Fourth Century: Aphraates; Constantine the Great and Shapur II; Persecution; the Bishops of Seleucia-Ctesiphon; Nisibis.

Chapter 9. The Church in the Fifth Century. 121
    The Nestorian Synods: 1. The Synod of Mar Isaac (410). 2. The Synod of Mar Yahbalaha (420). 3. The Synod of Mar Dadjesus (424). 4. Persecution. 5. Nestorianism. 6. The School of Nisibis: Its Early Years. 7. Monophysitism. 8. The Synods of 484 (Barṣauma) and 486 (Mar Acacius). 9. The Synod of Mar Babai (497).

Chapter 10. The Church in the Sixth and Early Seventh Centuries to 608/9. 135
    1. The Catholicos Shila (505–23) and the Subsequent Duality in the Catholicate. 2. The Synod of Mar Aba I (544). 3. The Synod of Mar Joseph (554). 4. The Synod of Mar Ezekiel (576). 5. The Synod of Mar Jesusyahb I (585). 6. The Synod of Mar Sabarjesus (596). 7. The Synod of Mar Gregory I (605). 8. Monophysitism.

Chapter 11. The Seventh Century to 643 A.D. 155
    1. The Later Years of the School of Nisibis. 2. The School of Seleucia. 3. The Nestorian Church during the Reign of Khusro II (591–628). 4. Jesusyahb II (628–43). 5. Monophysitism (after 628). 6. Asceticism and Monasticism in Parthia and Persia.

Conclusion. 177
Appendices. 179
    1. The Early Missionary Efforts of Syriac Christians.
    2. The Transmission of Western Science and Learning to the Arabs.
    3. Observations on the Syriac Liturgies.
    4. Canon Law of the Western Syrian Church.

Bibliography. 189
Index. 193–197

Abbreviations

Ant	*Jewish Antiquities* (Josephus)
Baumstark	*Geschichte der syrischen Literatur*
Bk of Gov	*The Book of Governors* (Thomas of Marga)
BLC	*Book of the Laws of Countries* (Bardaiṣan)
BSOS / BSOAS	*Bulletin of the School of Oriental (and African) Studies*
CAH	*Cambridge Ancient History*
ch	chapter
Chabot	*Littérature syriaque*
Chr de Michel	*Chronique de Michel le Syrien*
Chr de Séert	*Chronique de Séert* (Histoire nestorienne)
Christensen	*L'Iran sous les Sassanides*
CSCO	*Corpus Scriptorum Christianorum Orientalium*
d	died
Documents	*Syriac and Arabic Documents* (Vööbus)
Drijvers	*Bardaiṣan of Edessa*
Eccl Hist	*Ecclesiastical History* (of various authors)
ed	edited by
ET	English translation
Frend	*The Rise of the Monophysite Movement*
Frye	*The Heritage of Persia*
Gk	Greek
HASO	*History of Asceticism in the Syrian Orient* (Vööbus)
JA	*Journal asiatique*
Jalons	*Jalons pour une histoire de l'Église en Iraq* (Fiey)
JAOS	*Journal of the American Oriental Society*
JRAS	*Journal of the Royal Asiatic Society*
Labourt	*Le christianisme dans l'Empire Perse sous la dynastie sassanide (224–632)*
M	Mishnah
NT	New Testament
OC	Oriens Christianus
OT	Old Testament
p, pp	page, pages
PETSE	*Papers of the Estonian Theological Society in Exile* (Vööbus)
PO	Patrologia Orientalis

PS	*Patrologia Syriaca*
rev	revised (by)
sect	section
Segal	*Edessa 'the Blessed City'*
SNTSB	*Studiorum Novi Testamenti Societa Bulletin*
SO	*Synodicon Orientale*
Syr	Syriac
Tal	*Babylonian Talmud*
trans	translated by
vs, vss	verse, verses
War	*The Jewish War* (Josephus)
Wright	*A Short History of Syriac Literature*
Zaehner	*The Dawn and Twilight of Zoroastrianism*

Preface

The design of this work is to present a general survey of the subject which, it is hoped, will be of interest to those beginning the study of the Syriac language, to students of Church history, and to the general public. As I am writing for non-professionals, I have felt it might be useful for some readers to furnish them, in appropriate places, with some relevant background information. Those who are familiar with this material can readily skip what is here offered.

The contents of the volume indicate the two main divisions of the subject, viz., Syriac Christians living under the Romans (later, Byzantines), and those under the Parthians and Persians. As a terminal point for our study I have selected the rise of Islam. A more specific date could have been 643 A.D., the year of the death of the Nestorian Patriarch (or Catholicos), Jesusyahb II. Jesusyahb came to office in 628, completely unwaware, as everyone in his world seems to have been, of the ferment within Arabia centering in the prophet Muḥammad. The Muslim conquest of Sasanian Persia and of most of the Oriental provinces of the Byzantine empire, introduced a new political and religious order into western Asia, and Syriac Christians had to fit into this new order as well as they could. But to examine the fortunes of the Church in this Islamic era would open another chapter in ecclesiastical history which the present author does not wish to deal with here. Hence the rise of Islam in the seventh century is to serve as the terminus for this book.

In dealing with the Church in Persia, I have paid considerable attention both to the canons passed by the Nestorian Synods for the general guidance of clergy and laity and to the various regulations which attempted to control and shape monastic life. I have done so partly because these rules give us much insight into the day-to-day problems of the Church, and partly because the readers of this book are likely to be less familiar with the Oriental Church than with the Church of the West. For a brief account of canon law in the West Syrian Church, see section 12 of chapter 5.

The sources both primary and secondary for this subject are very extensive, but to supply a complete catalogue of them in a work intended for the general reader would serve no useful purpose. I am therefore furnishing a limited list of titles which will indicate the scope and nature of the material available. My citation of some modern authors, both in the bibliography and in the notes, should be taken as a very inadequate acknowledgment of what I owe to the numerous workers in this very large field.

February 1979   W. S. McCullough

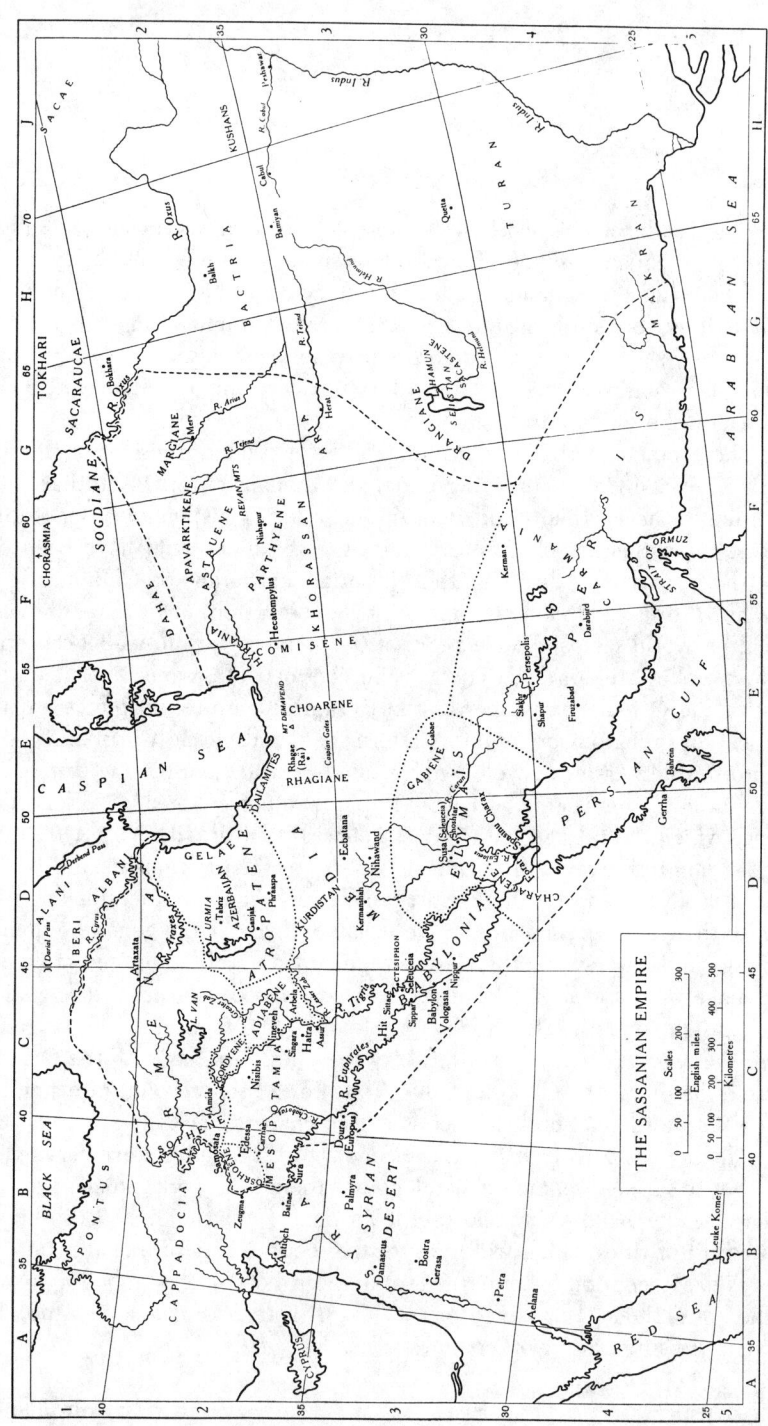

Part One
In the Roman (Byzantine) World

I.
In Parthian Times (to 224 A.D.)

Chapter 1.
The Milieu of Early Syriac Christianity

1. Parthia and Rome in Western Asia.

Parthia had arisen as an independent power in the eastern region of the Seleucid empire in the latter half of the third century B.C., and its subsequent westward expansion was at the expense of the Seleucids. It was c 121 B.C. that the Parthian king, Mithradates II, was able to take and hold Babylonia, thereby extending Parthia's western border to the Euphrates river.

About the same time that Parthia was expanding westwards, the Roman Republic was acquiring its first territory in the eastern Mediterranean. This process started when the former kingdom of Pergamum, through a bequest of its last ruler, Attalus III, became the province of Asia in 129 B.C. It was Pompey who played a considerable role in advancing this interest in the Orient. Operating under the terms of the *Lex Manilia* given him in 66 B.C., Pompey came down from the Black Sea coast into Syria in 64 B.C. and quickly put an end to the last vestiges of Seleucid power. Out of this disordered area he fashioned, as part of his settlement of the Near East, the Roman province of Syria. By the arrangement of 27 B.C. between Octavian (Octavius; from now on to be known as Augustus) and the Senate, Syria was made an "imperial" province, and was therefore under the direct supervision of the emperor. Its location made it the pivot of the eastern defences of the empire.

To the north of Syria lay the small kingdom of Commagene whose capital was at Samosata. Left alone by Augustus, Tiberius annexed this region in 18 A.D. and added it to the province of Syria, a move which made sense strategically for it extended the provincial border to the upper Euphrates. Gaius re-established the kingdom as a client state in 37 A.D. Its ruler supported Vespasian in his bid for the imperial power in 69 A.D., but this did not prevent the new emperor from re-annexing Commagene in 72 A.D. Henceforth Syria's eastern limits were those set by Tiberius.

That Rome and Parthia had the Euphrates as a common frontier did not make for peace. The existence of Armenia, theoretically a buffer state between the two rivals but a region in which both tried to exercise a preponderant influence, was an additional source of friction. A brief review of the Roman-Parthian clashes which occurred will illustrate the nature of the conflict and will also remind us of the unsettled political circumstances with which early Christian evangelists in this region would have had to cope.

The first century B.C. was notable in Roman military history for two major defeats of the legions at the hands of the Parthians. The first was experienced by Crassus at Carrhae in 53 B.C., and the second in 36 B.C. when Antony's Parthian expedition ended in a disastrous retreat. The advent of Augustus must have led many Romans to hope that these disasters would be avenged, but the new leader realized that what was needed was peace, not eastward expansion. In 20 B.C. he prevailed upon the Parthian king, Phraates IV, to restore to Rome the spoils, standards and surviving prisoners taken in 53 and 36 B.C., and to accept Tigranes, a Parthian prince, as client-ruler of Armenia under Roman supervision. Although in fact the Armenian situation continued to trouble Rome, peaceful relations with Parthia, at least in the Euphrates region, were to continue for almost a century. This was partly due to the fact that for much of this time the Parthian state was beset with internal turmoil.

The second century A.D., which is the period in which we find the earliest evidence for Syriac Christianity, witnessed a renewal of hostilities between Rome and Parthia. The first of these wars is associated with the emperor Trajan.[1] The immediate cause of the conflict was the deposition, without Rome's consent, by the Parthian king, Oroses (109–28), of the incumbent ruler of Armenia, an act which Trajan used as pretext for launching a campaign against Parthia. Probably his intent was to annex Armenia, and his hope may have been that this would end Rome's troubles in the East. Leaving Antioch in the spring of 114, he quickly overran Armenia and organized it as a Roman province. On his way back he occupied Nisibis and much of northern Mesopotamia, and confirmed Abgar VII (109–16) as ruler of Edessa. After wintering in Antioch, where he survived a terrible earthquake in December, in the spring of 115 he moved eastwards penetrating as far as Adiabene, which became the Roman province of Assyria. He then advanced south on the Tigris river while another force went down the Euphrates. Dura Europus was occupied in 115, remaining in Roman hands until 117, and probably Babylon was taken at the same time. The Romans reached Ctesiphon which was captured with little effort; Seleucia was evidently taken later. During the winter of 115–16, the emperor travelled south to Mesene (Characene), whose ruler became a tributary client-king.

When Trajan returned to Babylon in 116, he learned that Oroses was now counter-attacking in Adiabene, and that many of the Roman garrisons in the

---

[1] The question whether Trajan's Parthian War occupied two years or three is, for our purpose, unimportant. See R. P. Longden in CAH XI, ch VI; F. A. Lepper, *Trajan's Parthian War*, Oxford, 1948.

occupied areas were in grave difficulties. The emperor acted at once. Lusius Quietus recovered northern Mesopotamia; Edessa was burned, Nisibis was captured and pillaged, Seleucia was re-taken and burned. Adiabene, however, remained in Parthian hands, and the siege of the Arab city of Ḥatra had to be abandoned. The emperor's problems at this time were compounded by Jewish uprisings against Rome in various eastern parts of the empire. Beginning in 115 in Cyrene, Egypt and Cyprus, the insurgent mood, possibly with Messianic overtones, spread to the Jews of Mesopotamia. It is probable that there was some collusion between the Roman and the Parthian Jews, and doubtless the hope was that both parties would benefit from Rome's discomfiture. Trajan's immediate response to the local troubles was to send Lusius Quietus back to Mesopotamia where Jewish settlements suffered extremely ruthless treatment. Despite Rome's apparent successes, the general political situation east of the Euphrates remained unsettled. Trajan who had returned to Antioch in 117 now began, despite his deteriorating health, to plan a fresh campaign, but in the midst of these preparations he suffered a stroke. The project of further military action had to be abandoned, and on his way back to Italy, the emperor died in Cilicia (August 117). His ward Hadrian (adopted as his son only a day or so earlier), who had been acting as governor of Syria, was now proclaimed emperor by the army, and one of his earliest decisions was to abandon Trajan's recent conquests. Greater Armenia regained its king, and the Euphrates became once more the border between Rome and Parthia.

Fifty years of peace ended when, in the reign of Marcus Aurelius (161–180), Vologeses III (148–92) invaded Armenia in 162 and placed his own nominee on its throne. He then moved south to Mesopotamia where Edessa was taken, and into Syria where the local garrison was unable to repel him. Later the Parthians withdrew to their own territory. It was not until 163 that Roman forces from Cappadocia under Verus, the emperor's brother, advanced into Armenia and established it as a Roman dependency. In 164 a Roman army was finally able to reach upper Mesopotamia where battles occurred near Edessa and Nisibis and farther south at Dura Europus. The latter fortress was lost to Parthia permanently. Seleucia surrendered to the Romans in December 165, and Ctesiphon was taken by siege, both cities being partially destroyed. What seemed to be an almost total victory over Parthia was now vitiated by the onset of a plague. First experienced at Seleucia, the disease became so rampant that the Romans had no option but to retreat. This Roman withdrawal led to another Parthian advance into Mesopotamia, and this in turn in 166 provoked a Roman counter-attack. The only gains to Rome from these struggles of 162–67 were that henceforth Dura Europus was Roman, and Armenia, Osrhoene, and probably Nisibis were considered to be friendly to Rome. In fact in 166 Maʿnu VIII of Edessa became a *cliens* (dependent ally) of Rome.

When Commodus was murdered in 192, the resulting political struggle in the Roman world encouraged Vologeses IV of Parthia (191–207) to assert himself against Rome. Nisibis was besieged and Osrhoene was prevailed upon to renounce Roman suzerainty. These developments led the new emperor, Septimius Severus (193-211), to embark on the first of his two Parthian expeditions. He crossed the Euphrates in 194 and by early 195 he had reduced Osrhoene to a province and relieved Nisibis. The latter became the capital of an additional Roman province (Mesopotamia) between Osrhoene and the Tigris, and a force was sent across the Tigris into Adiabene. Later in the year Osrhoene was restored to its native ruler (Abgar VIII, 177-212). Another period of civil strife kept Severus out of the East for two years, and this incited Vologeses to resume his attack. The Parthians now overran northern Mesopotamia and laid siege again to Nisibis. Whether they penetrated Armenia is uncertain. When Rome's internal problems ended, Severus was free to strike again at Parthia. In the spring of 198 the Romans once more went into Mesopotamia, relieved Nisibis, and going down the Euphrates they reached Babylon and then Seleucia, which were taken in the fall of 198 without serious fighting, and even Ctesiphon's resistance was ineffective. When Severus returned to Syria in 199, having failed twice to reduce the Arab city of Hatra, he left behind a Roman province of Mesopotamia, with Nisibis, now a Roman *colonia*, as its capital. Osrhoene remained a client kingdom within this province. It was subsequent to this, and probably between 202 and 208, that Abgar VIII with a large retinue visited Rome at the emperor's invitation (Dio LXXX. 16. 2). Although Parthia had taken considerable punishment, the Roman gains from the campaigns of 194-98 were not impressive.

The Parthian war of Caracalla (211-17) seems to have been undertaken in the wild hope that Rome and Parthia might be united under a single ruler. One of the emperor's early moves in this enterprise was to arrest and imprison Abgar IX of Edessa (Dio LXXVIII. 12. 1). After a winter spent in Antioch (215-16), in the following summer Caracalla marched through Mesopotamia and crossed the Tigris into Adiabene, capturing Arbela and meeting no serious resistance, he may even have made forays into Media. He retired to Edessa for the winter, but he was murdered by his alienated troops near Carrhae in the spring of 217.

The last Roman-Parthian war is associated with Macrinus who was proclaimed emperor by the eastern legions in 217. It was begun by Artabanus V (c 213-24) who invaded Mesopotamia and defeated the Roman near Nisibis in the summer of 217. Macrinus's negotiations ended in the Romans paying a large sum for peace. This settlement, which caused considerable dissatisfaction among the Roman troops, was a factor in bringing a rival emperor on the scene, Elagabulus (218-22), who defeated Macrinus near Antioch in June 218. Macrinus was shortly afterwards captured and put to death. Affairs within Parthia did not permit Artabanus to follow up the advantage he had gained in 217. Serious political unrest had arisen, centering in Fars (Persis), and from this region there was to arise one, Ardashir, whose challenge to Parthian rule in Iran was to bring the Arsacid dynasty to an end. Within a few years a revived Persia was to arise under the hegemony of the Sasanians.

2. Trade between the Roman empire and the Orient.

As we have earlier seen, Syria became an imperial province in the Roman state in 27 B.C., and it proved to be so important a region that its governorship was the most honourable that the emperor could confer. One reason for Syria's primacy was economic. Its natural resources made it invaluable as a producer of food, and as a manufacturing centre it had no peer in the Roman world and its products were marketed widely throughout the empire.

The commerce in which Syrians were involved was not confined to the Mediterranean littoral. Very old trading patterns existed between Syria and Mesopotamia, and these seem to have been exploited and expanded in the Roman era.[2] Much of Syria's eastern trade was in the necessities of life, as we learn from Fronto (Vol. II, p. 215), who tells us that Trajan made "more stringent the ferry dues for camels and horses on the Euphrates and Tigris." This is further illustrated by the Palmyrene tariff of 137 A.D.[3] This decree covers such items as slaves, fleeces and skins, sweet oil, fat, salted fish, victuals, wheat, wine, wool, bronze statuary, salt and purple. Another staple food imported into Syria from Babylonia, but not mentioned in this tariff, was dates.[4] But the most lucrative part of this commerce was in luxury items, particularly in goods obtainable only from Arabia, Parthia (later Persia), and the Far East. A share of this trade entered the Mediterranean world through the Red Sea and Egypt,[5] but much of it came by other channels. Incense, myrrh, etc., from south Arabia often were brought overland to Gaza or Damascus.[6] Many imports from India were carried by sea to Spasinu Charax on the Persian Gulf,[7] and thence through Babylonia and Mesopotamia to either Palmyra or Zeugma on the Euphrates. Others came entirely overland from Iran, India and China, the most common route passing through Merv, Hecatompylos, Ecbatana (Hamadan), Adiabene (or farther south, Seleucia on the Tigris), Nisibis, Edessa and Zeugma. It was along such a route that silk and silk garments came from China, muslim, spices, metals, drugs and precious stones from India, and carpets from Iran. Pliny (first century A.D.) observed that India, China and the Arabian peninsula took from the empire every year one hundred million sesterces (*Nat Hist* XII. 84).

A trading route for which we have literary documentation is described by the geographer, Isidore of Charax (c 25 A.D.), in his work *Parthian Stations*

---

[2] On various trade routes in the Parthian period, see D. Oates, *Studies in the Ancient History of Northern Iraq*, Oxford, 1968, fig. 5, p. 76.

[3] The text of the tariff, see G. A. Cooke, *A Text-Book of North-Semitic Inscriptions*, Oxford, 1903, pp. 313-40.

[4] On the dates of Babylonia, see Herodotus I. 193; Strabo XVI. 1. 14; Ammianus Marcellinus XXIV. 3. 12-13.

[5] Strabo XVII. 1. 13; Pliny, *Nat Hist* VI. xxvi. 101-6.

[6] On the frankincense trade, see Pliny, *Nat Hist* XII. xxx-xxxii. 51-65: on merchant caravans, see Strabo XVI. 1. 27.

[7] The Hymn of Judas in A. F. J. Klijn, *The Acts of Judas Thomas the Apostle* (Leiden, 1962), refers to "Maishan (i.e. Mesene), the meeting-place of the merchants of the East," p. 121.

(ed. W. H. Schoff, Philadelphia, 1914). This four page document lists the caravanserais available on the overland trip from Zeugma on the Euphrates to Arachosia and the distances between the stations. The itinerary, after leaving Zeugma, passes through Anthemus, follows the Balik river to Nicephorium, on the Euphrates, and the Euphrates to Neapolis, where the road strikes east to Seleucia on the Tigris, and thence to Artemita, and through the Zagros mountains to Ecbatana, Rhagae, and points east. The highly romanticized account of the first century A.D. journey of Apollonius to India, found in Philostratus, *The Life of Apollonius of Tyana*, is influenced by the exploits of Alexander the Great and furnishes little reliable geographical data. The route starts at Antioch and ends at the Hyphasis river in north-west India.

These old trading practices continued long after the Parthian era ended. For instance we may note that in the treaty of 297-98 between the Romans and the Persian king Nerseh (293-302), it was agreed that Nisibis (now back in Roman hands) should be the centre for commercial dealings between the two powers. A half century later, Ammianus Marcellinus writing about events in 354, describes an annual trade fair held in early September at Batnae (south-west of Edessa), at which wealthy traders gathered to traffic in wares brought from India, China, and various other places (XIV. 3.3).

In view of the importance of trade in the life of western Asia, it is not surprising that merchants played a part in the dissemination of religious ideas. It was a Jewish merchant at Spasinu Charax, Ananias, who won over Izates, prince of Adiabene, to Judaism while the latter was staying temporarily in the town. At about the same time, the first century A.D., Izates' mother, Queen Helena, also adopted Judaism, being instructed by an unnamed Jew. Another Jew, Eleazar from Galilee, appeared at the Adiabene court, and he too was probably a merchant (Josephus, *Ant* XX, 34-48). We are further told in the *Doctrine of Addai* that when Addai first came to Edessa, he stayed with Tobias, the son of Tobias, who is said to have come from Palestine. The likelihood is that he was a merchant. Later, in the same story, some Jews who were silk merchants were added to Addai's converts.[8] It is a credible detail in an otherwise impossible tale, that in the *Acts of Judas Thomas the Apostle* Habban who had come from India by sea (presumably to Spasinu Charax) and had arrived at Jerusalem, is described as a merchant. The story goes that it was under the aegis of this Habban that Thomas reached India and began his ministry there.

In the nature of the case we would expect early Christianity to have traveled by known routes in its penetration of the Semitic-speaking world. Its earliest missionaries into these parts must have started from Antioch, and in the course of their journeys Aleppo (Beroea, Ḥaleb), Samosata, Edessa, Nisibis, Arbela, Seleucia on the Tigris, and perhaps even Spasinu Charax would have been exposed to the Christian message. It is therefore no mere accident

---

[8] *Doctrine of Addai*, Syriac text, p. 34, 11 16-19.

that all of the cities mentioned eventually became important centres for Syriac Christianity.

3. The Languages of Syria.

The indigenous language of Syria was a dialect of Aramaic, related to other dialects used in Nabataea, Jewish Palestine, Palmyra and Mesopotamia. When, however, Syria was overrun by Alexander the Great and when it presently came under the control of the Seleucids, Hellenistic Greek slowly became the second language and in some circles the first language of many people in the larger cities. Under Roman control this process continued and for a variety of reasons many must have found Greek indispensable. Thus Ignatius, bishop of Antioch (early second century), in writing his famous *Letters*, naturally used Greek. If he was a native of Syria, he presumably learned Greek in a school in the province's capital.

Despite the widespread use of Greek, large segments of the population continued to use Aramaic as their everyday tongue.[9] It appears that the farther people were away from the Mediterranean, the more likely they were to retain their native speech. There is no evidence, for instance, that Greek was ever widely used in the city of Damascus. One can only speculate about the language used by the Christians of Damascus, and by Saul, in the episode narrated in Acts 9. Similarly, when Josephus wrote his *Jewish War* (between 75 and 79 A.D.), which was intended for those Jews living beyond the Euphrates, and probably for those in northern Syria, it was written in Aramaic (*War* I, 3, 6). In the early second century Lucian of Samosata knew only Syrian Aramaic as the language of his boyhood and youth.[10] When he determined to get an education that would serve him in the Graeco-Roman world, he left Samosata, and took off, not for Antioch, but for Ionia where he gained eventually the superb command of the Greek language which has given his writings their claim to distinction. It seems that in Syria in the second century the native language had no strong literary tradition behind it, nor did it point to a future for an ambitious young man.

It was in Osrhoene (capital, Edessa), which became a client kingdom of Rome c 166 A.D. and as such was naturally associated with the Roman province of Syria, that the local dialect of Aramaic was to attain unusual prominence. Christianity came into this area probably in the second half of the second century, and subsequently Edessa became a city of importance in the eastern Church, and its dialect (to be known as Syriac) became the principal language of the Christian community. It was into Edessan Syriac that the Scriptures were translated, and this translation gave Christian writers and speakers a ready-made paradigm of both vocabulary and style for their native tongue. An individual who contributed much to this development of the Edessan

---

[9] So P. K. Hitti, *History of Syria*, 2nd ed, London 1957, pp. 256–57.
[10] L. Casson, *Selected Satires of Lucian*, Chicago, 1962, pp. xiii, 6.

language was Bardaisan (154–222), whose *Book of the Laws of Countries* has come down to us (although its text is due to his pupil Philip), and whose hymns were to have a great influence on all subsequent hymnody in the Oriental Church. When we meet Syriac in the Scriptures and in Bardaisan, it is a fully developed language, which is all the more surprising, for the occasional earlier appearances of Syriac, as in funerary inscriptions, give little indication of what the language could become.[11] As an early example of Syriac in a legal document, Dura Europus has given us a deed of sale, written in Edessa in the Estrangelo script of Syriac in 243 A.D.[12] Syriac is usually designated as belonging to the East Aramaic branch of the Aramaic family. Two other members of this branch are Babylonian-Talmudic and Mandaic.[13]

4. The Religions of Syria excluding Christianity.

The Imperial Cult in Syria.

The ruler cult in the Roman world, originally inspired by practices within Hellenistic society, went back to the deification of Julius Caesar in 42 B.C. It was furthered by Augustus who insisted that the city of Rome be associated with himself in any public rituals, as at Pergamum in 29 B.C. With Augustus's death and his subsequent deification, the ground was laid for the cult of the deified emperors, a cult which like the Roman religion was a series of formalized acts with little or no vital religious content. Participation in these acts was a patriotic gesture, an expression of loyalty to the mores and values of the empire. Any one holding a public office would have certain procedures to perform in connection with this cult, but this would affect only a minute part of the total population. If the ordinary Syrian had to confirm an oath, he might be expected to invoke the ruling emperor or his genius, and to refuse to do so might get him into trouble. The consequences could be quite serious as we know from the experiences of Igantius of Antioch and of the Christians of Bithynia. On the whole, however, and apart from public ceremonies in the cities, the ruler cult would be of limited interest or importance to most people.

The way the imperial cult worked out for the Roman army is illustrated by a document found at Dura Europus and dated 225–27 (or 225–35). This somewhat damaged papyrus was in the temple of Artemis Azzanathkono, which housed the archives of Cohors XX Palmyrenorum. Referred to as the Feriale Duranum, it is a list of festivals intended for observance by the army. One category of such celebrations is that of public festivals and rites of the gods (excluding non-Roman gods), and the second group is connected with the

---

[11] On Syriac inscriptions, see J. B. Segal (re two dated 6 A.D. and 73 A.D.) in *Edessa 'the Blessed City'*, Oxford 1970, p. 23, foot-notes 3 and 4; see also Segal in BSOAS, XVI, 1954, pp. 13–36; XX, 1957, pp. 513–22; pp. 23–40; XXX, 1967, pp. 293–304.

[12] *Excavations at Dura-Europos*: Final Report V, Part I, *The Parchments and the Papyri* (C. B. Welles, R. O. Fink, J. F. Gilliam), New Haven, 1959, pp. 142–49.

[13] R. Rosenthal, *Die Aramäistiche Forschung*, Leiden, 1939, pp. vii–ix.

deified Roman emperors. It is thought that in its essence, the Feriale goes back to the time of Augustus, though it was constantly updated as deceased emperors were added to the list of the gods. If this is so, the Feriale reflects in part the intention of Augustus to maintain and extend Roman traditions among all Roman citizens, in this case, among members of the armed forces.[14]

Native Cults in Syria.

As has long been known from both the literary and archaeological evidence, western Asia during the rise and expansion of early Christianity exhibited a very considerable variety of religions and cults. To avoid attempting an exhaustive description of these forms of worship and at the same time to give a representative account of them, our treatment will be confined to the data furnished by six centres.

Antioch (including its suburb Daphne).

Antioch was founded in 300 B.C. by Seleucus I, and as it was meant to be a Hellenistic city, Greek influencees were predominant in it from the very beginning. Even in the early Christian centuries its mosaics reflect classical traditions,[15] and most of its temples from the outset were dedicated to familiar Greek deities. Seleucus I, for example, built a sanctuary for Apollo in Daphne, and in Antioch he erected temples to Zeus Bottiaios, Zeus Keraunios, and Athene. Tyche, the Fortune goddess, was prominent from Antioch's foundation and appears on a silver coin as early as the mid-second century B.C. The earthquake in the reign of Claudius (51–54 A.D.) destroyed the temples of Artemis, Ares and Heracles. After the earthquake of 115 A.D., a temple of Zeus Soter and another to Artemis were built in Daphne. Following Trajan's death (117 A.D.), a small temple in his honour was constructed in Antioch. As late as 181 A.D. Commodus restored the temple of Athene and built a new temple to Olympian Zeus. On the oration of Libanius, a fourth century Antiochene rhetorician, on behalf of Artemis, see G. Downey, *A History of Antioch in Syria*, Princeton, 1961, pp. 681–88.

Of the non-Hellenic deities worshipped in Antioch, Isis seems to have been very popular, as might be inferred from some of the mosaics discovered in the city.[16] A cult such as this could stir a genuinely religious emotion, as Apuleius reminds us in his story of the conversion of Lucius to the worship of Isis.[17]

Dura (Dura Europus).

Dura was a Parthian frontier post and customs station on the Euphrates river, more or less due east of Palmyra. It was occupied temporarily by Trajan,

---

[14] Excavations at Dura-Europos, as in note 12, pp. 191–212.

[15] G. Downey, *Ancient Antioch*, Princeton, 1963, figures 25–31. This work is a condensed version of *A History of Antioch in Syria*, Princeton, 1961.

[16] D. Levi in *Berytus* VII, 1942: "Mors Voluntaria, Mystery Cults on Mosaics from Antioch," pp. 19–55.

[17] *The Golden Ass*, tr. by R. Graves, London, 1950, pp. 262–87.

115–17, but it was not until 164, in the time of Marcus Aurelius, that it was retaken by the Romans and it remained under their control until the next century.

Five major temples have been identified at Dura[18] for Atargatis (Dea Syria) and Hadad; for Artemis Nanaia; for Artemis (also called locally Azzanathkona); for a triad, Bel, Yarḥibol (the sun god), and ʿAglibol (the moon god); for Aphlad (or Apalad), built in 52 A.D. In addition to these structures, there was also at Dura a sanctuary dedicated to Mithras. Mithras, an old Iranian deity with a varying role in the different stages of Zoroastrianism, had earlier penetrated the Roman world and became with the passage of time the centre of a mystery cult which was surprisingly popular in the Roman army. Some of the soldiers stationed at Dura were evidently devotees of this god, for they were able to erect a Mithraic chapel. A wall painting from this Mithraeum depicting Mithras as a hunter is reproduced in M. A. R. Colledge, *The Parthians*, London 1967, plate 69, p. 233.

Palmyra.

This oasis in the north-west Arabian desert became an important caravan city only in the first century A.D., and sometime in the second century Rome established a measure of control over the city and its trade. Under this arrangement Palmyra retained its own militia whose primary task was to protect the caravans.[19] The following are the principal gods forming the pantheon of Palmyra: Bel, Baal Samin, Atargatis and Hadad, Ishtar-Astarte, Arsu and Azizu (caravan gods), Shamsh (an Arabian deity; cf. the Babylonian Shamash), the triad, found also at Dura, Bel, Yarḥibol and ʿAglibol, Allat, an Arabian goddess.

Hierapolis (Bambyce, Mabbog).

Hierapolis, west of the Euphrates and north-east of Beroea, was an ancient holy spot, at which Stratonice, the wife of Seleucus I, built, or rebuilt, a temple. This temple was to become famous throughout western Asia, and once in its history (54–53 B.C.) its accumulated treasures were to be plundered by Crassus the legate of Syria. Strabo knew of the temple as the place where the Syrian goddess Atargatis was worshipped (Geog. 16. 1. 27), but it is to the Syrian writer Lucian of the second century A.D. that we owe a first hand description of the temple and its procedures.[20] The chief gods were Atargatis and Hadad (whom Lucian calls Hera and Zeus), although there were statues of other deities in evidence, such as that of a bearded Apollo. Lucian describes the two enormous phalli at the entrance to the temple, the sacred zoo in the

---

[18] The data regarding temples are drawn from M. Rostovtzeff, *Caravan Cities*, tr. by D. and T. Talbot Rice, Oxford, 1932, p. 178, plates xxviii. 1: xxix. 1,2: xxx. 1,2; xxxii. 1,2. On Aphlad, see M. A. R. Colledge, *The Parthians*, London, 1967, fig. 67, and note on p. 233.

[19] See CAH XI, pp. 859–60.

[20] *De Dea Syria*, tr. by H. A. Strong, ed. by J. Garstang, London, 1913.

great court, the lake of sacred fish, the participation of three hundred white-robed priests at one sacrifice he witnessed, and the annual spring festival which attracted thousands of pilgrims, and at which young men, who were so minded, emasculated themselves to become Galli, eunuch priests of the goddess. A contemporary of Lucian, but born in north Africa, was Apuleius who traveled widely in the Near East, and who has left us his *Metamorphoses* or "The Golden Ass," in which he describes, among other things, the itinerant eunuch priests of the Syrian goddess. These priests, not averse to preying on men's fears and superstitions, would go from hamlet to hamlet with an image of Atargatis, playing their cymbals, tambourines and horns, and putting on dances and displays of self flagellation, and for all of this they would be amply rewarded with offerings (for the goddess!) of both money and food-stuffs.[21]

Sumatar Harabesi.[22]

This is now a deserted oasis south-east of Edessa. It is believed that in the mid-second century A.D. it was an area controlled by Edessa. A study of its ruins (seven and possibly eight buildings) indicates that in its heyday it was the centre of a cult of planet worship. About twenty miles away, in Carrhae, the veneration of the moon was still practised in the fourth century, as Ammianus Marcellinus observed (XXIII. 3. 1-2). Apparently the supreme god of Sumatar Harabesi was Marilaha, possibly to be identified with Baal Samin who appears at Palmyra. Three of the Syriac inscriptions found in this spot are dated 164 A.D., and two refer to Sin the moon god.

Edessa (modern Urfa).

Osrhoene was a small principality in northern Mesopotamia just east of the Euphrates river. It had come into existence c 132 B.C. as a result of the disintegration of the Seleucid kingdom, and about five years later an Arab family, destined to be the forbears of a long line of kings, had gained control of it. Its capital city (in later Syriac ʾ*wrhy*, Orhay) was one of the military colonies of Seleucus I and had been given the name of Edessa (after the Macedonian city bearing this name).[23] By reason of its location on one of the east-west trade routes, Edessa was of considerable economic importance, and we are not surprised that Mithradates II (c 123–87 B.C.) established control of Osrhoene, thus bringing the north-west border of Parthia up to the Euphrates river. This made inevitable Osrhoene's frequent involvement in the Roman-Parthian wars of the early Christian centuries.

---

[21] *The Golden Ass*, tr. by R. Graves, Penguin, London, 1950, pp. 198–211.

[22] J. B. Segal, "Pagan Syrian Monuments in the Vilayet of Urfa," in *Anatolian Studies* (the British Institute of Archaeology at Ankara), vol. III, 1953, pp. 97–119, and in *Edessa 'the Blessed City'*, pp. 56–60.

[23] In the later Syriac traditions, as recorded by Bar Hebraeus, Urhai (Orhay) was the smallest of the 180 cities built in the days of Enoch (*The Chronography*, tr. by E. A. W. Budge, Oxford 1932, I, p. 5).

Data on the paganism of Edessa before and after the arrival of Christianity are somewhat elusive.[24] *A priori* we might suspect that Edessene religion would be rather similar to what we encounter in Hierapolis, Dura and Palmyra, and such facts as we have and such inferences as we can make appear to support this supposition. The *Doctrine of Addai* (in its present form, c. 400 A.D.) has a reference to the temples (idols) of Nebu and Bel, as well as a great altar in the city, in Addai's time. There are numerous other allusions in this document to heathen worship, and we are told that after Addai's death the priests of Nebu and Bel were still held in esteem. For cult objects on coins, see Segal, Plate 28, a(i), (ii). Bardaisan in the *Book of the Laws of Countries* refers to the practice of self-castration in honour of Tarʿata (Atargatis). This must be the local variation of the emasculation of the Galli earlier noted at Hierapolis. The two large columns with Corinthian capitals which now stand on the citadel mount of Urfa (Segal, p. 26; plate 9 (a) (b)) may at one time have had a connection with some pagan temple. Probably the two pools of the city (of Abraham and of Zulha), whose fish to-day are sacred, may also like the sacred lake at Hierapolis have been originally dedicated to some deity (Segal p. 54; plates 8b, 10b). It is thought that the Orpheus mosaic, found in the Egup Mahallesi district of Urfa and dated 228 A. D., points to an active Orpheus cult at least in the early third century (Segal, p. 52; plate 44). As late as the fifth century one of the city gates was called Beth Shemesh, and on a coin the crescent moon appears on the head-dress of Abgar VIII; this limited evidence may indicate a solar or lunar cult, perhaps related to that at Sumatar Harabesi. A final bit of evidence for Edessa's paganism comes from the people represented in the mosaics and statuary of the city. These would appear to be from the upper classes of society, and as Segal notes, they were probably pagan for there is a notable absence of any symbols that can be identified as either Christian or Jewish (Segal, p. 41; plates 1–3, 12, 14–15).

These samples of the religion found in six selected areas in northern Syria are intended to portray the paganism which early Christianity encountered in this region. It is evdient that these religions were not essentially different from the pagan cults of the Graeco-Roman world. In the West, despite the efforts of the emperor Julian to invigorate it, paganism gradually disappeared under the impact of Christianity, partly because of its own internal weaknesses, and partly because the Christian Gospel offered superior answers to fundamental religious questions.[25] We might expect that the experience of the Oriental Church with paganism would be somewhat similar, *mutatis mutandis*, to that of the Western Church.

---

[24] For a detailed statement on this point, see Segal, pp. 50–61.

[25] The reasons for Christianity's success in the Roman empire have often been commented on, as for instance in A.D. Nock, *Early Gentile Chirstianity and its Hellenistic Background*, New York, 1928 (1964), pp. 100–104.

Judaism.

Josephus, writing in 75–79 A.D., claims that the Jewish race was particularly numerous in Syria, being largely congregated in Antioch (*War* VII. 43). Beloch estimated that in the time of Augustus there were about 45,000 Jews in the Syrian capital.[26] As we might suspect would be the case in a metropolitan city, the Jews attracted to themselves, so Josephus observes, multitudes of Greek-speaking pagans (*War* VII. 45). One such Antiochene proselyte from paganism, Nicolaus by name, is referred to in Acts 6:5. The relative peace and prosperity which the Jews of Syria enjoyed for a century or so under Roman rule[27] were largely terminated in the period 66–71 A.D., mostly due to repercussions in Syria of the rebellion of the Palestinian Jews, though, after the war, Titus refused to reduce any of the civic rights of the Antiochene Jews (Josephus, *War* II, 462–63; VII, 46–53, 100–11). The massacres and violence of these years greatly reduced the numbers and prominence of the Syrian Jews, and help to explain why the Jewry of Syria had no real share in the development of rabbinical Judaism.

Ignatius of Antioch has nothing to say about the Jews of that city, but in two of his letters he admonishes those addressed to beware of mixing Jewish practices with their Christian faith (*Magnesians* VIII, 1; X, 3; *Philadelphians* VI, 1). This may reflect some difficulties which the bishop had had in Antioch with converts won from the local Jewish community.

In Edessa there was a Jewish settlement which, although small, seems to have supported two synagogues, and was not averse to sharing a cemetery with pagans (Segal, p. 42). In the story of Addai, one Tobias, son of Tobias from Palestine, affords shelter to the Christian missionary when he reaches Edessa, and later acts as an intermediary between Addai and king Abgar. As the tale develops, we learn that some Jewish merchants who sold cloth and who were conversant with the Law and the Prophets, were won over to the Christian faith. But it is clear, even from this story, that not all the Jews of Edessa turned to Christianity, for at Addai's death, both Jews and pagans are said to have been among the mourners.

5. Early Christianity in Syria.

The NT tells us that after the death of Stephen (Acts 6:8–7:60), Jesus' followers were somewhat scattered, and a few of them ("men of Cyprus and Cyrene") came to Atioch "preaching the Lord Jesus" (Acts 11:19–20). So successful was their work that Barnabas was sent by the Jerusalem church to investigate it, and he was sufficiently impressed with what was taking place that he went to Tarsus and brought back Paul, and the two of them stayed in

---

[26] C. H. Kraeling, *The Jewish Community of Antioch*, New Haven, 1932, p. 136.

[27] There were some troubles in Antioch between Jews and Greeks c 40–41 A.D.; the emperor Claudius subsequently confirmed the tradition privileges of the Jews (Josephus, *Ant* XIX, 278–85; Kraeling (as in note 26), pp. 148–50).

Antioch assisting the church there for a whole year (c 40 A.D.). It was during this time that "the disciples were for the first time called Christians" (Acts 11:26). There is no evidence about either the size of this Christian community or its internal life. Of the subsequent history of the early Church in Syria, the NT tells us virtually nothing except that Antioch was seemingly the headquarters for Paul and Barnabas (Acts 13:1-3; etc.). Other towns mentioned in the NT as having groups of Christians are Damascus, Tyre, and Sidon, and of these only Damascus is likely to have had a Semitic-speaking population.

The Hellenistic character of the Church in Syria is illustrated by the letters of Igantius,[28] bishop of Antioch (late first and early second century). These famous seven letters were written in Greek to various churches in Asia Minor (except that the seventh is to the bishop of Smyrna) while the bishop was on his way to his death in Rome.[29] Igantius must have known that if any of these missives found their way back to Antioch, they would be fully intelligible to the Christians there. This conclusion receives some support from the *Didache*, a manual of instruction for Christians, found in Constantinople in 1875. If this document originated, as some scholars think, in Syria in the second century, its Greek text points to a Christian community whose members would understand Greek.

The letters of Igantius cast indirect light on the organization of the church in Antioch, and probably also of other churches under the supervision of the Antiochene bishop. Ignatius is very emphatic about the internal leadership of churches: at the head of each Christian congregation is a bishop, and under him are presbyters and deacons (Ephesians III. 2; IV, 1; Magnesians VII, 1; etc.). While this type of organization stands in some contrast to the apostles, prophets, teachers, etc. of whom Paul speaks (I Cor 12:28; cf. Acts 13:1), the references to bishops and deacons in Phil 1:1 and in the much later I Tim 3:1-13, indicate that some form of episcopal leadership was known in at least some other churches and was not peculiar to Antioch.

Ignatius also alludes to current problems in the churches, and while his remarks are addressed to Christian communities in Roman Asia Minor, there is every reason to suppose that these same issues confronted the Christians of Syria. He refers particularly to heretical preachers (Ephesians VII. 1, XVI, 1-2; Trallians VI. 1-2; etc.), Judaizers (Magnesians VIII, 1; X, 1-3), and docetism (Trallians IX. 1-2; X. 1; etc.). It is possible that under the category of "Judaizers," Ignatius may have ranked the followers of the prophet Elkesai (Elkhasai, Elxas, Alexis), who arose in East Jordan c 101 A.D. and whose

---

[28] These letters are available in *The Apostolic Fathers*, 2 vols ed. by K. Lake, (Loeb Classical Library), London and New York, 1913-14, vol I, pp. 166-277.

[29] The Syriac text of three of the letters, published by W. Cureton in 1845, is thought to be an abridgement of a Syriac translation of the "short recension." The latter attempted to establish which of the thirteen letters were the original seven (cf Eusebius, *Eccl Hist*, III, xxxvi. 1-11).

teachings were an amalgam of Judaism and Christianity. This movement, which featured baptisms in water, may have spread north into Syria in Ignatius's time. We know that in the late second century, one Alcibiades from Apamea brought the *Book of Elkesai* to Rome.

Ignatius's references to various dangerous movements in the Church suggest that the bishop was well informed about the religious climate in Syria. This region in the early second century seems to have been a hot-bed for various forms of speculative religious thought, both Christian and pagan, often termed Gnostic. Menander, for instance, a pupil of Simon Magus of Samaria, came to Antioch in Trajan's reign and may have been known to Ignatius. Some years later, in the time of Hadrian, Saturninus (Satornilus), a native of Antioch, became successor to Menander, and from this same circle came Cerdo (Kerdon), the teacher of Marcion in Rome. Basilides of the same generation, who became prominent in Alexandria, is also said to have emerged from this same Syrian coterie. Ignatius's warnings against heretical teachers are therefore no idle words. His reference in his Ephesians letter to the star that appeared at Jesus' nativity (Matt 2:1–12) and his comment that "all the other stars, with the sun and moon, gathered . . . round this star . . . By this all magic was dissolved and every band of wickedness vanished away" (Ephesians XIX. 1–3) may suggest that Ignatius was quite familiar with the current forms of planetary worship in Syria. His request that the Church in Syria should be prayed for (Ephesians XXI. 2; Magnesians XIV. 1; etc.) must reflect his concern for a Christian community faced with many challenges to its faith.

That variant forms of Christianity continued to trouble the Church in Syria illustrated by the experience of one of Ignatius's later successors, Serapion (d 211). Eusebius reports (*Eccl Hist* VI. xii 1–6) that Serapion discovered that the Christians in the town of Rhosus (on the coast, north-west of Antioch) were using a document known as the *Gospel of Peter*. On examining it the bishop found that it was mostly acceptable ("in accordance with the true teaching of the Saviour"), but that parts of it were docetic. This raises an important question, By what standard did Serapion identify "the true teaching of the Savior"?

An interesting side-light on Syrian Christianity, as seen by a pagan observer, comes to us from Lucian of Samosata (c 120–80). Lucian was in Antioch for a time, but he was widely traveled and most of his life was actually spent outside of Syria. In his *The Death of Peregrinus* there is an account of the life of this Cynic philosopher, and of his suicide at the Olympic Games of 165. It appears that for a short time Peregrinus belonged "to the priests and scribes of the Christians in Palestine and became an expert in that astonishing religion." . . . second only to "that man they still worship to-day, the one who was crucified in Palestine because he brought this new cult into being . . . The poor devils (i.e., the Christians) have convinced themselves that they're all going to be immortal . . . They worship the crucified sophist and live their lives according to his rules. They scorn all possessions without distinction and treat them as community property."[30] We conclude from these statements that in the mid-second century, Peregrinus had been involved in Palestine-Syria with an ascetic Christian sect which practised some form of economic communism (cf. Acts 4:32-7).

6. Christians *vis-à-vis* the Roman Government

For most of the first century Christianity seems to have been looked at as a sect of Judaism, and as such it profited from the general toleration extended to the Jews. Nero's action in 64 in persecuting the church in Rome was apparently short-lived, and was confined to Christians in the capital. But after the destruction of Jerusalem in 70, which involved the extinction of the Christian community in that city, it became clear to all Roman observers that Jews and Christians were quite distinct, and Christian groups now became unlicensed *collegia* (guilds, associations), often suspected of various clandestine rites. Further, most Christians made no secret of their contempt for the imperial cult and the worship of the traditional gods, and while they could not be censured on moral grounds, their attitude to accepted religious practices could hardly commend them either to the authorities or to the general public.

Pliny's well known correspondence with Trajan[31] indicates that the *modus operandi* against Christians in Bithynia, about 110-12, was by a private delation (by an informer), followed by a trial (*cognitio*) before a magistrate. The real test came when the defendant was asked to demonstrate that he was not a Christian by invoking the gods and making an offering of wine and incense before the emperor's statue. Those who would not renounce Christianity were executed forthwith, except in the case of Roman citizens who were sent off to Rome for punishment.

We may presume that the governor of Syria in Trajan's time followed the same procedures as Pliny did in Bithynia. In the case of Ignatius, an informer must have complained about him, and possibly the governor was glad to be able to make an example of such a prominent Christian. Whether the Christians in popular thought were held responsible for the earthquake which struck Antioch in December 116, and whether Ignatius was singled out for punishment in this connection we do not know. This view is tenable only if we suppose that Eusebius's date for Igantius's martyrdom (108) is incorrect. That other Christians were involved at the same time as the bishop is hinted at in Ignatius's *Romans* X. 2; *Philadelphians* XI. 1; *Smyrnaeans* X. 1. It is, however, clear that in the early second century, while Christianity was an offence, there was no general or systematic effort to repress it. Even Trajan said, "These people must not be hunted out." Such persecution as there was

---

[30] *Selected Satires of Lucian*, ed. and tr. by L. Casson, Chicago, 1962, pp. 368-69.
[31] Pliny, *Letters and Panegyricus*, tr. by B. Radice (Loeb Classical Library), Cambridge, Mass., 1969, vol. 2, X, xcvi-xcvii; cf. Eusebius, *Eccl. Hist*, III, xxxiii. 1-3.

depended upon the local situation and the whim of the individual governor. We suspect that Christians in Syria, whether Greek-speaking or Syriac-speaking, who did not live in the larger centres were free from any form of state interference in their reigious exercises. We should note that Hadrian, Trajan's successor, in a letter to the Roman legate in the province of Asia (124–25), ruled out accusations against Christians unless they could be supported in a law-court (Eusebius, *Eccl Hist* IV, ix. 1–3). W. H. C. Frend draws attention to the fact that in 177 Trajan's directive about not hunting out Christians was no longer being fully observed, at least in Gaul (*Martyrdom and Persecution in the Early Church*, Oxford, 1965, p. 6).

There was some deterioration in the Church's fortunes in the reigns of Marcus Aurelius and his brother Lucius (Eusebius, *Eccl Hist* IV. xiv 10–xv 3). A little later Septimius Severus (193–211) passed a curious edict in 202 which forbade conversion to both Judaism and Christianity. Whatever the motives behind this edict, it would seem to indicate that the emperor recognized both groups as largely unassimilable into the normal patterns of Roman society, and that both should be curbed as much as possible. This order from Severus led to a persecution of Christians in Alexandria, 202–03, and apparently in other centres as well. It was the next emperor, Aurelius Antoninus (Caracalla), 211–17, who had the distinction of issuing the *constitutio Antoniniana* in 212, which extended citizenship rights to all the free inhabitants of the empire. As the preamble to this law indicates, Caracalla's hope was that it would bring the state gods new worshippers, although the real motive may have been to increase the revenues derived from inheritance duties (cf Dio LXXVIII/LXXVII/9. 4–5). One by-product of Caracalla's edict would be to draw attention to Christians' unwillingness to participate fully as citizens in the Empire's religious life. The practical effects of the laws of 202 and 212 on Christianity in Syria and Roman Mesopotamia (the Romans as we have earlier seen were in and out of Mesopotamia 194–217) cannot be determined owing to the paucity of evidence. Eusebius tells us that bishop Serapion of Antioch (d. c 211) wrote to one, Domnus, who had abandoned his Christian faith "at the time of the persecution," and that Asclepiades, successor to Serapion, was involved in "the persecution," but he supplies us with no further details (*Eccl Hist* VI. xi.4; xii.1).

Chapter 2.
The Beginnings of the Syriac Church

It is curious that no NT figure seems concerned with taking the Gospel to the north-eastern part of Syria or to the lands beyond the Euphrates (the one NT reference to the Parthians is in Acts 2:9). This is all the more surprising in the case of Paul, who believed that "all Israel will be saved" (Rom 11:26), and who, as a student in Jerusalem of Gamaliel I, must have heard about Hillel's Babylonian origin and of the Jewish communities in Parthia. As there were no insurmountable barriers to travellers and merchants journeying eastward and crossing the Roman-Parthian frontier, we can only conclude that Paul felt that his missionary efforts would be more productive if he avoided the Aramaic areas and confined himself to the Hellenistic world in which he was probably more at home. It is possible that the destruction of Jerusalem in 70 and the extinction or dispersal of the Aramaic-speaking Christians in Judea may have been a factor which, for the time being, discouraged Church leaders from thinking in terms of a Christian mission to the East. When we turn to Ignatius of Antioch, we see from his *Letters* that his only concern was for the church in Antioch and certain Greek-speaking churches in Roman Asia Minor.

Although substantial evidence for it is lacking, some eastward extension of Christianity, perhaps in the late first or early second century, cannot be ruled out completely. Syrian merchants of Christian persuasion, travelling to Samosata, Edessa, or Nisibis could have brought to these trading centres scraps of information about the new religion which had sprung up in the West. It is also conceivable that some dedicated evangelists were involved in missionary efforts aimed at the Aramaic community. We cannot dismiss such a possibility out of hand, as the presence of Christians in Bithynia in Trajan's time should warn us. As we have earlier noted, Pliny testifies to a body of Christians there in the early second century, yet we do not know when or by whom it was established.

It is probable that political factors determined the timing of Christian missionary efforts in the East. When extensive regions were overshadowed by impending or actual warfare, Christian missionaries would find their activities seriously hampered or even impossible. For instance, Trajan's war against Parthia (114–17) and the uprisings of the eastern Jews against Rome (115–16) can hardly have created a climate favourable to the expansion of the Church. But with the advent of Hadrian as emperor, and despite the abnormal social and economic conditions which the rebellion of the Palestinian Jews against Rome (132–35) must have created in Syria and especially in Antioch, it is possible that the fifty years of peace with Parthia, initiated by Hadrian in 117, may have offered the most favourable conditions in this century for Christian missioners from Syria to proceed eastwards. We should expect such efforts to start from Antioch, but the personnel and the circumstances of such an enterprise are entirely conjectural. At a later date we find Christian churches in Beroea, Chalcis, Mabbog, Cyrrhus and Samosata, but when and by whom they were founded we do not know. The references in Bardaisan (d 222) to widespread Christian communities in Persia, Media, Edessa, Parthia and Hatra (BLC, p. 60, 11 4–13) may be rhetorical and may be influenced by Acts 2:9–11, but they do at least suggest that in the late Parthian era Christianity had moved not only into Osrhoene, but into other parts of the Orient as well. As far as Osrhoene is concerned, all the factors involved suggest that the Gospel came there from the west and probably from Antioch. But some scholars contend, partly on the basis of a reference in Abercius Marcellus (see later in this chapter), that the Christian faith was first established east of Edessa (in Nisibis or even in Adiabene), and that it reached Edessa from the east rather than from the west.[1] We must concede that if a sizable Jewish community was a desideratum for Christian evangelism, Nisibis, with its larger Jewish settlement, would appear to be a more encouraging goal than Edessa.

We turn now to more specific matters pertaining to the eastward expansion of the Church.

1. Abercius (Avircius) Marcellus.

Abercius was a bishop at Hierapolis (Hieropolis) in Phrygia, c 13 kms north of Laodicea, in the latter half of the second century. Eusebius refers to him as a participant in the Montanist controversy (*Eccl Hist* V. xvi. 1–3). Towards the end of his life he journeyed to Rome, and on his rather circuitous way back, he travelled through Syria and northern Mesopotamia before returning to his see. On his arrival at Hierapolis he composed his

---

[1] J. B. Segal, BSOAS, 28, 1965, pp. 144–45; *Edessa 'the Blessed City'*, Oxford 1970, p. 69; H.J.W. Drijvers, *Bardaisan of Edessa*, Assen 1966, p. 215; J. Neusner, "The Conversion of Adiabene to Christianity," *Numen* 13, 1966, pp. 144–50. For a discussion of this and other problems connected with the early Syriac Church, see R. Murray, *Symbols of Church and Kingdom*, Cambridge, 1975, pp. 4–24.

own epitaph, which is thought to date c 192. In this inscription, discovered in 1883, he records, "And I saw the land of Syria and all its cities—Nisibis I saw when I passed over Euphrates, but everywhere I had brethren."[2] As we have earlier noted, Nisibis came under Roman protection as a result of the war of 162-67, and about thirty years later in the time of Septimius Severus it became a Roman colony. So, despite the hazards of being a frontier fortress, the city might well have harboured a small Christian community, as the bishop's words suggest. The most favourable time for him to visit Nisibis would have been between 167 and 192.

2. The Flood in Edessa, 201.

The *Chronicle of Edessa*[3] records that in the year 201, a disastrous flood which Edessa experienced, destroyed the church of the Christians, which was apparently on low ground near the river Daisan and probably east of the royal palace. Floods were almost endemic in Edessa. Procopius, in recording the flood of April 525 which caused the death of one third of the population, tells us of the measures which Justinian took to cope with this situation (*Buildings* II, vii, 1-16). The Chronicle's passing reference to the Christian church supports the view that Christianity reached Edessa sometime before 201.

3. The Easter Controversy and Osrhoene.

Eusebius tells us (*Eccl Hist* V. xxiii-xxv) that the bishop of Rome, Victor I (189-98), found himself involved in a controversy over the date of Easter, the issue being whether this festival should be celebrated on the fourteenth of Nisan (the position of the Quartodecimans) or on the first Sunday following the fourteenth. Victor ordered the various parts of the Church to hold synods to deal with the problem, and Eusebius records that such councils were held in Palestine, Rome, Pontus, Gaul, Corinth and Osrhoene. The presiding bishops for all these councils are named, except for the one held in Osrhoene. Perhaps Eusebius or his source did not know very much about Christianity in Osrhoene, but the omission of the bishop's name casts some doubt on whether such a synod was actually held there at this

---

[2] W. M. Ramsay, *The Cities and Bishoprics of Phrygia*, 2 vols, Oxford, 1895, 1897; vol 1, part II, pp. 722-29; "Abercius" in vol 1 of *Dictionnaire d'archéologie chrétienne et de liturgie*, Paris, 1907, pp. 66-87; "Abercius, inscription of" in vol 1 of *The Catholic Encyclopaedia*, New York, 1913, pp. 40-41.

[3] The *Chronicle of Edessa*, an anonymous work, dates c 540. The Syriac text is found in CSCO, Scriptores Syri, 3rd series, tomus 4, *Chronica Minora*, ed. by J. Guidi, 1893, pp. 1-13. An ET is presented in the *Journal of Sacred Literature* V, new series, London, 1864, pp. 28-45.

time. If, however, it did meet, there must have been a Christian community in Edessa in the last decade of the second century.

4. The Story of Addai.

There are two literary sources dealing with Addai, Eusebius's *Ecclesiastical History* (I. xiii, 1–22; II. i.6–7) and *The Doctrine of Addai*.[4] Both of these writings, which come from the fourth century but which may rest on earlier sources, tax our credulity so much that some scholars treat this whole story as legendary.[5] The present writer's position is that behind the obvious fiction and didacticism of these narratives, there probably are some useful facts.

According to this tradition, critically examined, the Gospel was brought to Edessa in the second half of the second century by one, Addai (Thaddaeus in Eusebius), who came from Syro-Palestine. Presumably he was an Aramaic-speaking Christian. Since his second successor in the work at Edessa, Paluṭ, had to go to Antioch for episcopal ordination, we may infer that Antioch had something to do with Addai's original mission. Addai, on reaching Edessa, stayed with Tobias, a Palestinian Jew, who may have been in Edessa for business reasons, and subsequently the apostle was received by Abgar, the contemporary ruler of Edessa. Some have thought that the king's name in the story may be fictitious. The most plausible identifications of the king are, Maʿnu VIII bar Maʿnu, 139–63, 165–77, and Abgar VIII bar Maʿnu, 177–212. As there is some limited evidence that the healing ministry exercised by the first century Christians was still in evidence in the western Church in the second century,[6] we cannot rule out the possibility that Addai had the gift of healing and that this helped to make him *persona grata* in Edessa, as *The Doctrine of Addai* suggests. It must, however, remain an open question to what extent the account of Addai's acts of healing has been superimposed upon, or amplified by, local traditions pointing to Edessa as a healing centre (cf Segal, pp. 71–73). If the king in this story was Abgar VIII, it is improbable that he became a Christian until after his return from his visit to Rome, which occurred, as we have earlier noted, probably between 202 and 208.

Addai made many converts, and among them were certain pagan priests, and when they saw what Addai was accomplishing we are told that "they threw down the altars upon which sacrificed before Nebo and Bel their gods," although perhaps significantly, the great altar in the midst of the city was left intact. Addai erected a church whose building costs were paid by the king, and other churches were built in villages surrounding the

---

[4] G. Phillips, *The Doctrine of Addai the Apostle*, London, 1876.
[5] E.g., Baumstark, pp. 27–28.
[6] See L. D. Whitehead, *Psychology, Religion and Healing*, London, 1952, pp. 78–85.

city. When the apostle died in Edessa, the *Doctrine* concedes that there were still pagans and Jews in the city. Addai was succeeded in the headship of the Edessene Christians by Aggai, a royal craftsman and an early convert to the new religion. Aggai lost his life in a dispute with one of Abgar's sons who had remained a pagan, and as he died suddenly without an opportunity to designate his successor formally, the latter, the deacon Paluṭ, went to Antioch where he was ordained by the bishop Serapion. If this is a sound tradition, it gives us an approximate date for Addai, for Serapion was in the diocese of Antioch c 190–211. Addai's career might then be put somewhere in the period 150–90. If he flourished before Bardaisan he might be put in the sixties of this century. It is a curious twist in this Addai tradition that Palut gave his name to the orthodox Christians of Edessa, who, so Ephraim says, were called Palutians. This may have been to distinguish them from Arians or other heretical groups, but Ephraim strongly objects to the practice (Segal, p. 81).

It is of interest that in the *Doctrine of Addai* the apostle's mission in Edessa is not directed primarily to the Jews of that city but to its pagans. This suggests that Addai was not of Jewish extraction, for if he had been, he might, like the apostle Paul (in *Acts*), have used a local synagogue as a forum for proclaiming his message. Jews in fact, despite the claim that some Eddessene Jews became believers, are represented in the *Doctrine* as being at war with the Christians; Jews are labelled "the crucifiers," and Christians are urged not to be friends with them. These anti-Jewish sentiments may throw some light on the age in which the *Doctrine* took its final shape.

It is also noteworthy that twice in the *Doctrine* (Syriac text: p. 17, 11 19–24; p. 37, 11 2–9) reference is made to people from Mesopotamia and/or Assyria hearing the message of Addai, and in the second of these passages they are said to have taken it back home and to have established centres of worship there. This tradition would seem to support the view that Adiabene received the Gospel from Edessa rather that the other way round.

5. The Scriptures.[7]

The Scriptures must have played as vital a role in the growth of the Syriac Church as they did in the expansion of Christianity in the Roman world, but their early history in the Syriac community is obscure. In the Aramaic-using sections of the eastern Church, the Greek translation of the OT (the LXX) may have been known, but more probably the Scriptures of Israel were used in an Aramaic or Syriac version. The origin of this text, usually termed the Old Syriac, can only be conjectured. We might posit, for

---

[7] See also sect 8 in this chapter, "Tatian and the Diatessaron."

instance, that the Syriac OT was the work of Jewish Christians, and it can be argued that behind parts of it are clear signs of Targumic traditions. It is unlikely that in its early stages it was influenced by the LXX, though some scholars have found Greek influence in certain books.[8]

In addition to this Jewish heritage, the western Church had a number of Christian documents in Greek which were used in worship and for instructional purposes. In the latter half of the second century a selection of these, believed to be of apostolic origin, was in the process of becoming the NT. It is usually supposed that, about this same time, these Greek writings were being made available to the eastern Church in Syriac (the Old Syriac NT).[9] In this connection it is to be noted that in *The Doctrine of Addai*, the Scriptures to be read in the churches are described as "the Law, the Prophets, the Gospel, the Epistles of Paul and the Acts of the Twelve Apostles" (Syriac text, p. 46, 11 8–13).

This translation of the Church's Scriptures into Syriac was to have a profound effect upon the development of Syriac literature. A language which had hitherto been used in common speech, in business documents (cf the Deed of Sale, 243 A.D., found at Dura Europus, referred to earlier), and in inscriptions,[10] was now given, ready-made, a literature, which was to serve as a model for prose and poetry as long as the Syriac Church existed. All the important Syriac writers were, in fact, to reflect the language, idiom and thought of the Scriptures.

6. Marcionism.

As Bardaisan, Ephraim and Rabbula all felt obliged to combat Marcion's teaching, some notice of the latter must be taken here. Marcionism probably reached Syria and Osrhoene at the earliest only in the last decades of the second century, which explains why Bardaisan gave it his attention. Whether Marcionites were the first to bring Christianity to certain districts of the Near East, or whether their efforts were directed to reforming (as they would claim) existing churches, we do not know.

Marcion of Pontus first appeared in the western Church, coming to Rome as an orthodox Christian c 138–9. It was in Rome that he met a Syrian teacher, Cerdo, and it is believed that not a few of Marcion's later views were derived from this Cerdo. Valentinus, an Egyptian Gnostic, was in Rome 136–65, and he, too, may have influenced Marcion, as for instance by his denial of the goodness of the Creator and of the Creation. By c 144

---

[8] For a succinct treatment of the essential points of this uncertain subject, see B. J. Roberts, *The Old Testament Text and Versions*, Cardiff, 1951, pp. 217–23.

[9] This is a very involved subject of study, as is illustrated by J. Kerschensteiner, *Der Altsyrische Paulustext* in CSCO 315, Subsidia 37, 1970.

[10] Such as those referred to in ch 1, note 11.

the Roman church had decided that Marcion's ideas were totally unacceptable and he was excommunicated. Subsequently he carried on very successful propaganda in various parts of the Christian world. In fact he founded the Marcionite Church (with bishops, elders, deacons and catechumens), which in the course of its expansion penetrated into and beyond Rome's eastern provinces. When Tertullian wrote *Against Marcion* (the extant third edition was finished 207–08) Marcion seems to have been dead.[11]

Marcion's teaching (and what we know of it comes almost entirely from his opponents) has few of the marks of a carefully worked out position. Perhaps this is what we should expect from a shipmaster who was a layman in theology.

While Marcion could not claim to be a speculative thinker, he felt impelled to offer a view of the world that would support his religious ideas, but what he advocated must be described as a rather crude form of dualism. So he asserts that on the one hand there is the God of Creation, the God of the Jews and of the Jewish Scriptures. This just God fabricated the world out of "material obviously unbegotten and uncreated, and on that reckoning eternal." On the other hand there is a God of pure goodness and love, who has existed from the beginning of time, but who remained unknown until revealed by Christ. This dualism has a counterpart in the field of morality, for Marcion insisted upon a strict mortification of the flesh, implying some deep-seated distinction between flesh and spirit. It was part of his moral code that his followers should renounce worldly pleasures (circus, arena, theatre), abstain from sexual intercourse, and follow a vegetarian diet and a scheme of regular fasting. Marcionite church life was shaped by this code. Only those who followed these rules could be baptized and become church members; others had some lesser status, probably that of catechumens.

The Creator God at some time in the future is to send a Messiah, a warlike hero, who will set up an earthly kingdom. The Christ of history, however, was sent into the world by the God of goodness in the fifteenth year of Tiberius. He did not have a human birth but he assumed a phantom body, and after the crucifixion he returned to the good God. Such a docetic view of Jesus had earlier been known to and condemned by Ignatius of Antioch.

In Marcion's time most of the western Church accepted as authoritative both Israel's Scriptures, generally in the Greek version, and certain specifically Christian writings presently to be known as the NT. It is against this orthodoxy that Marcion's radical teaching about the Scriptures must be viewed. He claimed that the Jewish Scriptures, while a revelation of the Creator god, were useless for Christian purposes. But since Christians need some source of guidance, Marcion proceeded to draw up a canon of

---

[11] *Adversus Marcionem*, ed. and tr. by E. Evans, 2 vols, Oxford, 1972.

Marcionite Scripture. This consisted of (a) the Gospel, which was an edited edition of the Gospel of Luke (probably a form of the pre-canonical western text of Luke), and (b) the Apostolicon, which consisted of ten of Paul's letters, suitably revised to harmonize with Marcion's teaching.[12] Whether the *Antithesis*, a work composed by Marcion himself, using OT passages as a foil for his own views, had the status of Scripture in the same sense as the Gospel and the Apostolicon is not clear.

That Marcionism should have made the impact it apparently did on Syriac Christians in these centuries is testimony both to the religious vacuum of the age, and to the widespread longing for a satisfying over-all view of life.

7. Bardaisan (more accurately Bardaiṣan).

The principal sources for reconstructing the life and work of Bardaisan are (a) the *Book of the Laws of Countries*, written by his pupil Philip (hereafter BLC),[13] (b) various traditions about his cosmology found in several later writers, and (c) the writings of Ephraim (of Nisibis and Edessa), especially his *Hymns against Heresies* and *Prose Refutations*.[14]

Bardaisan was born, seemingly at Edessa, c 154.[15] Of his parents and of their background we have no certain information, although the tradition that they were from the east (Adiabene?) may rest upon a factual basis. From his rather sophisticated interests as reflected in BLC, we may infer that he was well educated, possibly with some exposure to Hellenistic philosophy, and that his private means were such as to give him leisure for religious and ethical discussions with friends (and pupils?). This may explain his traditional association with the court of Abgar VIII (177–212). He speaks of himself in BLC as a member of a Christian group, but when and under what circumstances he turned to Christianity we do not know. At one time he had accepted Chaldean astrology, but he dropped most of this when he became a Christian. The Christians he associated with met together on the first day of the week, fasted on appointed days, and observed the law of Christ. He spells out some of the precepts which Christians adhere to. He says nothing either about Addai or about the beginnings of Christianity in Edessa. His reference to "the new people of us Christians" suggests that the Church was a relative newcomer in the region. This is also implied when he

---

[12] For details of Marcion's treatment of Luke and Paul, see E. C. Blackman, *Marcion and his Influence*, London, 1948.

[13] The Syriac text, with ET, is available in *The Book of the Laws of Countries*, by H.J.W. Drijvers, Assen, 1965.

[14] These and other sources are critically examined by H.J.W. Drijvers in *Bardaiṣan of Edessa*, Assen, 1966, pp. 60–212.

[15] The material for Bardaisan's dates is dealt with in Drijvers, *op cit*, pp. 186–90.

states that Abgar the king was a recent convert to the faith, and when he further asserts that the king, because of his new loyalty, ordered the castration of males in Edessa to cease. Probably this was a part of a local pagan ritual in honor of Tarʿatha.

Bardaisan's religious outlook as reflected in BLC, can best be described as that of an ethical monotheist with a vigorous Christian conviction. He does not, however, elucidate his own Christology. But his faith was strong enough to make him wish to share it with others. According to Ephraim, he made much use of religious poetry to nurture his followers as well as to win converts and combat opponents. It is clear, however, that most of his religious efforts were directed not to the common folk of Edessa nor to the ordinary villagers, but to the educated and affluent segments of the population. When and where he polemized against the Marcionites as Eusebius reports (*Eccl Hist* IV. xxx) is not known. Eusebius also states that Bardaisan never completely freed himself from his earlier Valentinian Gnosticism, but it is impossible to substantiate this charge on the basis of what we know of Bardaisan's ideas.[16]

Political events in Edessa from 216 on must have ended the attractiveness of that city as a home, and the tradition that Bardaisan now went to Armenia is not incredible. If he made a contact with an Indian embassy heading for the emperor Elagabalus (218–22), it must have been c 218–19, but the place of meeting is not known.[17] Whether he had children and whether one was called Harmonius who carried on his father's work cannot be firmly established. He died c 222, but not before he had created a body of disciples, the Bardaisanites, who were to preserve his teachings, with various modifications, for over four hundred years.

When we turn to Bardaisan's teaching and in particular his psychology, we find that he uses in BLC the OT phraseology: man "is created after the image of God," but this is not explicated. He prefers another description: the individual is composed of a triad, spirit, soul and body. The spirit comes from God and joins the soul when the latter descends to the body at the moment of birth. The spirit which has cognitive and volitional functions is free and can do or not do what is true and right. The soul, whose origin is not specifically stated, in descending to its earthly body, passes through the spheres of the seven planets, and these endow it with various qualities, the precise mixture depending on the constellation at the natal moment, and this "fate" determines the person's outward fortunes in this world—wealth, poverty, length of life, degree of health, etc. Just how the process through the sphere of the planets affects the spirit is not clear. The body is of course subject to the laws of nature. But within the limitations imposed by his

---

[16] The opinion of Drijvers, *op cit*, pp. 183–84.

[17] O. de B. Priaulx, "On the Indian Embassies to Rome from the Reign of Claudius, to the Death of Justinian," JRAS 19 (Old Series), 1862, pp. 274–98.

physical nature and his horoscope, man is a free spirit. Bardaisan affirms that "good is natural to man," and in this sense his view of man is an optimistic one. Bardaisan's analysis of the constituent elements in man made it impossible for him to accept the commonly held Christian view that at the last day, the dead would be resurrected. His theory was that good and potential evil exist in the body, but only free will exercised by the soul (or by the spirit?) can cause evil to become an actuality. At death the body disintegrates, but the soul rises upward to God.[18]

Whereas in his psychology, Bardaisan offers a view of man which tallies to some degree with human experience, in his cosmology he presents a picturesque but entirely speculative account of the origin of the universe. It appears that he drew upon various strata of pagan mythology, including possibly some of Iranian origin, and in aiming at a synthesis of this disparate material, he did not resolve all its inherent contradictions and tensions.

In the beginning, so his scheme goes, there were four original and pure elements—light, wind, fire and water. Above them was their Lord. In the depths there was darkness. All this implies that the elements and the darkness eternally exist with God. Then by chance the four elements moved about and in the confusion darkness became mingled with them. The four elements then call upon the Lord for help, and in response he dispatches the Word of Thought to create order (cf Wisdom in Pro 8:22-31, and the Logos in John 1:1-3), but the Word was only partly successful in separating the four pure elements from the darkness. Our world, a mixture of pure elements and darkness, was thus created (another view of the creation, found in some lines quoted by Ephraim, will be ignored here).[19] At the same time the Lord created the seven planets that through them he could, in part, direct human fortunes. The human body is, like the natural world, a mixture of pure elements and darkness, and as we have earlier noted, it perishes at death. One cannot but wonder what happens to the pure elements and the darkness which the body is said to contain. The present world is to last for 6000 years and then there will be a new world with no darkness in it.

It is difficult to establish Bardaisan's view of Christ. In BLC Christ appears as a teacher or law-giver, but in the cosmology he seemingly has another role. He may be identical with the Word of Thought mentioned in the previous paragraph. Later Syriac writers, the earliest being Philoxenus of Mabbog, state that Bardaisan held a docetic view of Christ, and this opinion is endorsed by Drijvers.[20]

Apart from his role as a Christian leader, Bardaisan stands out as a formative influence in the development of Syriac as a langauge of both

---

[18] Drijvers, *op cit*, p. 154.
[19] Drijvers, *op cit*, p. 145.
[20] Drijvers, *op cit*, pp. 196-97, 221.

prose and poetry. While the BLC is the work of his pupil Philip, it is usually assumed that it faithfully reflects the teacher's literary style. Syriac now appears for the first time as an instrument for the rational exposition of religious and philosophical ideas. This use of the language in prose as well as Bardaisan's employment of it in his poetry, were to set a pattern to which all later Syriac writers were, in one way or another, to be indebted.

8. Tatian and the Diatessaron.

Tatian of the second century was a pagan from "Assyria," which probably means either northern Mesopotamia or Adiabene, and like his contemporary, Lucian of Samosata, he journeyed westwards in pursuit of a Greek education. From Athens he proceeded to Rome where he became a Christian, attaching himself to the school of Justin Martyr. He then returned to Athens and while there he wrote his *Address to the Greeks*,[21] a literary onslaught against all Greek culture. Apparently he went back to Rome, but left after the death of Justin in 165. It must have been about this time that he espoused encraticism, a somewhat extreme form of asceticism. His goal was now his old homeland, but en route he spent some time in Pisidia, Cilicia and Antioch. It is thought that he reached Mesopotamia or Adiabene c 172. He was still a Christian but his ultra-spirituality did not make his presentation of the Gospel an easy thing for most easterners to accept. Nonetheless he gained adherents, and through them, if not directly himself, he had a share in the development of asceticism in the Syriac Church.

Tatian's unique contribution to the Greek and Syriac Churches was his Diatessaron ("through the four"). The term Diatessaron suggests that four gospels were the basis for this work, though Baumstark maintains that a fifth source, the Gospel of the Hebrews, was also used.[22] As we have earlier noted, in the mid-second century the NT was in the making in the western Church, and it included the four Greek Gospels. The task which Tatian set himself was to turn these four documents into one continuous narrative.[23] This was doubtless intended primarily for the Greek-using churches, and it would be made from a current Greek text of the Gospels. A fragment of the Greek Diatessaron which was found at Dura Europus in 1933, and which

---

[21] ET by J. E. Ryland in *Ante-Nicene Fathers* 2, reprinted Grand Rapids, 1956, pp. 65–82; cf Eusebius, *Eccl Hist*, IV. xxviii–xxix.

[22] A. Vööbus, *Studies in the History of the Gospel Text in Syriac*, CSCO 128, Subsidia 3, Louvain, 1951, p. 19; Eusebius refers to Hegesippus's (second century) use of the Gospel according to the Hebrews (*Eccl Hist*, IV, xxii. 8).

[23] ET by H. W. Hogg from an Arabic text, thought to be a translation from the Syriac, in *Ante-Nicene Fathers* 10, reprinted in Grand Rapids, 1965, pp. 35–129. Tatian's probable procedure is reconstructed by P. Carrington, *The Early Christian Church*, Cambridge, 1957, vol 2, pp. 210–11. For a more recent study of the Diatessaron, see J. Molitor in OC 53 (1969), pp. 1–88, 54 (1970), pp 96–117, 55 (1971), pp. 1–61.

must belong to the early third century, is thought by many to support the view that Tatian's work was done originally in Greek.²⁴

Tatian's motives in compiling the Diatessaron can only be surmised. If he was liturgically minded, he may have hoped to produce something more suitable than the four separate Gospels for regular Sunday readings in church. Or he may have felt that if there was only one Christian Gospel (cf Gal 1:6-9), the literary records of its beginnings should also be one. It is also possible, since he lived during the early expansion of Marcionism, that he felt impelled to counter Marcion's "Gospel" by offering Christians the four traditional Gospels but in one unified presentation. A. Vööbus claims that Tatian edited his basic texts to make them conform to his own Encratite views.²⁵

This Greek Diatessaron was presently translated into Syriac for the benefit of the eastern Church. Whether this was done by Tatian himself or by some of his followers we do not know. It became known in Syriac as 'wnglywn d mḥlṭ', "the Gospel of the Mixed." As in the later part of the second century there was probably a translation into Syriac (the Old Syriac) of at least some of the books to be known presently as the NT, the question arises, Is the language of the Syriac Diatessaron indebted to the Old Syriac? This matter, however, is too involved to be pursued in this present study. What we do know is that the Syriac Diatessaron became widely used in the Syriac Church until the fifth century. In the *Doctrine of Addai* the one reference to the Diatessaron is obscure (Syriac text, p. 36, l 17). Later in the *Doctrine* (p. 46, ll 8–13), in a list of of books read in church, the "Gospel" appears in the singular, which suggests that the Diatessaron is indicated.

9. Julius Africanus.

Africanus, born in Aelia Capitolina (Jerusalem), was a lay Christian writer who enjoyed the favour of the emperors Elagabalus (218–22) and Alexander Severus (222–35). He is best known for his *Chronographies*, a synchronization of man's history from Adam to 221 A.D., a work extant only in fragments preserved in later sources.²⁶ He was in Adiabene in 195 and later in Edessa, where he became an intimate friend of Abgar VIII and of his son Maʿnu IX. He speaks of Abgar as a holy man, but he says nothing about the king's Christian faith or about any form of organized Christianity in Edessa.

---

²⁴ See B. M. Metzger in *Biblical Archaeologist*, 10.2, May 1947, pp. 42–44. For the text of this fragment see *The Excavations at Dura-Europos*, Final Report V, Part I, ed. by C. W. Welles, R. O. Fink, J. F. Gilliam, New Haven, 1959, pp. 73–74.

²⁵ *History of Asceticism in the Syrian Orient*, vol 1, CSCO 184, Subsidia 14, Louvain, 1958, pp. 40–45.

²⁶ H. Gelzer, *Sexture Julius Africanus und die Byzantinische Chronographie*, Part I, Leipzig, 1885, pp. 3, 8–9.

10. The Chronicle of Edessa.[27]

The *Chronicle*, edited c 540, made use of various documents no longer extant, but its data on the early period of Edessa's history are very sparse. It says nothing about Addai, gives only dates for Marcion and Bardaisan, and, as earlier noted, tells of the flood of 201 at some length, mentioned *en passant* the destruction of the church of the Christians.

11. The Odes of Solomon.

The *Odes of Solomon*[28] are forty-two hymns of varying lengths (27 has three verses, 7 has twenty-six verses), which come from an early Christian writer (or writers). Five of the *Odes*, in whole or in part, are in a Coptic manuscript which is dated in the third century. That part of a Greek codex (Bodmer Papyrus XI) which preserves number 11, is also thought to come from the third century. Certain features of the Greek suggest that it is a translation from a Semitic original. A Syriac manuscript, which dates tenth to thirteenth centuries, contains Odes 17:7b to 42:20. Another Syriac manuscript, in the John Rylands Library, which contains all of the Odes except 1, 2, and the beginning of 3, is not older than the fifteenth century. This textual evidence is usually taken to suggest that the Odes were originally composed in Syriac.

Many of the Odes are relatively simple compositions reflecting a genuine Christian piety, as in 5, 8, 9, 14, etc., while others are somewhat more contrived and wordy, as in 4, 7, 11, 23, etc. The language is that of the Scriptures, with, at times, a special interest in Johannine terminology. Just as the Lord God sometimes speaks in the Psalter (e.g., Ps 91:14–16), so in these Odes Christ is occasionally the speaker (e.g., 8:9–19; 10:4–6; 17:6–16; etc.). The theology of the poems is basically that of the NT (cf Father, son and Holy Spirit in 19:2; 23:22); an unusual concept is that of milk coming to the faithful from the breasts of Christ (8:14), or from the breasts of the Father (19:2–3); I Cor 3:1–2 and I Peter 2:2 do not offer a true parallel to this uncommon idea. Curiously, for a Christian writer, there are only a few minor references to Jesus' life (7:12; 17:13; 24:1–2; 28:18; 31:8–13; 42:5–6), and none to the sacraments, to any form of asceticism, to the Church (unless the virgin of 33:5 is the Church), or to its organization (cf 20:1 where the odist claims to be a priest). The "singer" of 7:22 may be an allusion to a choral group in a service of worship; cf. "Glory to you our head" in 17:17; "Let all the Lord's offspring praise him" in 41:1. The only

---

[27] See note 3 above.

[28] A critical edition of the Syriac text of the Odes, with ET, is found in J. H. Charlesworth, *The Odes of Solomon*, Oxford, 1973. A bibliography on the Odes, down to 1971, is included in pp. 149–67.

allusion to anything that can be identified with the milieu of the odist is to "persecutors" in 5:4; 23:20, which may refer to the Roman persecutions of Christians in the second or third centuries (cf "seducers" in 23:20; "adversaries" in 25:11; "corruptor" in 33:1; 38:9; "deceiver" in 38:10, 16).

It would seem to be consonant with the limited evidence available to conclude that the Odes belong to a Syriac-speaking group of Christians in north-east Syria living probably in the latter half of the second century. H. J. W. Drijvers in *Bardaisan of Edessa* (p. 209) suggests the date of c 125, and Antioch or Edessa as the place of origin.

The data marshalled above point to the conclusion that Christianity had reached Edessa and probably other centres in Osrhoene in the latter half of the second century. But of the organization and structure of this nascent Syriac Christianity we know very little. Ignatius, as we have ealier seen, was concerned about leadership in the Church, and if we assume that the first Christians to reach Osrhoene were from Antioch, we might suppose that they would try to set up structures for the new churches similar to what they had known at home. The *Doctrine of Addai* makes references to deacons and elders (presbyters), and to the priesthood, but how far this nomenclature corresponds with the situation in the late second century it is impossible to say. The *Acts of Thomas*, which seems to belong to the third century, may reflect in some respects a second century situation in which the Church is not yet fully structured, and where one type of believer can be portrayed as a wandering Christian who is a doer of miracles and a preacher of a somewhat truncated version of the Gospel.

The statement of Eusebius that "from that day (when Thaddaeus worked in Edessa) to this the whole city of the Edessenes has been dedicated to the name of Christ" (*Eccl Hist* II. i. 7) appears to be a gross exaggeration. The Christians about 200 A.D. were probably a very small minority in the city's population. Even the *Doctrine of Addai* acknowledges that there were pagans and Jews in Edessa at the time of Addai's death. This is confirmed by a limited number of tomb inscriptions found in the neighbourhood of modern Urfa. Some of these are dated (one in 201-02 and another 208-09), and insofar as they contain no allusions or symbols that are specifically Christian or Jewish, it can be assumed that they are pagan (Segal, pp. 27-8).

If Christianity reached Edessa in the second half of the second century, it is likely that soon after this the Gospel was taken to various centres in the east, particularly to Nisibis. This in fact is suggested in the *Doctrine of Addai*. We have earlier noted that Abercius Marcellus found Christians in Nisibis in the late second century. Nisibis, at one time a city under the control of Adiabene (Josephus, *Ant* XX. 66-8), was by reason of its location inevitably drawn into the recurring border wars between Rome and Parthia. After the struggles of 162-67 (in the reign of Marcus Aurelius), Nisibis emerged as a friend of Rome, and thirty years later, at the end of the war of 194–98 in the time of Septimius Severus, Nisibis became the capital of the new Roman province of Mesopotamia. Under both Caracalla and Macrinus Nisibis was again involved in the Parthian wars, and in fact the last battle between the Roman and Parthian forces was fought near the city in 217. We can only speculate on the effects of this fighting on the Christian cause in Nisibis.

Part II.
In Sasanian Times (224-651 A.D.)

Chapter 3.
The Milieu of the West Syriac Church

1. The Roman East to the Reign of Diocletian (284-305).

The poor documentation for Roman history in the third century gives us only limited information about the Roman East in this period. We know that the murder of Alexander Severus and his mother, Julia Mamaea, in 235 ushered in a period of political anarchy in the Roman world, as is illustrated by the fact that between 235 and the accession of Diocletian in 284, at least eighteen emperors held power, thirteen of whom were murdered to make room for a successor. In what ways these recurrent crises adversely affected the administration of the Roman Orient can readily be imagined.

One specific example of what could happen in the Roman East is supplied by Palmyra. This small Arab state became a beneficiary of the breakdown of Roman authority in the eastern provinces. Under its ruler, Odenathus, Palmyra extended the territory under its control, and when the Palmyrene king gave his support to Gallienus against a rival, the emperor gladly accepted this helping hand and bestowed on the Arab prince the title of *imperator*. Odenathus, with a well-trained army, attacked Persian forces that had penetrated Syria and Asia Minor, and he actually took the offensive against Persia. After his murder in 267 in Syria, Odenathus was succeeded by his widow, Zenobia, who, acting as regent for their young son, continued the policy of her late husband. When Aurelian came to the throne in 270 he had to accept the fact that Palmyrene forces were now in Egypt. It was not until 272 that the emperor was able to move against these Arab colleagues whose fall was almost as dramatic as their rise. The Palmyrene forces were defeated in 272 near Antioch and a little later that year Palmyra itself was taken, and in retaliation for a rebellion two months later, destroyed so completely that it never regained its commercial importance. Zenobia was taken prisoner and she subsequently graced Aurelian's triumph in Rome.

The Accession of Diocletian in 284 brought back for a while settled government to a troubled Roman world. This was facilitated by the emperor's appointment of another Augustus (Maximian), and a little later two Caesars were chosen (Constantius and Galerius) to assist the Augusti. Connected with this sharing of the imperial power, a number of administrative changes were made. Mesopotamia was the name given to an

38 / HISTORY OF SYRIAC CHRISTIANITY

area east of the Khabur river, and it included five small provinces east of the Tigris, ceded by the Persians in 298. Its capital was at Amid. To the west lay the principality of Osrhoene.

It was in the third and early fourth centuries that Roman emperors mounted their first serious persecutions of the Christian Church. These began with the emperor Decius (249-51), who, faced with a troubled Roman world, concluded that the strengthening of Rome's traditional religion was essential to the preservation of the state. Those who would not acknowledge the old gods were treated mercilessly. The most serious trial to which a Roman emperor subjected Christians was due to Diocletian who was an enthusiast for Roman traditions, religion, and discipline, and who felt that only in loyalty to these values was there any future for the empire. So, beginning in 303, and probably encouraged by his Caesar, Galerius, he passed a series of edicts unfavourable to Christians. The worship of the gods was savagely enforced; Christian books were burned, church buildings looted and destroyed, etc. (see Eusebius, *Eccl Hist* VII. xxx. 22; VIII. v.1-vi.10; xiii. 9-11; CAH XII, pp. 665-71). It was a baptism of fire for the Church, but happily its full force began to diminish with the retirement of Diocletian from the emperorship in 305.

2. Persia: the Founding of the Sasanian Dynasty.

It seems ironical that at a time when the Parthian king, Artabanus V, was having considerable success against the Romans in Mesopotamia, a movement was under way in the province of Fars (Persis) which was to lead to the downfall of the Parthian state. Of the details of this rebellion and the background of its leader, Ardashir, we need only note that in Fars the old Persian traditions appear to have been kept alive, and that they finally inspired Ardashir, whose ancestor was one, Sasan, and whose family connections were in Istakhr (near Persepolis), to assert himself against his Parthian overlord. The ensuing military struggle ended when Artabanus was killed in battle in 224. Two years later Ardashir was crowned king,[1] which meant that after a lapse of five and a half centuries, the Persians had regained power in Iran. Ardashir had to do considerable fighting to consolidate his position, but when he died in 241, he left a strong kingdom to his son Shapur I.[2] The dynasty thus established was to retain its position in Persia until the seventh century.

The half century spanning the reigns of Ardashir I and Shapur I (241-72) proved in some respect to be an augury of the life of the new dynasty. Many things which appeared or developed in these years were to become

---
[1] For the bas-relief depicting Ardashir's investiture, see A.U. Pope (ed), *A Survey of Persian Art*, VII, Oxford, reissue 1964-65, plates 154 A, 162 C.

[2] On the uncertainty regarding the dates of Ardashir I and Shapur I, see R.N. Frye, *The Heritage of Persia*, London, 1962, pp 208-09.

features of the Sasanian world down to the rise of Islam. Of the internal developments of the third century, the most important was the revival of Zoroastrianism. As, however, this renaissance of Zoroastrianism did not affect Syriac Christians in the Roman empire, our treatment of it is to be found later in this study in chapters 7 and 8.

Another result of the advent of the Sasanians was political and concerned Persia's western frontier. The wars which Parthia had so frequently waged with the Romans were now to be continued by the Persians. From the vantage point of a later age we can see that these conflicts settled nothing and in the end they were to prove catastrophic for both sides. Ardashir lost little time in renewing this struggle. In 230 he invaded northern Mesopotamia, and while the siege of Nisibis was unsuccessful, cavalry detachments penetrated both Syria and Cappadocia. The situation was serious enough to demand the Roman emperor's action. After a vain attempt to negotiate with Ardashir, Alexander Severus moved his forces out of Antioch in 232, but of the three divisions of his army, only the one which headed for Atropatene recorded limited success. The fighting terminated in 233 (Severus had to go to the Roman West against the Germans), but Ardashir resumed it in 237–38, overrunning Mesopotamia and taking Nisibis and Carrhae. In 241 the Persian king died, but his son, Shapur I, carried on the war with Rome. In 242 (or 243) the Persians penetrated Syria and threatened Antioch, but the Romans under the young emperor Gordion (238–44) counterattacked and recovered both Carrhae and Nisibis. There was actually peace in the time of the emperor Philip (244–49), but after the latter's death, Shapur invaded and occupied Armenia, and about the same time another Persian force attacked Mesopotamia and points west; in 254 Nisibis was captured, but Edessa resisted the Persians successfully. Hatra was taken, Syria was devastated and Antioch burned,[3] and in 256 the fortress at Dura Europus was taken and never again held by the Romans. In this deteriorating situation the details of Roman action are somewhat uncertain. It is probable that it was in 256 that the emperor Valerian came to Antioch, and after some inconsequential campaigning against the Persians in Cappadocia, in 260 he attempted to meet a Persian attack against Edessa, but in some way which is not clear, the Roman emperor was taken prisoner as was a large part of his army. Valerian died in captivity some years later.[4] Shapur was now able to take Antioch again (260), while he sent other Persian forces into Cilicia and Cappadocia. Much booty and many prisoners are reported to have been taken. On his return march to Persia, Shapur was attacked near Carrhae by Odenathus of Palmyra and lost many of the spoils of war which he had acquired.

---

[3] On the date of Shapur's first capture of Antioch, see G. Downey, *A History of Antioch in Syria*, Princeton, 1961, Excursus 5, pp 587–95.

[4] The capture of Valerian is commemorated in no less than five Sasanian bas-reliefs. For the one at Naqsh-i-Rustam, see A.U. Pope (ed), *op cit*, VII, plate 155 A.

3. The Era of Constantine: the Beginnings of the Byzantine Empire.

Constantine, undisputed master of the Roman world, 324–37, is rightly associated with a complete reversal of Rome's attitude towards the Christian Church, but the recorded details of this change are somewhat confused. It is clear that the persecution initiated by Diocletian had failed to break the Church, and it appears that even Galerius realized this, for in 311, a few days before his death, he issued an edict giving Christians a legal right to exist as Christians (cf Eusebius, *Eccl Hist* VIII. xvii. 1–10). Constantine and Licinius were also aware that the persecution of Christians was ineffectual, and they therefore determined to come to terms with the Church. Whether or not there was ever a formal Edict of Milan, the fact remains that in 313, the two emperors, Constantine and Licinius, agreed that the persecution of Christians should cease, and that the principle of religious toleration should be observed throughout the empire (Eusebius, *Eccl Hist* X. v. 1–14). In the years which followed, Constantine showed himself increasingly favourable to the Christian cause, and shortly before death he received Christian baptism.

The advantages to Christianity of religious toleration do not need to be spelled out here, but it is important to note one serious disadvantage. All of Constantine's successors except Julian (360–63), were nominal Christians, and they used their authority to further the interests of the Church. Thus slowly Christianity and the State were increasingly intermingled, and the toleration of dissent, whether within the Church or outside of it, was gradually eroded.

What was to happen frequently in the future is illustrated by Constantine's summoning of a Council of the Church to meet at Nicaea in Bithynia in 325 to deal with the Arian controversy. This dispute, which began in Alexandria (the main point raised by Arius being whether Christ was a created or an eternal being), set the eastern parts of the Roman world by the ears. It was primarily a theological issue, but Constantine was concerned with it principally as a political problem which caused unacceptable tumults in the eastern provinces. When the Council produced the Nicene Creed, it seemed to settle the matter, but in fact Arianism lived on until the Council of Constantinople in 381. Furthermore, subtle theological issues had been raised which were to engender deep-seated divisions in the eastern Church in the next century.

Next to his toleration and support of the Church, Constantine's chief claim to fame is his choice of Byzantium as the new eastern capital of the Roman world. "New Rome" (later Constantinople) was dedicated on May 11, 330, and in the years that followed, it became in fact the political, economic, cultural and religious centre of the empire. When the western provinces were lost to the various Germanic invaders, the eastern regions, centering in Constantinople, survived to preserve the legacy of Rome, and this legacy, compounded with Christian and oriental elements, was to produce the unique phenomenon known to us as Byzantine civilization.

4. Rome and the Barbarian Invasions.

The details of the long series of events whereby various tribes, mostly Germanic, moved or forced their way into the western parts of the Roman empire do not concern us here. The results of these invasions were that Roman power in the West came to an end and that in its place there arose independent barbarian states. Although Justinian, through a series of wars from 533 to 555, won back some of this territory (as it turned out, only temporarily), we can see that it was impossible at this point in history to check the disintegration of the western half of the empire.

Rome's eastern provinces fared better in meeting the invaders than did the western ones. It is true that there was great trouble around the Danube and later in Illyria and Greece with Avars, Slavs, and Bulgars, and that in 617 the Avars in a series of destructive raids reached Constantinople and took back with them 270,000 captives. On the whole, however, Constantinople and most of its European territory and all of its Asiatic provinces emerged intact from these assaults. This meant that the Greek Church, and this includes the Syriac Christians under the patriarchate of Antioch, suffered no disruption in its life comparable to what the Latin Church experienced.

5. Persia's Confrontation with the Roman World from Varahran I (273-76) to Khusro I (531-79).

The three centuries under review exhibit a replay, with minor variations, of the struggle which Ardashir I and Shapur I had earlier initiated with Rome. The net gains of these wars to either party were negligible. To illustrate this political seesaw we cite a few examples. In 296 the Persian king Nerseh (Narses, 293-302) invaded Syria, and Galerius, Diocletian's Caesar, was called from Illyricum to drive him back. It was not until 298 that a peace was worked out. Its terms included the acknowledgement of Roman control over both Mesopotamia and five small regions east of the Tigris. Shapur II (309-79) commenced another war by an attack on and capture of the Roman fortress of Amida (359), and this in turn provoked the invasion of Persia by the emperor Julian in 363. The death of Julian in June of this year ended the Roman campaign, and Julian's successor, Jovian, concluded a peace which gave up most of the gains of the treaty of 298, including the city of Nisibis. It was the emperor Theodosius I (379-95) who realized that these frequent wars were senseless, and who made a treaty with Varahran IV (388-99) c 389, whereby Armenia—usually a source of contention—was partitioned between the two empires.

After a long period of peace, marred only by brief conflicts in 421-22 and 440-42, hostilities were once more renewed in the reign of Kavad I

(488–531) when the Persians invaded Roman Armenia. This was the first of a series of wars which continued into the sixth century. The struggle in the time of the emperor Anastasius (491–518) has given us the Syriac *Chronicle of Joshua the Stylite* (ed W. Wright, Cambridge, 1882), which is a contemporary account of the years 495–507, with special reference to the districts in which Edessa and Amid (Amida) were situated, and which ends with a reference to the truce made in 507. The *Chronicle* notes that Arab tribesmen, irrespective of whether they were pro-Persia or pro-Byzantium, generally found these wars between the two empires quite profitable (LXXXVIII). Another war began in 528, but the death of Kavad and the accession of Khusro I in 531 led to a treaty in 532 known as "the Endless Peace" (Procopius, *Wars* I. xxii. 1–19). This treaty was broken in 540 when Persian forces raided Syria (*Wars* II. v. 1–xiii. 29). Many cities, including Edessa, ransomed themselves with payments of gold and silver, but Antioch refused to do so and was almost completely destroyed and the usual prisoners were sent back to Persia (*Wars* II. viii. 1–ix. 18; x. 6–9; xiii. 1–6). For Procopius's account of Justinian's rebuilding of Antioch, see *Buildings* II. x. 1–25). On Khusro's good treatment of the Syrian prisoners, who were settled near Ctesiphon in a new site called "Antioch of Khusro," see *Wars* II. xiv. 1–4. In 544 Khusro led another attack upon Syria, his primary objective being the capture of Edessa. Procopius devotes much space to the siege of the city (*Wars* II. xxvi. 1 to xxvii. 46), a siege which terminated when the Persian king accepted a large ransom from the citizens and agreed to leave the city unharmed. A five-year truce was signed in 545, and renewed in 551 and 557, and finally peace was agreed upon in 562. But the emperor Justin II broke the agreement in 572 and besieged Nisibis. Khusro relieved the beleagured city and proceeded to invest the Roman fortress of Dara (Daras), a stronghold greatly strengthened by Justinian (Procopius, *Buildings* II. i. 4–27). Another Persian force invaded Syria, sacked Apamea, and returned to its base with much booty and thousands of prisoners. The fall of Dara in November 573 was an appalling disaster for Constantinople (see John of Ephesus, *Eccl Hist*, VI. 5), the shock of which led to Justin's death in 578. John of Ephesus states that the prisoners taken by the Persians at Apamea, Dara and other centres numbered 275,000 (*Eccl Hist*, VI. 19). Justin's successor, Tiberius II (578–82), obtained a truce from Khusro for which he paid the Persian king three talents of gold a year, but when the truce ran out, the indecisive hostilities were resumed.

6. The Arabs of Northern Arabia.

The Ghassanid Arabs of north-west Arabia.

The Ghassanid Arabs, who claimed descent from a South Arabian tribe, moved to the north-west of the Arabian peninsula towards the end of the third century A.D. The region in which they settled was south of Damascus (Gaulanitis in Josephus), and one of their better known cities was Bostra

(Bozra, Busra). Over a period of time they became Christians of the Monophysite stamp. They attained some importance in the Byzantine world in the sixth century. Their king Ḥarith II (Aretas, c 530-72) was appointed by Justinian as lord over all the Arab tribes on the eastern borders of Syria (Procopius, *Wars* I. xvii. 47-8), and fought with Belisarius on the Byzantine side against the Persians (*Wars* I. xviii. 7, 26, 35-6; II. xvi. 5; xix. 11-12, 15-49). Ḥarith's son, al-Mundhir, was an influential figure in the Byzantine world, and in any struggle with Persia, his Arab forces played an important role. But the Arabs as allies were somewhat volatile and they could get out of hand, and in an attempt to deal with this, we find the following paragraph in the peace treaty between Justinian I and Khusro I, negotiated in 562: "The Saracen allies of either state shall on their part, too, abide by the terms, and neither shall those of the Persians take arms against the Romans, nor those of the Romans against the Persians" (Menander Protector, quoted by P.N. Ure, *Justinian and His Age*, Harmondsworth, 1951, p 97).

The cooperation between the Ghassanids and Constantinople terminated c 580 for reasons that we need not go into here. Al-Mundhir was seized by the Byzantines, condemned for treason, and exiled to Sicily. His son, al-Nuʻman, who later ventured to raid Byzantine territory, was also apprehended and removed to Constantinople. Continuing Ghassanid attacks on Palestine and Phoenicia, really plundering forays, posed great difficulties to the Byzantines, who were committed to traditional ideas of warfare and could not cope effectively with the Arab tactics. Michel the Syrian tells us of a situation in 610 when Arabs pillaged many parts of Syria (*Chr de Michel*, 2, XI. i, p 401). The emperor Heraclius must have made some reconciling gesture to the Ghassanids, for Jabalah, the last of their rulers, fought on the side of the Byzantines in the battle of Yarmuk in 636 against the Muslim invaders. Jabalah survived the battle, adopted Islam but later renounced it, and spent his remaining days in Constantinople.

The Lakhmids of north-east Arabia.

In the early third century A.D. a number of Arabs calling themselves Tanukh moved into the region west of the Euphrates and settled in and around al-Ḥirah, which soon became their capital. One of their early leaders was ʻAmar . . . ibn-Lakhm, and it was from him that the Lakhmids took their name. They are often referred to as Ṭayyaye (Syr *ṭyyʼ*). Their location in southern Iraq made it prudent for them to cooperate with the Persians, and their fifth century leader, al-Mundhir I (418-62) fought beside the forces of Varahran V against the Byzantines. In the sixth century al-Mundhir III (c 505-64) was the outstanding Lakhmid king, and his raids on Syria caused much devastation (Procopius, *Wars* I. xvii. 1, 29-46, etc.). Al Nuʻman III (c 580-602) was the last of the Lakhmid dynasty and the only Lakhmid king to embrace Christianity (of the Nestorian variety). While the Lakhmids still had their own head from 602 on (he was actually a Ṭayyiʼ

Arab), he also had beside him a Persian official who represented the Sasanian king. This dimunition of Lakhmid independence doubtless caused some resentment, and may have been a factor which facilitated the Muslim conquest of lower Iraq by 637.

7. The Final Struggle between Persia and Byzantium.

The death of Hormizd IV (590) put an end temporarily to Persia's war with Constantinople, but it ushered in for Khusro II, Hormizd's son and successor, a very turbulent year. One of Persia's great generals, Varahran Chobin, refused to acknowledge the new king, and a civil war began, with Khusro getting the worst of it. The king fled for refuge to Roman Circesium and wrote to the emperor Maurice (582–602) seeking his aid. Maurice, despite criticism from the Senate, decided to assist Khusro. According to Michel the Syrian (*Chr de Michel*, 2, X, xxiii, pp 371–72), Khusro then went to Edessa to await the forces being sent by Maurice. With additional help from Persian Armenia, Khusro was now able to invade his own country, and by 591 he had captured Ctesiphon and was established as Persia's legitimate ruler. This same year a peace treaty was signed with Maurice.

This comparatively stable situation in the relations between Persia and Byzantium might have continued if Maurice could have kept his throne. But he lost his popularity with all sections of Byzantine society, and in 602 a revolution occurred, with Phocas, an army officer, being proclaimed king and with Maurice and at least five of his male children being murdered. When Khusro heard of the death of Maurice, he was so enraged that he determined to avenge his benefactor's death (*Chr de Michel*, 2, X. xxv, p 377), and so began another struggle between Persia and Byzantium. As matters turned out, it was a fateful contest for both parties.

Khusro did not act hastily, and it was not until the spring of 604, after careful preparations, that he invaded Byzantine territory. The great Byzantine stronghold of Dara fell in 606 and Edessa in 609. It was only in 610 that the Persians crossed the Euphrates and captured Hierapolis and Aleppo. In 611 they took Antioch (weakened by internal dissensions), and retained control of the city until 629.

The inability of Phocas to stop the Persian advance was only one of the circumstances that led to his downfall, which was brought about by a revolt started in Africa, the upshot of which was that Heraclius was crowned emperor in Constantinople on October 5, 610. It was not a propitious time to become head of the Byzantine world, for the continuing war with Persia was but one of the many problems to which Heraclius fell heir. His first effort on the eastern front was made in 612 when the Byzantines recaptured Caesarea in Cappadocia, but their attempt to retake Antioch was unsuccessful. The Persians responded to these actions by advancing into Syria, Palestine and Egypt. Damascus was captured and early in 614 the

Persians entered Palestine. Jerusalem was only taken after a siege, and among its spoils of war which went to Persia was Christendom's Holy Cross. From Palestine the Persian forces proceeded to Egypt. Their occupation of Egypt was completed by 620, and they remained in control of it until 629. Another Persian force under Sahin entered Asia Minor in 615-16 and reached Chalcedon. Heraclius is said to have agreed with Sahin to negotiate a peace settlement, but Khusro turned down this overture.

In the meantime Heraclius was preparing for an invasion of Persia. He first made peace with the Avars who were a perennial threat to Constantinople, and at the same time collected, organized, equipped and trained a new army, a task which took all of 620 and part of 621. Heraclius, who was to lead the campaign himself, left the capital in April 621 and in the fall of 622 he set out from Caesarea in Cappadocia and presently had his first engagement with the enemy.

Heraclius's operations against the Persians have been extensively studied,[5] but here we shall treat them only in summary. There were three campaigns, 622-23, 624-26 and 627-28. In the third of these, Heraclius moved into the Caucasus region, taking Tiflis in Iberia in the summer of 627. He then advanced southwards and in December he fought a successful battle near Nineveh. At this point Heraclius suggested a peace settlement, but Khusro stubbornly rejected the proposal. The Byzantine forces subsequently crossed the Great Zab, the Little Zab and the Diyala rivers, and reached the Persian royal residence, Dastagird, from which Khusro now fled and which was taken by Heraclius in January 628.

Meanwhile dissatisfaction with Khusro's handling of the war broke into an open revolt, and on February 24, 628, the palace at Ctesiphon was overrun and Khusro was captured and later killed. The next day, Kavad II, Khusro's eldest son, was crowned king (on these events, see *Bk of Gov* 2, I. xxxv, pp 112-16). Kavad, determined to make peace, sent a letter to this effect to Heraclius. The latter accepted the proposal but we do not know what terms were agreed upon. Heraclius then turned homewards, leaving his brother Theodore in charge of the army. The emperor received a tumultuous welcome when he reached Constantinople in September 628.

Back in Asia, Sahrbaraz, who had administered Syria and Egypt, presented a problem, and it looked as though Theodore would have to use force to take the eastern provinces from him. Heraclius, however, was determined to negotiate with Sahrbaraz, and in April 629 he went to Caesarea which he made his headquarters. The two men met in July, and it was agreed that all Byzantine territory occupied by the Persians should be given up and the Holy Cross returned to Christian custody.

---

[5] See V. Minorsky, BSOAS XI, 1943-46, "Roman and Byzantine Campaigns in Atropatene," pp 248-58; A.N. Stratos, *Byzantium in the Seventh Century* (tr by M. Ogilvie-Grant), Amsterdam, I, 1968, covering the years 602-34.

At the beginning of 630 Heraclius left Edessa, where he had been checking on the Persian withdrawal, and came to Hierapolis where he was given the Holy Cross. When he reached Jerusalem he restored the Cross to its place in the church of the Holy Sepulchre (March 21, 630). From Jerusalem Heraclius went to Damascus and then to Aleppo where he had a meeting with Jesusyahb II, the Catholicos of the Nestorian Christians in Persia.

Meanwhile in Persia there was political chaos. Kavad died, probably of the plague, in September 628, and he was succeeded by his young son, Ardashir III. Sahrbaraz, who had returned to Persia, was a party to a coup which resulted in the young king being killed, and Sahrbaraz himself, who had seized the throne, lasted only forty-two days. Boran, daughter of Khusro, became queen c 629–30, but presently she too was murdered. And so on. It was not until 632 that the struggle for power came to an end, when one Yazdagird from Istakhr, supposedly a descendant of Khusro II, proclaimed himself king and at the end of 632 he was crowned as Yazdagird III.

This quarter century of armed conflict, like most of the Byzantine-Persian wars, settled nothing, and in addition left both parties in a state of exhaustion. This situation, bad enough at any time, was disastrous in this instance, for seemingly neither the Byzantines nor the Persians had any inkling of what was going on within Arabia, nor any premonition of the nature of the Arab forces that were about to be unleashed against them.

8. The Early Expansion of the Muslim Arabs.

This is an oft-told tale, and only its highlights will be mentioned here. After Muḥammad's death in 632, Abu-Bakr was elected his successor (Caliph), most of his two years in office (632–34) being taken up with wars within Arabia, whose object was to win recalcitrant tribes over to Islam and to end fratricidal fighting within the peninsula. This task accomplished, the Muslim fighters turned their attention to the northern borders of Arabia, and thus they came into contact with both the Byzantines and the Persians. It does not appear that at this stage 'Umar (Caliph 634–44) had any deliberate plan to conquer the whole of the Near East. The fighting spirit of the tribesmen was simply directed to immediate objectives. In some of the Arabs there may have been genuine religious motivation behind this expansion, but there can be no doubt that in all of them the love of adventure and the prospect of acquiring better living conditions as well as booty were equally important considerations.

In Palestine and Syria as well as in Byzantine Mesopotamia the existing Greek forces were simply unable to cope with the Arab armies. Sergius, the patrician of Palestine, was defeated south of the Dead Sea in 634 and his men in retreat were almost annihilated. Damascus fell in 635 (it had to be retaken in 637), and in August 636 the battle of the Yarmuk river was a crushing defeat for the Byzantines. It was after this battle that Heraclius, who was then in Antioch, realizing that Syria was lost to the Arabs, returned to Constantinople. As he entered Cilicia, he is reported to have said, "Peace be with you, Syria; what a beautiful land you will be to the enemy".[6] Antioch fell in 638. In Palestine Jerusalem held out until 638 and Caesarea on the coast until 640. In Mesopotamia, Edessa like most of the cities capitulated without a fight in 639, but others such as Constantia (Tella) and Dara had to be besieged.

In the western provinces of Persia the story was essentially the same as in the Byzantine West. To begin with, the Muslim Arabs aided by the Lakhmids, undertook razzias into the Persian borderlands which brought coveted booty to the participants. Al Ḥira changed hands twice before it was finally captured by the Arabs in 635. Such raids were presently followed by large scale military movements. The first major battle between the Muslims and the Persians was fought in May-June 637 near Ḥira at Qadisiyah, when the Persian general, Rustam, was killed and his large army dissolved in panic. A few weeks later the Arabs entered Ctesiphon whose garrison and king had deserted it. Another ineffectual stand was made by the Persians at Jalula (north-east of later Baghdad). Four years later at Nihavend (south of Hamadan) the Arabs fought their last great battle with the remnants of Yazdagird's army, resulting in a disastrous defeat of the Persians. The chief city of Fars, Istakhr, was occupied by the Muslims in 649-50. Yazdagird took refuge in flight, being finally murdered in 651 near Merv. Thus ended somewhat ingloriously the Sasanian dynasty which had ruled Persia for over four hundred years.

9. Troublesome Theological Movements in the Greek Church.

Arianism, supposedly disposed of at the Council of Nicaea in 325, lived on to disturb the Church. Constantine in his later years, his son Constantius II (337-61), and the emperor Valens II (364-78) were all supporters of the Arian cause. The first Council of Constantinople (381) reaffirmed the doctrine of Christ as set forth by the Council of Nicaea, and from this time on Arianism in the eastern Church rapidly declined.

A more serious issue for the Church was the rise of Nestorianism. Nestorius, a native of north Syria, became prominent in the church in Antioch, and in 428 he was selected by Theodosius II as the archbishop of Constantinople. His criticism of the use of the term *theotokos* ("mother of God") as a reference to Jesus' mother roused popular resentment, but his real trouble stemmed from his views on the person of Christ. It appears that he taught that Christ was one person, with two complete natures, one

---

[6] A.N. Stratos, *op cit*, II, p 73; cf *Chr de Michel*, 2, XI, vii, p 424.

human and the other divine. In an age when popular piety looked upon Christ as God and gave little thought to his manhood, Nestorius's emphasis upon the Lord's humanity was not well received. Cyril, archbishop of Alexandria (412-44), actively opposed the views of Nestorius, and at a synod held in Rome in 430, Pope Celestine I formally condemned Nestorius, and this judgement was confirmed by a council held at Ephesus in 431 which deposed Nestorius from his see, condemned his doctrines and excommunicated him. Four years later he was banished to Egypt where he subsequently died.

More disruptive than either Arianism or Nestorianism of the unity of the Greek Church was the appearance of Monophysitism.[7] Arising out of the opposition to Nestorius and given its basic formulation by Eutyches, abbot of a monastery near Constantinople, Monophysitism claimed that in the Incarnate Christ there was but a single nature. In effect Eutyches denied that the humanity of Christ was cosubstantial with that of mankind. His views were now supported by Dioscorus, archbishop of Alexandria (444-51), whose dictum was "two natures before the union, one afterwards," and they were endorsed by the emperor Theodosius II (408-50), and by the "Robber Council" held at Ephesus in 449, though they were opposed by Pope Leo (440-61) and Flavian archbishop of Constantinople (446-49).

The new emperor, Marcian (450-57) would not tolerate Monophysitism, and called a council to meet at Nicaea in 451.[8] The council, which in fact met at Chalcedon, and which was considerably influenced by the "Tome of Leo", a clear and precise statement of the Latin Church's theological views, produced the Creed of Chalcedon, confirming the main doctrines of earlier councils.[9] In it Christ is described as "perfect in Godhead. . . . perfect in manhood, truly God and truly man." Although Chalcedon's statement about Christ seemed to the dissidents to be vitually an endorsement of what Nestorius had argued for, the council approved the condemnation of Nestorius by the council of Ephesus in 431, and it also condemned Eutyches, deposed him from office and sent him into exile. Dioscorus of Alexandria was similarly disposed of.

Although the Council of Chalcedon hoped to end theological controversy, it failed to do so, for the supporters of Nestorius thought he had been badly treated, and the followers of Eutyches continued to think in Monyphysite terms. To the latter the Nicene Creed was the basic Christian document, and the Creed of Chalcedon was an aberration. Hence the Monophysites consistently referred to themselves as the "orthodox" (i.e., the

---

[7] See W.H.C. Frend, *The Rise of the Monophysite Movement*, Cambridge, 1972.

[8] Of the 365 bishops in attendance, nine were from Syria I, eight from Euphratesia, eight from Osrhoene, and six from Mesopotamia (*Chr de Michel*, 2, VIII, x p 62).

[9] For a summary of the proceedings of the Council of Chalcedon by a sixth century writer, see Evagrius, *Eccl Hist*, II, iv, xviii.

supporters of Nicaea), and their opponents were dubbed variously Nestorians, Diophysites or Chalcedonians. Their hope was that just as Eutyches had been supported by the emperor Theodosius II, so another emperor might arise who would endorse their position. Initially, therefore, the Monophysites had no desire to wreck the unity of either the Church or the empire.

All thoughtful Christians deplored the differences within the Church, and attempts were made from time to time to bring the Monophysites and the orthodox together. The emperor Zeno (474-91) for instance, tried to unite the two groups, in this case by his Henoticon of 482,[10] which made some concessions to the Monophysites. The real effect of this document was to occasion a schism between Rome and Constantinople when Pope Felix III excommunicated Acacius, patriarch of Constantinople, an interdict which lasted until 518. Zeno's successor, Anastasius (491-518), was also friendly to the Monophysites, and it was he who approved of the selection of the Monophysite, Severus, as patriarch of antioch. But the next emperor, Justin I (518-27), was a supporter of Chalcedon and was determined to undermine the Monophysite cause, and he instituted a persecution of Monophysites in an effort to persuade them to change their ways. Severus of Antioch was deposed and fifty-three other Monophysite bishops were expelled from their sees and numerous monks from their monasteries. Justin's successor, Justinian I (527-65), vacillated in his policy, sometimes persecuting the Monophysites and sometimes favouring them. It was his consort, Theodora, who was their constant friend. But the various efforts in this century, in 532, 548, 558, ad 563, to reconcile the two parties were fruitless. The controversy of 544-53 over the Three Chapters[11] was largely due to Justinian's belief (a mistaken one, as it proved) that a condemnation of the Chapters (this was done in 553) would make the Creed of Chalcedon more palatable to the Monophysites.

10. The Monophysites as a Dissident Sect within the Church.

By the late sixth century it had become clear to the Monophysites that they had little hope of controlling the Church in the Byzantine world. They had to accept the status of a schismatic movement, and they therefore took steps to develop their own leadership. It is in this connection that we must understand the work of John, bishop of Tella, Jacob Baradaeus, bishop of Edessa, and John, bishop of Ephesus, all of whom were extraordinarily

---

[10] The text of the Henoticon is found in Evagrius, *op cit*, III, xiv: Frend, *op cit*, pp 360-62.

[11] The Three Chapters were: (1) the person and writings of Theodore of Mopsuestia; (2) the writings of Theodoret, bishop of Cyrrhus, directed against Cyril of Alexandria; (3) a letter of Ibas of Edessa written in 433 to the priest Maris, censuring the Council of Ephesus, 431, denouncing the twelve anathemas of Cyril of Alexandria, and repudiating the views of Rabbula his bishop.

successful as Monophysite missionaries, and who in fact laid the foundation for the Monophysite Church of the future.

John of Tella and Jacob Baradaeus will be dealt with later in this study. Here we shall glance briefly at John of Ephesus, who is important both as a Monophysite leader and as a Church historian. He was born in Amid c 505-7, and at the age of fifteen he joined a local convent and in 529 he was ordained deacon by John of Tella. It is probable that down to 534, when he was in Palestine, his movements from one convent to another were an attempt to avoid the persecution to which the Monophysites in Syria were being subjected. In 535 we find him in Constantinople where he had the support of Theodora, but where, curiously, he also gained the favour of Justinian. It was the latter who appointed him "teacher of the heathen" in the provinces of Asia, Caria, Phrygia and Lydia, a task at which he worked most successfully for four years. In 546 he was back in Constantinople searching out, at Justinian's behest, the various forms of paganism which still lingered both in the city and in outlying regions. He had now become one of the leading spokesmen for Monophysitism in the capital, and in addition he had "the administration of the entire revenues of all the congregation of believers" (Wright, p 103), both in the city and elsewhere. In 558 Jacob Baradaeus made him bishop of Ephesus. John's fortunes changed, however, with the death of Justinian, and when Justin II (565-78) began his persecution of the Monophysites in 571, John's tribulations began (see his *Eccl Hist* II. 4-7). He died in Chalcedon after a year's incarceration c 585.

Of John's two principal historical works, both in Syriac, one is his *Ecclesiastical History*, of which only part III has come down to us, with some lacunae. Some excerpts from part II are also extant. Part III commences with 571 and continues to the end of John's life.[12] It is an invaluable record of the times as seen through John's perceptive eyes. His other work, *Lives of the Eastern Saints*, has been published by E.W. Brooks.[13]

Serious divisions among the Monophysites appeared in the sixth century, mostly concerned with the patriarchate of Alexander, but into these troubles we need not enter here. It is more to our purpose to note that the continuance of Monophysitism as a sect within the Church not only destroyed the ideal of a unified Church, but it also had divisive political results. The efforts of Justin I, Justinian I (spasmodically), and Justin II, to enforce Chalcedonian orthodoxy in the Church, meant that the political arm of the empire was used to suppress religious differences, and this evoked strong reaction in the eastern provinces of the empire. The Monophysites who suffered directly from the policy of Constantinople were the clergy and

---

[12] *The Third Part of the Ecclesiastical History of John, Bishop of Ephesus*, tr by R. Payne Smith, Oxford 1860.

[13] PO 17(1923), pp i–xiv, 1–307; 18 (1924), pp 511–698; 19 (1926), pp 151–282.

the monks. The monks, however, often represented the piety of the countryside (Sozomen VI. xxvii), and their opposition to the imperial policy helped to develop a regional loyalty which eventually became sharply critical of everything connected with Constantinople. This was especially evident in Syria and Egypt. To what extent this strong undercurrent of hostility to Constantinople facilitated the Persian attack on the Roman East in the early seventh century, and a few years later the Muslim conquest of the same areas, is a matter that we cannot here explore.

The last serious attempt to bring the Chalcedonians and the Monophysites together belongs to the very end of the period which this volume covers. The emperor Heraclius was fully aware of the practical wisdom of uniting the two groups, and with the Persian war ended, the times seemed propitious to work towards such a union. Conversations were held at Hierapolis in 631 between the emperor and Athanasius, the Jacobite (Monophysite) patriarch of Antioch, but when later in the year, the patriarch died, nothing came of the effort. In Egypt there was seemingly more progress, and at a synod held in Alexandria in 633, a Tome of Union was drawn up and agreed upon: its chapter 7 referred to Christ as "having a single acting force." But the optimism expressed in the Tome was short-lived, one of its vigorous opponents being Sophronius, patriarch of Jerusalem (from 634). Nonetheless Serguis the orthodox patriarch of Alexandria decided to present a confession of faith binding on all the faithful. It was entitled "Statement (Gk *ekthesis*) of the Orthodox Faith," and in it Christ is said to have had a single will. This statement was approved by Heraclius and published in October 638; it was endorsed by two synods in Constantinople in 638 and 639. Pope Honorius, who had supported Heraclius's conciliatory moves and had approved the "one will" idea, died in October, but his successor roundly condemned the Ekthesis and its Monothelitism (one-will-ism). The debate on this matter continued for some years until the Sixth General Council held in Constantinople in 680 declared that Christ had two wills, and it condemned all those who had taken a contrary position, including Pope Honorius. By this time the Monophysite regions of Syria and Egypt had long been in Muslim hands, and there was no longer any point in the orthodox Church trying to appease them.

Chapter 4.
Syriac Christians in the Third and Fourth Centuries

1. The Dearth of Information.

We know virtually nothing about Syriac Christians in Roman Syria in the third century. Sozomen (VI. 34) notes the slow growth of the Church in Coele-Syria and Upper Syria, which is somewhat surprising if this observation applies to Osrhoene, where, as we have seen, the Christian tradition appears to have been established, at least in Edessa, in the late second century. On the other hand, Dionysius, bishop of Alexandria 247-64, affirms that in his time there were churches in Syria, Arabia (i.e., Arabia Nabataea), and Mesopotamia, although he supplies no names of bishops in these areas except Demetrian of Antioch (Eusebius, *Eccl Hist* VII. iv.1–v. 1-2). The only datum of a religious character which the *Chronicle of Edessa* records in this century, after the flood episode of 201, is the year of Mani's birth which is erroneously given as 551 (239 A.D.). Nothing is said in the *Chronicle* about the Roman persecution of Christians in the time of Decius (249-51), but since we know that prominent individuals in Palestine and Syria were its victims, such as Alexander of Jerusalem, Origin of Caesarea and Babylas of Antioch (Eusebius, *Eccl Hist* VI. xxxix. 1-5), it is probable that the writ of Decius was enforced in Osrhoene. If this was so, it can be theorized that the highly coloured stories of the martyrdoms in Edessa of Sharbil and his sister Babai, which in an old Syriac document are placed in the time of the emperor Trajan (98-117), belong, if they have any historical basis at all, to the time of Decius.[1]

One of the reasons for the meagreness of our information about Syriac Christians in this century must be those wars whose theatre was northern Syria and Mesopotamia. As we have seen in Ch 1, Caracalla's expedition against the Parthians started from Antioch in 216 and reached as far east as Abiabene. Not long after this the new Sasanian ruler of Persia began a series of wars against the eastern Roman world, and these of course called forth a Roman response, and so the years 230, 232, 237-38, 242, 254, 260, 296-98 witnessed full-blown hostilities between East and West. These recurrent conflicts, which can only have played havoc with normal social and economic life, must also have made the expansion of Christianity in this area very difficult. To what extent the Persian practice of sending prisoners of war back to Persia weakened such churches as existed we do not know. Most of the statements about such captives relate to the larger cities.

[1] W. Cureton (ed), *Ancient Syriac Documents*, London, 1864, pp 41-62.

2. Dura Europus.

It is archaeological information, in this case from Dura Europus, which sheds a little light on this obscure period. This fortress town (hereafter Dura), located on the Euphrates more or less due east of Palmyra, is only marginally related to the Syriac-speaking world to its north, but what we learn from it helps to fill out our limited knowledge of the eastern Church in the mid third century.

Dura was taken by Rome from the Parthians c 165, and after ninety years of Roman occupation, the Sasanian Persians overran and destroyed it in 256. We know from the excavations of the site that there was a Christian community there, and that sometime between 232 and 256 these Christians acquired a private house and converted it into a place of worship.[2] The partition between two rooms was removed and the single room thus obtained became an assembly hall which could accommodate 65-75 persons. On the other side of the house a smaller room was made into a baptistery. A striking feature of the latter was that its ceiling and walls had painted decorations, the walls displaying pictorial compositions inspired by stories from the Scriptures.

Whether Edessa had a hand in the founding or expansion of this Christian group in Dura we do not know. The coins that have been found in the ruins include quantities of small change minted at Edessa from 195 on; others are from the mints at Carrhae and after 230 from Nisibis.[3] These coins suggest that there were, as we might expect, economic links between Dura and the northern cities. Whether these channels would lead to some fraternizing between the Christians of Edessa and those of Dura is conjectural. While there was a Jewish group in Dura who had a synagogue, there is no evidence that the Christians in Dura were recruited from the local Jews. It is much more likely that the members of the Roman garrison, most of whom are known to have come from regions where there was some form of Christianity (Palestine, Syria, Arabia Petraea),[4] formed a large proportion of the Christians in Dura. The rest might well be merchants from Edessa and elsewhere, resident in Dura.

The linguistic finds at Dura are almost exclusively in Greek or Latin. A striking exception is a deed of sale, written in Syriac at Edessa in 243.[5] The sale is that of a female slave, Amath-Sin, to a man, Tiro of Carrhae. One copy of the document was for the archives of Edessa, the other, the present

---

[2] *The Excavations at Dura-Europos*, Final Report VIII, Part II, *The Christian Building*, by C. H. Kraeling, ed by C. B. Welles, New Haven, 1967.

[3] *The Excavations at Dura-Europos*, Final Report VI, *The Coins*, by A. R. Bellinger, New Haven, 1949, pp 205-09.

[4] As in note 2, p 109.

[5] *The Excavations at Dura-Europos*, Final Report V, Part I, *The Parchments and Papyri*, by C. B. Welles, R. O. Fink, and J. F. Gilliam, New Haven, 1959, pp 142-49.

text, was for Tiro. What circumstances led to the latter's copy being found in Dura we do not know. This document at least testifies that there were close relations in some matters between Edessa, Carrhae and Dura.

The linguistic graffiti of the Christian building in Dura are almost all in Greek. One exception is what appears to be the Syriac alphabet found on the wall of the courtyard, although in the same building there are no fewer than five Greek alphabets.[6] This suggests that the local Christians were mostly from a Hellenistic background, a supposition which finds support in the fact that the fragment of Tatian's Diatessaron (see ch 2), found in some rubbish some distance from the church, is in Greek, and would be of use only to those who knew Greek.

3. The Last of the Roman Persecutions of Christianity.

The early fourth century is marked by Diocletian's persecution of the Church, which was continued in the East for some years after the emperor's retirement (305) by Galerius and Maximian and later by Licinius. Eusebius supplies us with only a few details of Diocletian's persecution with respect to Christians in Mesopotamia (*Eccl Hist* VIII. xii. 1) and in Antioch (VIII. xii. 2–5; xiii. 2–4). A Syriac document describes the martyrdom between 308 and 316 of three persons, Shamuna, Gurya and Habib a deacon, all of whom were villagers from the vicinity of Edessa, and who were buried together outside the northern wall of that city.[7]

Constantine's toleration of the Church (see sect 3 of Ch 3), a policy followed by all his successors except Julian, was to prove to be a somewhat mixed blessing for the Christian community. For Christians within the Roman world it meant of course the end of persecution. The Gospel could now be preached without let or hindrance and the Church therefore expanded. We have no details of this expansion in north-east Syria, but it is a fact that in the fourth and following centuries Christian communities are to be found in Amid, Beroea (Ḥaleb, Aleppo), Callinicus (Raqqa), Chalcis (Qen Neshrin), Ḥaran (Ḥarran), Mabbog (Hierapolis), Martyropolis (Maiperqaṭ) Samosata, Serug (Batnae), Tella (Constantia) and Theodosioupolis (Resaina). The circumstances surrounding the beginnings of Christianity in these centres are hidden from us. But the cessation of persecution also meant, as we have seen in ch 3, and as the fourth to seventh centuries illustrate, that the secular power could be used to support one particular theological position. Inevitably this led to the harassment and even persecution of those Christians who opposed that position.

---

[6] id. pp 89–97.
[7] W. Cureton, *op cit*, pp 72–106; *Ante-Nicene Fathers*, ed by A. Roberts and J. Donaldson, rev by A. C. Coxe, Grand Rapids, 1951, vol VIII, pp 690–701.

4. The Persistence of Paganism down to the sixth century.

It must be recognized that neither in the fourth nor in the following centuries did Christianity make a clean sweep of Roman Syria and neighbouring regions. Jews on the whole appear to have retained their own traditions, and Jewish converts to the Church were the exception rather than the rule. Paganism, however, faded out of the picture, but rather slowly. Although Julian's attempt to revive a state-supported cult failed, much older local pagan practices, which were often yoked to magic and superstition, lived on, and this despite the fact that they had no widespread organization linking them together. Libanius of Antioch (314–93), a very distinguished rhetorician, who lived from 354 onward in his native city, where he was the teacher of John Chrysostom, remained a pagan all his life, as is illustrated by one of his orations which is on behalf of Artemis. His autobiography is, in part, a personal confession of faith in the religious traditions of Hellenism.[8] In view of the witness of Libanius regarding Hellenism in Antioch, we are not surprised that when Ephraim first settled in Edessa (after 363), most of the inhabitants were still pagan. In the next century a wealthy sophist of Antioch, Isocasius, was accused of various offences including paganism before Leo I in Constantinople in 468; the trial ended when Isocasius agreed to be baptized. It is of interest that both Ephraim (c 306–73) of Nisibis and later of Edessa, and Rabbula, bishop of Edessa 412–35, are reported to have been from families whose fathers were pagan priests. Later in the fifth century, Joshua the Stylite in reporting in his *Chronicle* on the year 807 (495–96 A.D.), describes a pagan festival in Edessa of which he highly disapproves.[9] Two years later the same festival is said to have received only a mild rebuke from Philoxenus, bishop of Mabbog, who was in the city at the time (*Chronicle* XXVII, XXX). In the next century, Justinian felt it needful in 529 to close the University of Athens, "the last rampart of effete paganism" (A. A. Vasiliev), the decline of which had been hastened by the organization of the University of Constantinople by Theodosius II. It is the *Ecclesiastical History* of John of Ephesus which tells us of the paganism in the Asiatic parts of the Byzantine world in the sixth century, specifically in the provinces of Asia, Caria, Phrygia and Lydia (III. 36–37); it also describes the heathenism in the reign of Tiberius II (578–82) at Baalbek which Rabbula had earlier exposed himself to, as well as the paganism practised by some individuals both in Antioch and Edessa (III. 27–34). In the latter city the governor-procurator, Anatolius, was found to be involved in heathen practices, and on being sent to Constantinople, he was tried and put to death. About this time a great many other people, including some clergy, were accused and convicted of taking part in various forms of paganism.

---

[8] *Libanius' Autobiography (Oration I)*, the Greek text ed and tr by A. F. Norman, Oxford, 1965, sects 119, 155, 201, 222, 233–35.

[9] *The Chronicle of Joshua the Stylite*, tr by W. Wright, Cambridge, 1882, xxvii, xxx.

According to Procopius, most of the citizens of Carrhae were pagans as late as the sixth century (*Wars* II. xiii. 7; cf *Chr de Michel*, 2, X. xxiv p 375).

5. Arianism.

As we have earlier noted (ch 3), Arianism did not die at the Council of Nicaea (325). On the contrary, thanks to the support of Constantine, Constantius II, and Valens, it seemed to be quite vigorous in the middle years of the fourth century. Syria was a strong supporter of the Arian cause, and Sozomen (VI. 21) claims that Arians were in the majority in the city of Antioch. It illustrates the theological turmoil of the age that in the Syrian capital from 361–78 there was an Arian bishop, Euzoius, as well as two rival bishops who supported the Nicene creed. The life of Ephraim records how Valens visited Edessa c 372 with the intention of forcing Arianism on the city, but the protests of the non-Arian Christians forced him to change his mind. The *Chronicle of Edessa*, however, states that in 373 an Arian group took possession of the church in the city and held it for five years (31–33). A vigorous fight in Syria against the Arians was waged by Apollinarius (Apollinaris), c 310–90, who became bishop of Laodicea in 360. Actually the bishop championed a view of the person of Christ which proved unacceptable to the Church and which was condemned at the Council of Constantinople in 381.

6. Ephraim of Nisibis and Edessa.

Ephraim is the most widely celebrated figure in the Syriac Church, but it is not easy from the available data to reconstruct the details of his life.[10] The tradition is that he was born in or near Nisibis in the reign of Constantine. Nisibis had been under Roman control since 298, and Shapur II's first three attempts to seize it (337–38, 346(?), 350) were unsuccessful. Most of Ephraim's life was therefore spent in a city where war or the threat of war must have frequently overshadowed all normal activities. The Syrian biographies state that Ephraim's father, a native of Nisibis, was a pagan priest, and that his mother, a Christian woman, came from Amid. There were Christians in Nisibis at this time, and when Ephraim's father discovered his son talking to some of them, he expelled him from his home as "an enemy of the gods." Ephraim found friends among the Christians whose bishop was Mar Jacob (d 338) and who appears to have taken a special interest in the young man. The Christian community was one in

---

[10] For references to Ephraim in the Greek Church historians, see, for example, Theodoret, *Eccl Hist*, IV, xxix; Sozomen, III, xvi. See also R. Duval, "Le Testament de saint Ephrém" in *Journal Asiatique*, Nouvième serie IX, 18, 1901, pp 234–319. For a critical examination of these and other sources, see A. Vööbus, *Literary, Critical and Historical Studies in Ephrem the Syrian*, PETSE 10, Stockholm, 1958.

which celibacy was much favoured, and we are not surprised, when Ephraim became a catechumen, that Jacob was able to induce him to embark on an ascetic way of life. It seems quite improbable, as one story has it, that he accompanied Jacob to the Council of Nicaea in 325. That he had some share in repulsing one of the Persian attacks on Nisibis is not an impossibility.

Ephraim's catechumenate must have revealed unusual intellectual gifts, and he was evidently encouraged to continue his studies and to write on behalf of the Christian cause. The Nisibene hymns, for instance come from these years in Nisibis. Ephraim may have acquired a smattering of Greek, but there is no evidence in his works of any real acquaintance with the theological thought of the western Church. It was in this Nisibis period of his life that he first became a popular preacher, and his hymns, which initially followed the pattern set by Bardaisan, were widely acclaimed.

In 363 by a treaty which Jovian made with Shapur II, Nisibis was handed over to the Persians. Many Christians now left the vicinity of Nisibis, and among them was Ephraim who, after a stay in Amid, came to Edessa. According to the *Chronicle of Edessa* (25), the bishop of the city in the days of Ephraim was Barsai (Barses). It was in the environs of Edessa, a city which housed the great church of Thomas the Apostle, that Ephraim spent the remaining nine or ten years of his life, mostly in his cell, close to other male and female celibates, who had settled in the hills north of the city. Here he continued the writing he had engaged in at Nisibis. Although he must have spent most of the time in his cell, he seems to have participated in the formal worship of the Christian community, and his sermons on these occasions created a deserved reputation as a great preacher and his fame spread far beyond the Syriac-speaking community. One source tell us that in these Edessene years he also had something to do with the choral training of young women for the services of the church. While the tradition that Ephraim visited bishop Basil of Caesarea (in Cappadocia) has frequently been dismissed as worthless, such a visit cannot be ruled out completely in view of the interest of both men in asceticism and in combatting Arianism, though their views on the relative merits of cenobitism and anchoritism would have been radically different. Part of this story about Basil tells us that it was the bishop who persuaded Ephraim to accept the diaconate, but he was unable to prevail upon him to become a priest. One of the last public acts credited to Ephraim is his leadership in organizing famine relief in Edessa in 372-73. He died in his adopted city on June 9, 373.

Ephraim was an extraordinarily prolific writer; Sozomen (III. 16) reckoned that he had written 300,000 verses.[11] As a secluded ascetic for most of

---

[11] Ephraim's writings have been extensively published. For a full list of these (down to 1922), see Baumstark, pp 32-52; cf Chabot (1934), pp 25-30. On Ephraim as a writer, see A. Vööbus, HASO II, pp 394-99.

his life, Ephraim doubtless devoted a portion of his time to appropriate expressions of private devotion, but it is clear that he could never have written as much as he did if he had not made economical use of the remainder of each day. This must go back to rigorous study habits acquired in his youth and maintained throughout his life.

Ephraim's extant works fall into three groups: biblical commentaries, homilies, including controversial writings, and hymns and odes. It is not practicable in the present study to survey these writings with any degree of thoroughness. We shall therefore here ignore the biblical commentaries, and offer only a few remarks on the homilies and the hymns.

One of the homilies translated by A. E. Johnston[12] is entitled "On the Sinful Woman," and is an exposition of Lk 7:36-50, the incident concerning Simon the Pharisee and the sinful woman. It is a highly imaginative but basically sound treatment of the biblical material. The theme, the gracious compassion of the Lord, is a simple one, and Ephraim's presentation of it in this twenty to twenty-five minute sermon must have been very effective. It concludes, "May our Lord account us worthy of hearing this word of his, 'Come, enter you blessed of my Father, inherit the kingdom made ready for all who shall do my will.' . . . To him be glory, on us be mercy, at all times. Amen."

While we have no reliable data about the extent of heretical activity at this time within the Syriac Church, we can infer from the fact that Ephraim felt obliged to engage in a verbal battle with heretics, that they presented a serious challenge to orthodoxy. His approach to this situation is illustrated by his *"Prose Refutations of Mani, Marcion and Bardaisan."*[13] These five discourses, dedicated to one, Hypatius, are clearly meant for perusal by the better educated members of the Church, for they offer a type of sustained argument which the average church member could probably not follow. It is impossible to summarize these Refutations here, but it is obvious that Ephraim had considerable knowledge of what he was talking about. In his treatment of Manichaeism he spots very acutely, and sometimes with a touch of irony, the inherent weaknesses of the system. The conclusion of the fifth discourse, although a kind of *non sequitur*, is not without interest. "He who prays with the Manichees, prays with Satan, and he who prays with the Marcionites (?) prays with Legion, and he who prays with the Bardaisanites prays with Beelzebub, and he who prays with the Jews prays with Barabbas the robber."

Ephraim, taking a cue from Bardaisan, turned to poetry as a vehicle for teaching, exhortation and worship, and in the course of his life he produced

---

[12] *Three Homilies*, tr by A. E. Johnston, *Nicene and Post-Nicene Fathers*, Second Series, XIII, New York, 1898, pp 303-41.

[13] S. Ephraim's *Prose Refutations of Mani, Marcion and Bardaisan*, C. W. Mitchell, I London, 1912.

a large number of poems for the Church. We surmise from the fact that most of them include a response in the text, that they were primarily intended for liturgical use. The response appearing at the end of each strophe was sometimes the same for all the strophes of the poem. Typical responses in the Nisibene hymns are:

> "Stretch forth your bow against the flood,
> for lo it has lifted up its waves against
> our walls"(1);
> "From all that have mouths, glory be to
> your grace"(2);
> "Our hope, be you our wall!"(4)
> "Give peace, O Son, to our land!"(7).

In other instances a different response appears at the end of each strophe. The strophes of the poetry exhibit a large variety of structure, length and number. Even the metre varies, though Ephraim seems to have had some partiality for the seven syllable line. Normally the pattern established in the first strophe is followed throughout the poem.

Western readers, schooled in the traditions of English poetry, are unlikely to rate Ephraim's poems very highly, whether they read them in Syriac or in translation. They are, admittedly, theologically orientated, which is apt to make dull reading; their purpose is often didactic or inspirational, and the parallelism, which is a feature of most Semitic poetry, can if it is overused, make the poems tedious and verbose. We can only argue, in defence of Ephraim, that poetry, as he wrote it, was evidently acceptable to those for whom it was intended. If the text of a poem in certain details was beyond the ken of the average worshipper, the latter at least could usually appreciate the simplicity of the response.

As one group of poems out of the many that could be referred to, we cite the nineteen Hymns of the Nativity.[14] These poems use the celebration of Jesus' birth to present devotional matter drawn from the OT and the NT. Hymns XI and XII represent Mary speaking to her son. The Feast of the Epiphany, as in the Eastern Churches generally, celebrates Jesus' baptism, and we have fifteen hymns written for this occasion. It seems implied in several of them that the day was used for the baptism of neophytes, and this conclusion is supported by XIII. 1-22, which is termed "The Hymn of the Baptized."

The popularity of his poems and sermons, and the careful elucidation of the text displayed in the biblical commentaries, ensured Ephraim of a permanent place among the great figures of the Syriac Church. While much of his work shows little originality of thought, he was a master of the Syriac language, and he helped to make that language the accepted medium of communication for Christians both in north-east Roman Syria and in the

---

[14] *Nicene and Post-Nicene Fathers*, as in note 12, XIII, pp 223-62.

Sasanian empire. Ephraim has the additional distinction of being the only Syrian writer to be publicly recognized by the Western Church. In 1920 Pope Benedict XV declared him to be a "Doctor of the Church."

Although the names of some of Ephraim's disciples are known, none ever reached the stature of the master.[15] But two writers, who belong to the next generation, deserve a brief notice here. Balai (or Balaeus) was seemingly the chorepiscopus in the diocese of Aleppo. He wrote poetry and homilies, five of the poems being in praise of his superior, Acacius the bishop of Aleppo. As the latter died in 432, this gives us an approximate date for Balai. The other writer was Cyrillona[16] of whom we know little excpet that one of his poems dealt with the invasion of the Huns. This event is referred to in the *Chronicle of Edessa* (40), the latter giving it the date 395.

7. The School of Edessa.[17]

The beginnings of the celebrated School in Edessa are obscure, though its designation as "The School of the Persians" suggests that Persian Christians had something to do with its foundation. If this was so, then the event most likely to throw light upon its early history was the transfer of Nisibis to Persian control by the emperor Jovian in 363. One result of this was that many of the Christians of Nisibis moved westwards into Roman territory where their Christian faith could be freely practised,[18] and with this in mind, it is theorized that some of these settled in Edessa and founded later in the fourth century a school for the training of the clergy.[19] It is doubtful if Ephraim, one of the refugees from Nisibis and who lived in a cell outside of Edessa until his death in 373, had much if anything to do either with the establishment of the School or with its daily activities, although doubtless he looked upon the project with favour.

Eventually the School consisted of a group of buildings near the Pool of Abraham. Its first known director was Qiiore who shouldered all the responsibility within the School, but Narsai (Narseh), who directed the School from 451 to at least 471, only accepted the post on the condition that he would do biblical exposition exclusively, and that the necessary administrative duties

---

[15] Wright, pp 38–39; A. Vööbus, HASO II, pp 399–400.

[16] On Balai and Cyrillona, see Wright, pp 39–42, Baumstark, pp 61–63.

[17] A. Vööbus, *History of the School of Nisibis*, CSCO, Subsidia 26, Louvain, 1965, pp 7–31. For the Syriac tradition, see Barhadbshabba, "Cause de la Fondation des écoles," ed by A. Scher, PO IV. 4, 1908, pp 327–97.

[18] Cf Ammianus Mercellinus, XXV. 9. 1–12.

[19] The Greek derivation of the Syriac word for "school" ('*skwl*': Gk *schole*) suggests that the idea of a school was taken by the Syrian Christians from the Greek Church. As is well known, there was a famous school in Alexandria of which Eusebius speaks (*Eccl Hist* V. x), and of which Pantaenus, Clement and Origen were the successive heads. It is also possible that the Edessan School owed something to the presence in Babylonia of Jewish academies.

would be performed by others. Instruction was given in reading and writing, the former having in mind particularly what was required in the liturgy. Biblical studies were central in the School's programme. The chief of the teachers was the "interpreter." At first the commentaries of Ephraim were the principal aids to scriptural study, but later the writings of Theodore of Mopsuestia (bishop of Mopsuestia 392–428) came into use. Theodore had been a pupil of Diodore of Tarsus (bishop of Tarsus 378–90), who had laid stress on the literal and historical exegesis of the Scripture, with the result that through Theodore this method of approaching the Scriptures became the standard treatment of the Bible in the School. Theodore's works were now translated into Syriac, which indicates that the School was attracting to itself a number of bilingual scholars who could undertake the necessary translation, not only of Theodore's writings but also those of other scholars who wrote in Greek. In addition to biblical studies, the curriculum included philosophy, history, geography, and even astronomy, but whether these were optional courses for students is not clear. Their availability suggests that translation efforts were not confined to commentaries on the Scriptures. It is of interest that one of the primary manuscripts for the text of Eusebius's *Ecclesiastical History* is a Syriac version, thought to have been made early in the fifth century.[20]

[20] Vol I of Eusebius, *Eccl Hist*, ed by K. Lake, London, 1926 (1959), p xxviii.

Chapter 5.
The Heyday of the West Syriac Church: The Fifth to Seventh Centuries

These three centuries are of considerable importance for the history of Syriac Christianity. In the fifth century, as have seen in Ch 3, the Greek Church produced Monophysitism, and a great deal of what we know about Syriac Christians is related to the Monophysite controversy. At the end of the period we are considering, there was a totally unexpected change in the political climate in which Oriental Christians lived, when Muslim Arabs replaced Byzantine Christians as the masters of most of what had constituted the Oriental parts of the Byzantine world. In what follows, the history of the Syriac Christians in this period will be presented, for the most part, in and through the lives and work of their leading representatives.

1. Marutha of Maiperqaṭ.

While we know nothing of Marutha's home or early life or when he became a bishop, he appears to have been a man of considerable culture, well versed in both Greek and Syriac, and with some pretension to be a doctor of medicine. It is doubtful if he was present at the Council of Constantinople in 381, although Socrates (VI. 15) and Sozomen (VIII. 16) record his attendance at a synod held in Chalcedon. He was used by the emperors Arcadius (395–408) and Theodosius II (408–50) as Constantinople's ambassador to the Persian king, Yazdagird I (399–421). Probably his first mission was in 399 to represent Arcadius at the accession of Yazdagird to the Persian throne, and his second in 408 to advise Yazdagird of the accession of Theodosius II (cf Socrates VII. 8). On one of these occasions he is said to have cured the Persian king of a troublesome malady. How long the bishop remained in Persia on either occasion is uncertain. He played an active role, as we shall see in ch 9, in the reorganization of the Persian Church, and he seems to have improved the time spent in Persia by collecting data on the Persian martyrs, which he subsequently issued in Syriac as the *Book of Martyrs*, only portions of which survive. The city in which his see was located came to be called Martyropolis. He died about 420.

2. Acacius, bishop of Amid.

About 419–20 Acacius, bishop of Amid, was sent as an envoy to the Persian king Yazdagird II by Theodosius II, and while in Persia the bishop had a share in a Council, the details of which are obscure, called at that time by the Catholicos, Yahbalaha I. According to Socrates (VII. 21) this same Acacius, who had returned to Amid, about two years later ransomed 7,000 Persian prisoners who had been taken in Arzoun in the Persian war of 421-22 conducted by Theodosius II. The men were in a state of semi-starvation, and the bishop obtained the necessary funds by selling some church vessels. After keeping the prisoners a short while, he sent them back to Persia. Whether Acacius was a member of the Byzantine delegation that negotiated peace with Persia in 422 is not known.

3. Rabbula of Edessa.[1]

Rabbula, a contemporary of Marutha, bishop of Maiperqaṭ, was born in the fourth century in Chalcis (Qen-neshrin). The tradition is that his father was a wealthy pagan priest and that his mother was a Christian. He became a Christian under the influence of Eusebius, bishop of Chalcis and Acacius, bishop of Aleppo, and subsequently retired to the monastery of Abraham at Chalcis. One of the ruined churches which Butler examined in north Syria was the mud-brick structure, erected after 313, at Zebed, a few miles east of Chalcis. Here on one panel of a throne were found the words in Syriac "Rabbula made the throne." Possibly this church was the chapel of the monastery of Abraham where Rabbula lived until he was made bishop of Edessa, and the throne may have been one of his gifts to the institution.[2]

Whatever his earlier education, Rabbula was sufficiently bilingual for his biographer to credit him with translating the NT from Greek into Syriac. P. Peeters doubts if he had enough training to undertake such a task, and while he concedes that the bishop may have sponsored the work, he suggests that the actual translation was done by others.[3] When Diogenes, the bishop of Edessa died, Rabbula was selected by a synod at Antioch as his successor, a post which he held from 412 to c 435.

These were difficult times for any eastern bishop, and not less so for a bishop in Edessa, for, so his biographer claims, Rabbula found that he had to contend with Bardaisanites, Arians, Marcionites, Manichees and Messalians. This situation was further complicated by the controversy centering in Nestorius, who had become patriarch of Constantinople in 428. Rabbula at first had sided with Nestorius, and at the Council of Ephesus (431) he had

---

[1] A highly laudatory Syriac account of Rabbula's life appears in C. Brockelmann, *Syrische Grammatik*, 5th ed, Leipzig, 1938, pp 69°-101°. Two relatively recent studies of Rabbula are, P. Peeters, *La vie de Rabboula, évèque d'Édesse*, in *Recherches d'histoire et de philologie Orientales*, SH 27, Bruxelles, 1951, pp 139-70; G. G. Blum, *Rabbula von Edessa*, CSCO 300, Subsidia 34, Louvain, 1969.

[2] H. C. Butler (ed E. B. Smith), *Early Churches in Syria*, Princeton, 1929 (Amsterdam, 1969), p 39, illustration 38.

[3] Peeters, *op cit*, pp 153-54.

supported John of Antioch, a friend of Nestorius, but a few months later he decided that Cyril of Alexandria, a critic of Nestorius, was right. A visit to Constantinople, 431–32, only confirmed him in this position, and from this time on he was a violent opponent of Nestorianism. This made the work in his own see all the more difficult, for Edessa was traditionally sympathetic with Theodore of Mopsuestia, and Rabbula's public burning of the works of Theodore and of Diodore of Tarsus, only added to his troubles, especially when his own clergy, headed by Ibas, were increasingly discontented with his leadership.

Rabbula is credited with a strict administration of his diocese. He established firm rules of conduct for priests and monks, some of which have come down to us and have been edited, most recently, by A. Vööbus.[4] The canons for monks are of special interest because they indicate that the coenobitical monasticism was expanding within the Syrian Church at this time, and that the bishops recognized it needed guidance. Rabbula's work and actions respecting the Scriptures are discussed in section 12 of this chapter. That this austere and scholarly monk had his human side is shown by his constant concern for the poor. From the time he disposed of his private property when entering Abraham's monastery until his establishment in Edessa of hospitals for the sick and needy of both sexes, his social conscience was very much alive, and helps to explain why his death was an occasion for general grief in the city.

4. Ibas (Hiba) of Edessa.

Ibas was born in the closing years of the fourth century. We suspect that he must have received a good linguistic education in either Edessa or Antioch, for when he became a teacher in the School of Edessa, he was able to assist in translating the works of Theodore of Mopsuestia, Diodore of Tarsus, Theodoret of Cyrrhus, and Nestorius into Syriac. About 435 he succeeded Rabbula as the bishop of Edessa. He became involved in the continuing Nestorian controversy, and he had to face the fact that a growing number of both the clergy and laity in Edessa were antagonistic to Nestorianism and to their bishop's apparent support of it. Furthermore, Ibas's ecclesiastical and moral conduct offended many people, as is illustrated by the variety of charges brought against him (see Segal, pp 130–32). This criticism of Ibas was sufficiently strong to warrant the establishment of no fewer than three commissions to investigate various accusations against him. These bodies met successively at Antioch, Tyre, and Beirut, but the charges could not be sustained and Ibas was found innocent. The malcontents, however, continued to press their case, and when the matter came before the Robber Council of Ephesus in 449, Ibas, like several

[4] *Documents*, pp 24–50.

other bishops, was deposed from his see as a Nestorian. When the Council of Chalcedon met in 451, he was allowed to plead for a reconsideration of his case, with the result that by anathematizing both Nestorius and Eutyches, he was restored to his see, dying in Edessa six years later in 457. The *Chronicle of Edessa* (59-60) tells us that he built a new church in the city, subsequently called the House of the Apostles, and that in 438 a gift, from one, Senator, of a great silver table (720 pounds of silver) was put in the Old Church. A letter which Ibas wrote in 433 to a Persian bishop, Maris (who had visited Edessa), and wherein he discussed current theological issues, was to become famous a hundred years later as one of "The Three Chapters" condemned by the Council of Constantinople in 553.

5. Isaac of Antioch.

Although the Isaac we are here concerned with was often confused in later Syriac sources with two other Isaacs (both of Edessa in the late fifth and early sixth centuries), the main facts of his life are reasonably certain. He was born in the late fourth century in Amid, studied at Edessa, and subsequently went to a convent near Antioch of which in due course he became the abbot. Sometime, apparently in the early fifth century, he visited Rome (which may point to some private means), and related to this visit are his poems on the secular games held in Rome in 404 and on the capture of the city by Alaric in 410. Returning to his monastery in Syria, he avoided public involvement in the theological disputes of his age, although his own position appears to have been orthodox. His writings in Syriac, "nearly as voluminous and varied as those of Ephraim" (Wright), have been published by G. Bickell.[5] One of these on the earthquake, followed by fire, which destroyed much of Antioch in 458, was probably one of his latest efforts. He is thought to have died 459-60.

6. Theodoret of Cyrrhus.

Although Theodoret cannot be reckoned among Syriac writers, the location of his see, Cyrrhus, in a predominantly Syriac region, and his involvement in the thelogical disputes of the fifth century, justify a brief notice of him here. Born in Antioch c 393, he was educated in that city. Theodore, bishop of Mopsuestia, and Nestorius were among those who influenced his early days. After the death of his parents, he retired to a monastery some miles from Antioch. In 423 he was, against his personal wishes, made bishop of Cyrrhus, where he is said to have had 800 villages under his jurisdiction. He was inevitably drawn into the Nestorian controversy, and when Cyril, archbishop of Alexandria (412-44) issued his

---

[5] Baumstark, pp 63-66.

twelve anathemas against Nestorianism, Theodoret was asked to refute them.[6] As the dispute dragged on, Theodoret found himself in 449, first of all, confined to his own diocese by the emperor, Theodosius II, and later in the year the Robber Council of Ephesus deprived him of his see. After the lapse of two years, the Council of Chalcedon restored him to his post, he having now publicly anathematized Nestorius. The rest of his life was spent peacefully in his diocese (d c 458). His best known work is his *Ecclesiastical History* (in Greek), which covers the years 322-427. An equally important work is (in the French translation by P. Canivet) *Histoire des moines de Syrie* (Paris 1977). This presents the biographies of thirty celebrated ascetics in Syria.

7. The Closing of the Edessan School.

The School of Edessa might have had a long and useful life if Syriac Christians had not become involved in the theological disputes of the western Church in the fifth century. As we have seen in ch 3, Christians were now divided over Christological questions, particularly by those raised by Nestorius and Eutyches, and it did not take long for these controversies to reach the School of Edessa. In particular, the theological positions of the bishops of Antioch and Edessa were bound to affect the fortunes of the School, for these sees as well as the School itself were traditionally devoted to the teachings of Theodore of Mopsuestia, and were therefore predisposed to support Nestorianism. But as we have seen, Rabbula the bishop of Edessa (412-35) became a strong opponent of Nestorius, a change which did not augur well for the Edessene School, most of whose teachers were out of sympathy with their bishop's views. Matters improved somewhat when Ibas, who was also a teacher at the School, became bishop in 435, and who retained that position, save for the years 449-51, until his death in 457. But the forces of Monophysitism were growing in strength, and at the death of Ibas, they were able to secure the see of Edessa for one of their number, Nuna (Nonnus), who had had an earlier term there as bishop 449-51, and who died in 471. Although this appointment made a difficult situation for the School, the latter continued to function. It was Nuna's successor, Cyrus, who rightly judged that the School, a thorn in the flesh to the Monophysite cause, would have to be closed. It seems that after the accession of Cyrus in 471 there was a further loss of teachers who were sensitive to the winds of change and who sought asylum across the border in Persia. Finally the bishop obtained from the emperor Zeno (474-91) permission to shut the famous academy. This was carried out in 489, and such teachers and pupils as were considered heretical were expelled from the city. On the site of the

---

[6] The twelve anathemas and Theodoret's rebuttal of them are found in *Nicene and Post-Nicene Fathers*, III, New York, 1892, pp 25-31.

School there was dedicated a church, dedicated, ironically, to Mary the Mother of God. While the School was thus liquidated, its former graduates continued to enrich the life of the Syriac Church for the next two generations.

8. The Chronicle of Joshua the Stylite.[7]

This Chronicle was written by one, Joshua, who is described by a copyist as from a convent near Amid, and whose sobriquet, "the Stylite," suggests that for part of his life he had been a pillar saint. At the time of his writing he was evidently in Edessa, which he refers to as "our city." He had been requested by one, Sergius, the abbot of a monastery in or near Edessa, to write a record of the times in which they were living. Possibly Joshua had some post within this monastery which would make the complying with such a request feasible. In consequence he has given us a record of the years 495–507 insofar as it pertains to the regions of Edessa and Amid. His narrative sheds invaluable light on the Persian-Byzantine war of 502–5, as well as on the social, political, economic and to a lesser extent, the religious affairs of these years. The reference in his title to "the time of affliction" points to the unbelievable suffering through war, earthquake, famine, pestilence, and the brutality of Gothic mercenaries in the Byzantine army, which people had to endure. Joshua's work ends with an expression of the hope that he will in the future be able to continue his narrative beyond its present conclusion, but apparently he was unable to fulfill this expectation.

9. The Early History of Asceticism and Monasticism.[8]

This subject sends us back briefly to the first and following centuries. In the first century the Church assumed that the Christian life could be lived within ordinary society, and that the moral perfection which Matt 5:48 inculcated could be understood as an approximation, as close as humanly possible, to wholeness and integrity. The Devil was the chief antagonist (Eph 4:27; James 4:7), and Christians had to be constantly on the alert against his wiles, and at the same time exercise self-control in all things (I Cor 7:5; 9:25). This view is reflected in second century sources, such as Ignatius of Antioch, the Didache, and Bardaisan of Edessa. Clement of Alexandria (150–215) in his *Paedagogus*, belongs to this tradition. The Christian life, in this work, is simple, modest and chaste, and is compatible with the marriage relationship.

There are, however, in the Gospels (in addition to the narratives about John the Baptist) a number of passages whose general tenor is that Christian

---

[7] Tr by W. Wright, Cambridge, 1882. The full title of the Syriac text is, *A History of the Time of Affliction in Edessa and Amid and throughout all Mesopotamia*.

[8] A. Vööbus, HASO II.

discipleship involves some degree of self-abnegation (Matt 10:37–38; 19:10–12; Mk 8:34–35; 10:21; Lk 9:57–62; etc.), and when these words are taken in what seems to be their ordinary sense, they encourage various degrees of self-sacrifice. Even Paul's sensible statement on marriage (I Cor 7) does not conceal his own view that virginity is superior to marriage (vss 1, 38), though Paul does not go as far as the author of Revelation who claimed (according to one interpretation) that marriage in some way defiles (14:4). This may be related to the OT view that sexual intercourse causes temporary uncleanness (Lev 15:18). There is clearly some relation between all this and the Jewish Essenes or Qumranis, whose distinctive way of life was characterized by celibacy (for the majority) and a common purse.

It was only in the second century that the incipient asceticism of first century Christianity began to take on more perceptible forms, at least in western Asia. We cannot here attempt to identify all the influences that brought about this development. The fact is that in this century there was a visible outburst of asceticism in the Christian communities in the Roman Orient. This growth was, apparently, indigenous for it is difficult to find in it traces of outside influence. It was not, as far as can be determined, under the direction of the bishops, and its development was therefore somewhat anarchic. What happened is illustrated in the careers of both Marcion and Tatian, whose ascetic ideas were not favourably received by the Church as a whole. Whatever the growing numbers of proponents of asceticism might claim, the bishops of the Church seem to have viewed asceticism as an option for Christians, although it was conceded that it conferred special merit on those who practised it. Probably the *Didache* of the second century expresses the point of view of many of the bishops. "If you can bear the whole yoke of the Lord, you will be perfect, but if you cannot, do what you can" (6.2).

It is impossible to determine to what extent asceticism in Syria in the third and early fourth centuries was affected by the Roman persecutions of the Church. We can only observe that as the persecution appears to have been staged mostly in urban centres, the countryside would have offered many suitable places where various forms of asceticism could still be practised without state interference. Strong central leadership in the ascetic movement continued to be lacking, and so the movement developed of itself, and as we might expect, it took many forms and produced a generous share of fanatics and eccentrics. A sidelight on what could happen is found in the *Acts of Thomas*,[9] an apocryphal narrative written probably in Edessa in the early third century, and detailing Thomas's various activities in India. We note in this work that, apart from the performance of various miracles by Thomas, there is much emphasis on the wickedness of sexual intercourse.

---

[9] A. F. J. Klijn, *The Acts of Thomas* (Supplements to *Novum Testamentum*, 5), Leiden, 1962.

In section 84 fornication is said to be "the head of all evils," and later we read of "hateful intercourse." It is clear that in these *Acts*, celibacy is the great virtue. It is Sozomen who comments on the anchorites in Syria and neighbouring regions, and who notes that some carried the principle of self-denial to extraordinary lengths (VI. 34). One part of Syria which was a natural habitat for those who wished solitude was the mountainous zone which surrounds Edessa on three sides. Two fourth century figures, who belong to this area, both known to Ephraim of Edessa, illustrate the asceticism of the period. One was Juliana Saba who died about 366–67.[10] Born in a peasant family, he established himself as an anchorite in a cave north-east of Edessa, and he presently permitted a community of like-minded persons to grow up around him, all of them living in near-by caves. Juliana practised severe mortification as well as absolute poverty, and at a very minimum of food. After morning worship, the members of the group went, two by two, on journeys of varying lengths, their time being spent in prayer and worship. Juliana is said to have spent fifty years in his particular kind of asceticism. The other example is Abraham Qidunaia, who probably came from Edessa, and who was converted to Christianity during a wedding festival. He settled in a deserted house east of Edessa, and became quite famous locally for his fasting, his vigils, and his ruthless treatment of his body.[11] He, too, died about 367.

The famous Ephraim of Edessa belongs to this anchorite tradition.[12] When he left Nisibis and settled in Edessa, his living quarters were in a cell in the hills north of the city, and it was here that he did his extensive writing. He seems to have been somewhat ambivalent about asceticism. He frequently addressed ordinary people as though the Christian life were a real possibility for them. Yet others he encouraged to take the path of the anchorites. To him anchoritism was the ideal ascetic life, allowing those who practised it to recover man's wholeness, through penitence, virginity, fasting, prayer, poverty, mortification of the body, and primitive habitation. Such wholeness was conceived by Ephraim to be the end of all asceticism. Although this was more by example than by precept, Ephraim did much to stimulate the intellectual life of the anchorite movement. His own writings were a challenge to other ascetics to both study and write, and in the long run this made for an enrichment of the monastic ideal.

If the *Doctrine of Addai* comes from the fourth century, as is commonly thought, it is noteworthy that its message, as outlined both in the apostle's sermon before an audience in Edessa, and in his address on the eve of his

---

[10] On Juliana Saba and Abraham Qidunaia, see A. Vööbus, HASO II, pp 42–60. Juliana's death is recorded in the *Chronicle of Edessa*, 28.

[11] Although Abraham was essentially a recluse, he had an active part in the conversion of the nearby village of Qidun, in whose needy he showed particular interest.

[12] For a recent study of Ephraim, see A. Vööbus, HASO II, pp 70–110.

death, does not present an ascetic interpretation of the Christian faith. Only once, in the last-named speech, does Addai, in refusing to accept from the king costly garments in which he might be buried, seem to downgrade all gifts from men: "Receive not anything from man and acquire not anything in this world."

Theodoret in his *Ecclesiastical History* (IV. 26–8) mentions the names of some of the more important monks of the fourth century who were found in the vicinity of Antioch. In another work, translated by P. Canivet, *Histoire des moines de Syrie* (Paris, 1977), he gives biographies of thirty celebrated ascetics in Syria. Only thirteen of these appear in Canivet's volume. Presumably the remaining seventeen will appear later. Theodoret tells us that most of these monks spoke Syriac (A. Vööbus, HASO II, p 122). For the situation in the region of Edessa, we have the evidence supplied by one, Sylvia (or Egeria), who was a minor figure at the court of Theodosius I (379-95) and Arcadius (395-408). She was interested in the Oriental Churches, and c 390 she began a pilgrimage to the holy places.[13] On coming to Edessa she wrote, "I visited in the city many shrines of martyrs and many holy monks, some living near the shrines, others living far from the city in secluded places where they had cells" (G. E. Gingras, *Egeria: Diary of a Pilgrimage*, New York, 1970, p 77). It would appear that at this time the solitary religious life was still the ideal for most ascetics in Osrhoene.

For an excellent example of an anchorite with a flair for showmanship we have the famous Simeon Stylites.[14] Simeon was a Greek-speaking Christian, but insofar as he represents a certain type of asceticism in the eastern Church he is being noticed here. He was born c 390 to a Christian family near Nicopolis in north Syria. As a youth he gave himself up to asceticism, and presently he entered a monastery near Antioch where he spent about ten years and became known for his severe mortifications, but from which he was expelled because of his queer behaviour. He then went to a village (Telneshin, Telneshe) between Aleppo and Antioch where in a small monastery he had an enclosure (Gk *mandra*) built for himself, and where he is said to have wrought miracles while sitting on the ground. His fame was greatly furthered when he had a nine-foot pillar made and on the top of which he now lived. The height of the pillar was increased by stages to about forty feet, the area at the top being about six feet square, and on this pillar he spent a total of thirty-seven years. Presumably his physical needs were met by persons on the ground who must have operated with some kind of a ladder or hoist. Most of his time was spent in prayer,

---

[13] *Corpus Scriptorum Ecclesiasticorum Latinorum*, XXXIX, 1898, *Peregrinatio Silvae* xix. 4. George E. Gingras, *Egeria: Diary of a Pilgrimage*, New York, 1970.

[14] On Simeon Stylites, see F. Lent, JAOS 35, 1915-17, pp 103–98 (ET of Bedjan's Syriac text of the life of St. Simeon Stylites); Evagrius, *Eccl Hist*, I, 13–14; T. Nöldeke (tr by J. S. Black), *Sketches from Eastern History*, London, 1892, ch VII, pp 207-35; A. Vööbus, HASO II, pp 208-23.

meditation or sleep, but in the afternoons he spoke to the crowds below and dictated letters to a disciple. His novel form of austerity attracted countless visitors, and through his contacts with people on the ground, by his preaching to them (mostly, it seems, about the monastic ideal), and by the correspondence, he exercised a considerable influence upon the Church of his age. In the theological disputes of the fifth century, he was a champion of the Council of Chalcedon. He died after a short illness in September 459. The convent and the church (Qal'at Sim'an) built on the site of the famous pillar before 470 are described by H. C. Butler (ed E. B. Smith) in *Early Churches in Syria* (Princeton, 1929, pp 97–105).

Simeon Stylites is a shining example of an anchorite who maintained, in his own peculiar way, the ascetic ideal, and yet who remained in touch with the problems of the world. Even the great Anthony of Egypt had briefly left the solitudes of the desert to go to Alexandria and declaim against the doctrines of Arius. Other solitaries seem to have been accessible for limited periods of time to those who remained in the wicked world but who were in need of guidance and comfort. The ministration of the monks to such troubled souls was a form of pastoral care which supplemented what was normally exercised by the parish priests.

It must strike an observer as curious that it was not until the fourth century that it was realized by many ascetics that their basic ideals of poverty and chastity did not necessarily demand isolation from like-minded Christians, and out of this awareness cenobitism was born. It is probable that the end of the Roman persecution of Christians in the early part of the century was a factor in encouraging asceticism to take more visible forms in society. Other considerations may have stimulated the growth of cenobitism within the Church, such as the practices of the primitive Church (Acts 2:44–7; 4:32–7), traditions stemming from the Jewish Essenes (Qumranis), the ideals and discipline of the Manichees (see ch 7). That the monastic ideas of Buddhism helped in the development of Christian monasticism seems to the present writer to be highly doubtful. In any case, Christian monasticism was a slow development, but the two names that stand out in connection with its early history are those of Pachomius in Egypt (290–346) and Basil of Caesarea in Cappadocia (330–79). The latter was a strong advocate of cenobitical asceticism, and his organization of and rules for the monks were to have a permanent influence on monastic life within the Greek Church.

It will not serve our purpose to attempt to trace in detail the growth of monasteries in Roman Syria, but a few examples of the early ones will illustrate what was happening. In northern Mesopotamia, in the mountainous region of Tur 'Abdin, there were many monastic foundations, one being that founded by Samuel in the village of Qartamin about 397. Harsh mortifications were a feature of its life, but these were somehow combined with the administration of a complex of buildings and with the necessary care of fields and gardens. In the vicinity of Amid many monasteries were established, a neighbourhood in which John of Ephesus spent his early life. One of the largest of these foundations, that of Mar Mama, whose inmates numbered several hundred, was in the village of Hazin. To the south-west of Amid in the region roundabout Edessa, once as in Ephraim's time the home of numerous anchorites, many monastic establishments were now to be found. Here we meet, among others, the monastery of the Orientals, the monastery of Mar John the Evangelist, the monastery of Mar Jacob of Naphshata, etc. When Theodoret, bishop of Cyrrhus, wrote his *Ecclesiastical History* about 444, he noted that monasteries had greatly multiplied, and that monks now seemed to prefer the cenobitic life to the solitary one. Many monasteries appear to have been founded by individual monks or by groups of monks, while others were due to the interest of bishops or of devout laymen. Evagrius records (I. xxi) that the empress Eudocia, wife of Theodosius II, who visited Jerusalem in 438, founded monasteries, mostly in Palestine.

The growth of monasteries was not without its opponents. A representative of this group was Isaac of Antioch (d c 460), who found great dangers to the traditional values of anchoritism in the advance of cenobitism. When monasteries were built they demanded the attention and care of their inmates. Physical work, worry and responsibility were now common experiences of the brethren in monastic establishments, and this was a situation that seemed to Isaac and to those who sided with him, to be a betrayal of the ideal of true asceticism. On the various types of ascetics who eschewed cenobitical life, see Evagrius I. xxi.

The establishment of monasteries was bound to lead to the growth of traditions and canons related to the life of the monks and to the administration of monastic property. As an example of what was developed, we summarize below some of the monastic rules attributed to Rabbula, bishop of Edessa 412–35.[15] It appears from these regulations that a monastery had two leading officials, the overseer (*Syr sʿwr'*), and the abbot (*Syr rysh dyr'*), but the precise relationship between these two personages is not clearly indicated.

1. No women are to enter monasteries.
2. Only the overseer may enter the (nearby) villages.
4. Monks shall not drink wine.
5. Monks shall not grow hair (long hair?).
6. When the overseer goes out on monastery business, he shall not wear the monastic garb, nor shall the brothers when they are outside the monastery.
7. No monk shall distribute (lit "make") oil, nor give it to the women. If the latter need oil, it shall be sent to them through their husbands.

---

[15] Ed and tr by A. Vööbus, *Documents*, pp 24–33.

8. Commemoration feasts in the monasteries are to be attended only by the monks.
9. Work animals are limited to one donkey or one yoke of oxen (per monastery?).
10. Heretical books are not to be found in monasteries.
11. Buying and selling in the monasteries is forbidden except for needful things.
12. No monk shall own private possessions (there is evidently a community of possessions, controlled by the abbot).
13. The monks are not to meet with relatives.
14. Sickness is to be endured within the monastery, and is not to be used as a pretext for visiting the village or town.
15. Monks shall not leave the monastery to act as attorneys for the laity.
16. Attendance at the hours of worship is compulsory and no excuses for absence are accepted.
17. Strangers are to be received kindly.
18. Dwelling in isolation (within the monastery?) is allowed to a monk only rarely.
19. (This seems to mean that a monk will not normally answer the queries of the laity regarding the Scriptures).
20. Only a priest or a deacon can administer the Eucharist.
21. Monks who are priests or deacons may be entrusted by the abbot with the care of churches in the villages.
22. (This deals with what is to be done with real and alleged bones of martyrs).
24. If a monk dies, he is to be buried quietly by the monks without the presence of outsiders.
25. When a crop, presumably grown on monastery land, is sold at the threshing-season, it is to be sold at the current price.
26. An itinerant monk is to be received only if he is recommended by the abbot of the last monastery he was in.

In A. Vööbus's *Syriac and Arabic Documents*, there appear some rules for nuns.[16] Their author or compiler is unknown. The date of the Syriac MS is between the mid-fifth and the eighth centuries, and its provenance is probably the western part of Syria. Among its regulations we find the following:

[16] Id pp 62–68.

1. It is not lawful for a sister to go out from the monastery alone.
4. It is not lawful for a sister to drink or eat anything in the town except water.
5. It is not lawful for a sister to eat with a man. But if the abbess approves, she may eat with certain male relatives. A man, however, must not enter the main building of the convent.
6. It is not lawful for a sister to enter a house alone with a man.
7 and 14. It is not lawful for a sister to enter a monastery for monks. Only an old priest is allowed to enter the convent on Sundays to consecrate the Eucharist.
9. It is not lawful, without the approval of the abbess, for a sister to borrow from or lend to anyone (certain exceptions are specified).
10. It is not lawful for a sister to neglect daily prayers or the Eucharist on Sunday.
11. The permission of the overseeing sister must be obtained if a sister wishes to go on a journey longer than one mile.
12. (This rule relates to altercations between sisters, and to the penalties to be imposed on the guilty party).
13. A sister shall not go out of the convent except on necessary business.

It is a paradox of monasticism that those who cut themselves off from normal human society frequently displayed a deep concern for the poor of the world which they, the monks, had left behind. In the story of Ephraim, we read that in the year before his death he worked energetically in Edessa to cope with a local famine and to improve the lot of the sick. When cenobitism came to the fore, this ascetic tradition of helping the world's dispossessed and needy lived on, and guest houses, hostels and/or hospitals were frequently to be found associated with monasteries.

Monasticism was also important in the literary culture of the Syriac Church. For it was a part of the ascetic tradition that even when the world and its possessions were abandoned, it was permissible for an anchorite to own a codex or book, especially a biblical text or a biblical commentary. When monasteries were established, they became the heirs of this tradition, and the books of individual monks often became the nucleus of a monastic library. It was recognized that the study of approved books was a means for strengthening the religious life, though as Rabbula's canon 10 indicates, books "outside the faith of the Church shall not be in the monasteries." The monastic establishments thus became centres for preserving and re-copying both biblical codices and sundry works on biblical exegesis and Christian theology, and in this way they helped to perptuate some of the intellectual traditions of the School of Edessa. It should be noted, however, that monastery libraries on the whole seem to have confined their holdings to works of a religious character. Writings of a purely secular nature, such as some used in the School of Edessa, were not generally available in the monasteries.

A somewhat minor activity of the monasteries was in the area of primary education. If, as one of Rabbula's canons for "the sons of the Covenant" states, "the sons of the Covenant must learn the Psalms" (20), and if, as Maruta's canon XXVI. 2–4, enjoins, the sons of the Covenant "shall be given to the churches and monasteries. . . . and they shall be educated in doctrine and instruction," there must have been some elementary teaching in reading and writing available in monasteries (and apparently also in some churches), but how this activity was actually organized we do not know. While this arrangement was intended primarily for "the sons and daughters of the Covenant," it is probable that other members of the Christian community were able to take advantage of it.

A striking feature of the life of many (but not all) Syriac congregations was the presence in them of clergy of lower rank than priest and deacons, and known as "the sons (or daughters) of the Covenant" (*Syr bny / bnt/ qym'*).[17] As they appear to be an off-shoot of the ascetic movement, a brief account of them is given here. We shall look at them through the rules, said to be the rules of Rabbula, for the priests and "the sons of the Covenant." It is assumed by the present writer that in what follows "the sons of the Church" designates all the clergy, including "the sons of the Covenant."

1.	They are to know the true faith of the holy Church.
2.	A son of the Covenant shall not live with a woman, except when he is in the house of his mother, sister or daughter (cf 28 regarding a daughter of the Covenant).
9.	A son or daughter of the Covenant shall take no interest on a loan (this suggests that they were allowed to maintain control of some private property).
10, 18, 42.	They are to live with relatives, or with one another, or in the church.
11, 27.	They are to be faithful in fasting, concerned about the poor, and diligent both in prayer and in attendance at church services.
12, 19.	If they are poor, the priests and deacons must take care of them.

[17] Id pp 34–50.

20.	They shall all learn the Psalms, and the daughters of the Covenant shall in addition learn hymns.
21.	They are not to swear by the name of God.
23, 46.	They are to refrain from wine and meat except in cases of illness. Drunkenness or patronage of a tavern will entail expulsion from the Church. They shall not drink wine at a funeral feast.
25-6.	They may not be employed as watchmen of granaries or vineyards, nor as stewards or taskmasters for laymen, nor take on lawsuits for relatives.
29.	When guilty of misconduct (not defined), both the sons and daughters of the Covenant shall be sent to monasteries (and convents?) for repentance, and along with their parents they shall be suspended from the benefits of the Church.
32.	They are not to place ordinary vessels side by side with sacred vessels in a chest or shrine.
37.	If sons of the Covenant go to a gathering (of the congregation?), they must be accompanied by priests, and the daughters of the Covenant by deaconesses.
38.	The bishop's permission is necessary for a son of the Covenant to do any travelling, even on congregational or village business.
41.	He must not go surety for anyone.
45.	A son of the Covenant shall normally serve as steward of the congregation.
48.	He is to have no relations with heretics.
55.	He must not castrate himself.
58.	He shall not ascend to the raised platform of the altar, nor bring any food into the apse.

As the Christological disputes of the fourth to sixth centuries were to show, monks either as individual ascetics or as members of monasteries were the heart and soul of popular Christianity in the Roman Orient, and as spokesmen for a cause their influence could carry much weight. Although there were some strong monasteries in Syria and Palestine which favoured the Council of Chalcedon, most of the monasteries in these regions seem to have championed some form of Monophysitism. To such monks, salvation could only come from One who was truly God and whose sacrament guaranteed them against the power of the Devil. Nestorius and the Council of Chalcedon were therefore anathema to them.

All monasticism, whether it be eremitical or cenobitical, whether it be Oriental, Greek or Roman, can be censured on various grounds as an inadequate and lop-sided expression of the Christian faith. But it is important to remeber that it has a number of things to its credit. It helped, for instance, to preserve the spirituality of the Church, to insist that a man's true life does not consist in the abundance of his possessions, and to maintain that the Gospel must be expressed in a life of high moral quality. While monasticism served to safeguard and perpetuate these emphases in the Church, it also kept alive through its libraries and through the labours of the devoted monks who worked in them, the ancient Hebrew tradition that knowledge and instruction are handmaids to the fear of the Lord.

10. Monophysitism in Syria and the Orthodox Reaction.[18]

The beginnings of Monophysitism in Syria go back at least to the time of Peter the Fuller. Peter was a Monophysite monk and priest who came to Antioch with Zeno (c 470), when the latter held the office of *magister militum per Orientem*. He seems to have found certain elements in Antioch congenial to his Monophysite views, and when Martyrius, the patriarch of Antioch, was absent in Constantinople, he contrived apparently with Zeno's support and with the strident assistance of monks brought into Antioch for the purpose to have himself declared bishop of Antioch. This was quite an irregular proceeding and Peter's term in office lasted only a year, but as matters turned out, it was the first of the four times he held the see of Antioch, the others being in 471, 475, and 484. His last appointment was due to Zeno (now emperor), to whose Henoticon he agreed to subscribe. Peter died in office in 488, but not before he left a Monophysite party in Antioch firmly established.

The patriarchate of Flavian II in Antioch (498–512) did little to advance the Monophysite cause, for although Flavian had assented to Zeno's Henoticon, he came to his office from a background in a pro-Chalcendonian monastery in Syria. As we shall see later in this chapter, Philoxenus, bishop of Mabbog, was determined to oust him from office, and this he accomplished in 512. The next Antiochene Patriarch was Severus (512–18), a staunch Monophysite, but when Justin I, an equally staunch Chalcedonian, became emperor, he brought about the deposition of Severus, which may be thought of as the beginning of the persecution of Monophysites in Syria. This was carried out by the Patriarchs of Antioch, such as Paul the Jew (519–21) and Euphrasius (521–26). The latter, killed in the earthquake that hit Antioch in 526, was succeeded by Ephraim of Amid (527–45) whom

---

[18] See E. Honigmann, *Évêoues et Évêchés Monophysites d' Asie Antérieure au VIe Siècle*, CSCO 127, Subsidia 2, Louvain, 1951; W. H. C. Frend, *The Rise of the Monophysite Movement*, Cambridge, 1972. A. Vööbus, "The Origin of the Monophysite Church in Syria and Mesopotamia," *Church History* 42 (1973), pp 17–26.

John of Ephesus describes as "a worse pesecutor than either Paul or Euphrasius" (*Eccl Hist*, I. 41). For some details of these persecutions, especially as they affected convents and monasteries, see *Chr de Michel*, 2, IX. xiv. The leading Monophysites of the early and mid sixth century, all of whom except Jacob of Serug were involved in the persecution enforced by emperors determined to support Chalcedon, are dealt with separately in what follows.

Jacob of Serug.

Jacob of Serug who came to be known as "the flute of the Holy Spirit and the harp of the believing Church," was born c 451 in Kurtam, a village on the Euphrates, in the district of Serug. Since his father was a priest in the Church, he was exposed from his earliest days to the beliefs and traditions of the Christian community. After training in Edessa, where he appears to have been in 470, presumably at "the School of the Persians," he entered the priesthood, and c 502–3 he became periodeutes of Haura in the district of Serug, and in 519 he was made bishop of Batnae (Batnan), also in Serug. He died 520–21.

Although Jacob seems to have been a Monophysite, he kept clear of the theological wrangles of his day. If he had lived a little longer, he probably would have become a victim of the persecution of the Monophysites by Justin I. As it was, he led a quiet life, devoting himself to his ecclesiastical responsibilities and using the rest of his time and energy for literary work. It was his writing as well as his preaching that gave him so wide a reputation. He is said to have begun his writing at the age of twenty-two, and to have written more than 700 poems and to have employed seventy amanuenses. In addition to poems, odes and hymns, he wrote numerous letters and both metrical and prose homilies. His output of writing was such that in 1922 Baumstark required pp 148–58 in his *Geschichte der syrischen Literatur* to describe it. Very little of this material has been translated into English (cf W. Cureton, *Ancient Syriac Documents* (London, 1864), pp 86–107). A. Vööbus has put all students of Jacob in his debt by issuing in 1973 (Louvain) his *Handschriftliche Überlieferung der Memre-Dichtung des Ja'qob von Serug* (CSCO, Subsidia 39 and 40). The abbreviations in Subsidia 39 (pp vii-xxvii) serve also as an extensive bibliography of the subject.

As an example of Jacob's poetry, we quote from the beginning of his metrical homily concerning the holy Mar Simeon the Stylite.[19]

> Grant to me, O Lord, that I may depict
>   an image which is full of grace,
> Of Simeon the chosen one, whose graces
>   are more exalted than (human) speech.

---

[19] The Syriac text is found in Brockelmann, *op cit*, p 102°.

Through you I will speak of his exploits
> while I am lost in wonder
That only through you is the grace
> of your servant ineffable.
For his sake, speak O Lord
> through me in all your fullness,
That I may speak concerning him
> who is a champion, replete with exploits.
I am your flute, breathe on me
> your spirit, O son of God,
That I may give out wondrous sounds
> concerning the excellent one;
May your strength stir me up,
> as the spirit stirs up the pen,
And speaks through it sweet
> music with a sublime voice.

Philoxenus.

A figure of great importance in Syrian Monophysitism is that of Philoxenus (Aksenaya).[20] Born in Persia in the province of Beth Garmai, seemingly of Christian parents, Philoxenus fled to Roman territory from Persia under the persecution of Christians launched by Yazdagird II (439–57), and eventually he became a student at the School of Edessa when Ibas was the bishop of that city. It would appear that the young student had early given himself to a religious vocation, and in the theological disputes of the age he became a fervent Monophysite.[21] The orthodox Patriarch of Antioch, Calandion (481–84), chased him from his diocese, but when the Patriarch, who refused to endorse the Henoticon, was exiled to Egypt, his successor, Peter the Fuller, singled out Philoxenus for ecclesiastical preferment, appointing him chorepiscopus of Mabbog, and in 485 bishop of that city, which made him metropolitan bishop of the province of Euphratesia. This region had hitherto been largely pro-Nestorius, but under Philoxenus it slowly was won over to Monophysitism. Philoxenus was a very energetic Monophysite. Perhaps more than anyone else, he helped to wreck the emperor Anastasius's policy of uniting the Roman Orient on the basis of Zeno's Henoticon. He encouraged Cyrus, bishop of Edessa, to obtain from the emperor Zeno an edict to close the School of Edessa because of its Nestorian sympathies (489), and he worked hard to get Flavian, Patriarch of Antioch (498–512), who had declared himself to be a supporter of Chalcedon, removed from his see. Not being able to dispose of Flavian by more approved methods, Philoxenus brought Monophysite monks into Antioch and organized demonstrations against him.[22] When some of the Antiochenes resisted the intruders, there were violent scenes in the city, and

---

[20] See A. de Halleux, *Philoxène de Mabbog, sa vie, ses écrits, sa théologie*, Louvain, 1963.

[21] For a brief statement of his Monophysite views, see "The Creed of Philoxenus" in *The Discourses of Philoxenus*, ed and tr by E. A. W. Budge, 2 vols, London, 1894, vol 2, pp xxxi–xlviii.

[22] On the disputes between Philoxenus and Flavian, see Evagrius III. 31–2.

Flavian left the city, he supposed temporarily. These disorders prompted the emperor to get rid of Flavian, who was formally deposed by a synod which met at Laodicea in 512. In this year a synod at Hierapolis, headed by Philoxenus, chose Severus as Flavian's successor. Philoxenus's fortunes went into an abrupt decline after 518. In that year Justin I was acclaimed emperor and he was determined to enforce Chalcedonian orthodoxy in the empire. In 519-21 all bishops were required to subscribe to the Creed of Chalcedon, the result being that 55 Monophysite bishops, including Philoxenus, were deprived of their sees.[23] Philoxenus was banished to Thrace and later to Paphlagonia, where he died (apparently murdered) in 523.

The Discourses of Philoxenus (ed E. A. W. Budge, 2 vols, London 1894) illustrate most of Philoxenus's interests, although they are lacking in Monophysite polemics. They are addressed to the newer members of the monastic community, and they present Philoxenus as a champion of the ascetic ideal who speaks in a fatherly way and as an experienced monk to his younger brethren. It is also evident from these discourses that Philoxenus was a careful student of the Scriptures from which he quotes freely. This concern with God's Word sheds light on his desire to make available a better Syriac version of the Scriptures, a task undertaken at his behest in 505-8 by his chorepiscopus Polycarp. This translation covered the NT and possibly part of the OT; the latter must have been based on the current Septuagint. It seems to have been in use for about a hundred years, and it was then displaced by a new version attributed to Paul, bishop of Tella, and Thomas of Ḥarkel (Heraclea), bishop of Mabbog.

Severus.

Severus was Greek-speaking, but as most of his writings are preserved only in Syriac, we are including him in this survey. He was the successor of Flavian in Antioch, and he was, in fact, the most illustrious and the most erudite of the Monophysites of the early sixth century. Born of a wealthy family in Pisidia c 465, he studied rhetoric at Alexandria and law at Berytus, and in the latter city he became a Christian of Monophysite persuasion, and also a monk who at one time nearly killed himself with his privations. His natural gifts led him to a position of leadership in the ascetic world, and in 508 he came to Constantinople with 200 monks to support the emperor Anastasius who had strong Monophysite leanings. When Flavian was deposed in 512, Severus was a natural choice as his successor. If we count Peter the Fuller as the first, then Severus was the second of the Monophysite Patriarchs of Antioch. During his six years in office it seems indisputable that the Monophysites employed physical violence against Chalcedonians in influential places (Evagrius III. 33), though they were not able to suppress all opposition to Severus and his views, especially outside of Antioch.

[23] For some details of the persecution, see W. H. C. Frend, *op cit*, pp 247-49.

The emperor Justin I, a stout Chalcedonian, looked upon Severus as a danger both to the orthodox Church and to the state, and he ordered Severus's removal from office. In July 518 a synod in Antioch deposed him, and to avoid arrest Severus fled to Alexandria. For several years he was obliged to live in hiding. He writes in his letters, "no man has known our place of abode:" "I have been hiding in corners" and "in the desert where I am dwelling unseen."

The hopes of the Monophysites were raised when Justinian came to power (527), mostly because his consort Theodora was a known Monophysite sympathizer. The years 530–36 saw a virtual truce between the Orthodox and the Monophysites. Monophysite monks were permitted to return to their monasteries, but the deposed bishops could not return to their sees. As we noted in ch 3, conferences were held with the aim of bringing the two sides together. In the winter of 534–35 Severus was invited to the capital by the emperor and received by him with honour, probably because of the influence of Theodora. Anthimus, the new Patriarch of Constantinople, and Severus seemed to be on good terms and even in communion with one another. But Anthimus was not a genuine Chalcedonian, and when this became apparent to Justinian, he had him removed from office. A synod in Constantinople in May-June 536 then renewed the ban on Severus, and an imperial edict ordered the burning of all copies of Severus's writings. Severus, thus condemned afresh, left the capital and died eighteen months later in 538, an exile in Egypt.

A good deal of Severus's energy was spent in combatting divisive forces within Monophysitism itself, but these struggles with the Julianists and the Eutychians do not concern us here. His letters,[24] however, are of considerable interest for they not only reflect the tense theological atmosphere of the sixth century, but they also give us a glimpse into the day to day problems of a Syrian bishop, both before and after his deposition. In these letters Severus reveals his expert knowledge of the Scriptures, and he himself comes through as magnanimous (except when dealing with opponents), sensible, and temperate in his judgments.

John of Tella.[25]

John bar Cursus was born in Callinicus c 483. After a short period in the army, he became a Monophysite monk and in 519 he was elevated to the bishopric of Tella (Constantia). In 521 he was one of fifty-four

---

[24] The original Greek text of the letters is lost, but many are extant in Syriac translations: see *The Sixth Book of the Select Letters of Severus, Patriarch of Antioch*, ed and tr by E. W. Brooks, 3 vols, London, 1902–4; other letters, also edited by Brooks, are found in PO 12 (1919), pp 163–342; 14 (1920), pp 1–310. On Severus's life, see "The Conflict of Severus," tr E. J. Goodspeed, PO 4, pp 571–725.

[25] See E. W. Brooks, "Life of John, Bishop of Tella, by Elias," CSCO ser III, vol 25, Paris 1907 (Syr pp 29–95; Latin, pp 21–60).

Monophysite bishops expelled from their sees by Justin I, but his enthusiasm for Monophysitism was not thereby dampened. He spent the next several years propagating his faith, travelling widely, often in secret, and ordaining many deacons and priests who were tested for their basic literacy and knowledge of the Scriptures. One of those ordained deacon c 529 was John of Amid, later the famous bishop of Ephesus. John in fact did a great deal to consolidate Monophysitism in north-east Syria and north-west Mesopotamia. In 537 he was seized by the authorities in the mountains of Singara and confined to a convent near Antioch were he died in 538.

    Jacob Baradaeus.

    Jacob was the son of one, Theophilus, a priest in Tella. After a good education he entered a monastery in Mount Izla, near Tella, and apparently it was during these days that he wore as his ordinary garment a saddle- or horse-cloth (*Syr brd't'*), presumably signalizing his devotion to personal poverty. He continued to be clothed in this manner throughout his later life, and hence he was called Baradaeus (*Syr bwrd'y'*). It is not known at what point in his life he espoused Monophysitism.

    About 527-28 Jacob and another Monk, Sergius, were sent to Constantinople in the interests of the Monophysites, and here they lived for fifteen years enjoying the protection of the empress Theodora. This rather quiet life changed c 542-3 when the empress was importuned by Harith, the Arab ruler of Ghassan, to send some bishops to Syria to help the Monophysites who had not recovered from the earlier persecutions of Justin I. In response to this plea, Theodora had Theodosius, the exiled Patriarch of Alexandria, then living in Constantinople, consecrate one, Theodore, of Arab origin as bishop of Bostra, and Jacob as bishop of Edessa, with jurisdiction over Syria and regions to the west. Jacob now left the relative security of Constantinople, and for the next thirty-five years he spent himself in ceaseless toil and innumerable journeys on behalf of the Monophysite cause. Early in this enterprise he had to visit both Alexandria and Constantinople to obtain other Monophysite bishops, so that the minimum of three bishops would be available for episcopal ordinations. During these missionary years Jacob is said to have consecrated (down to 566) 27 bishops and to have ordained 100,000 priests (the latter figure excites suspicion). So successful were John's efforts in reviving Monophysitism that the Monophysite Church in Syria and even in Persia came to be popularly known as the Jacobite Church. John died in 578 on his way to Alexandria. His few writings have survived mostly in Arabic and Ethiopic translations.

    Syrian Monophysitism in the latter half of the sixth century had once more to face persecution, in this case initiated by Justin II (565-78), who was abetted by John III Scholasticus, Patriarch of Constantinople (566-77). Actually Justin had worked hard to reconcile the two factions of the Church. Several attempts were made between 566 and 571 to find common ground between the orthodox and the Monophysites. One of these meetings, held at Callinicus c 568, was attended by a vast throng of monks and clergy. In 569-70 conversations were held in Constantinople involving among others John of Ephesus and Paul of Antioch. Further, the emperor issued his Henoticon (Henoticon II)[26] in 571 in the hope that it would be found acceptable to both parties. When it was not, Justin in exasperation authorized a persecution of the Monophysites, and except for the early part of the reign of Tiberius II (578-82), persecution of Monophysites, sometimes desultory, was to become almost standard procedure in the Byzantine world. Monophysite bishops were expelled from their sees, and Monophysite monks and nuns, who seem to have been a special target, were driven from their monasteries and convents (John of Ephesus, I. 10). It was this persecution begun by Justin that John of Ephesus himself experienced (see ch 3, sect 9). In 599 the persecution of Monophysites broke out afresh, the chief instigator being Domitian (d 602), bishop of Melitene, a cousin of the emperor Maurice. In his own diocese the measures taken were ruthless, and equally so when Domitian extended them to the province of Mesopotamia. Monasteries and churches of the Monophysites were seized and given over to the orthodox, Monks in Edessa were massacred by soldiers when they refused to leave their monasteries (*Chr de Michel*, 2, X. xxiii). Michel informs us that when Khusro II of Persia overran Mesopotamia and Syria (various years between 606 and 611), all the Chalcedonian bishops were expelled from their sees, and the orthodox churches and monsteries were put under the Monophysites (X. xxv). But when the tide of war changed and when these areas in the time of Heraclius (610-41) reverted to the control of Constantinople, and after the emperor had a set-to with Isaiah, the Monophysite bishop of Edessa, Byzantine orthodoxy was once more dominant (*Chr de Michel*, 2, XI. iii). At this point in his narrative Michel, who is about to describe the Arab invasion, permits himself some reflections on the divine retribution which comes on those who treat the orthodox (the Monophysites) so pitilessly.

Well might Michel philosophize on these matters. The persecution of Monophysites by the Byzantine authorities naturally aroused bitter resentment against Constantinople and its religious policy. At this particular moment in history, when, unknown to all concerned, the Muslim Arabs were about to break out of the confines of the Arabian peninsula, such resentment in the eastern provinces was something that the emperor in Constantinople could have done without.

Other vexations of the Syrian Monophysites were of an internal nature. They commenced in 564 when the aging Monophysite Patriarch, Theodosius (residing in Constantinople) consecrated an Alexandrian, Paul the Black, as Patriarch of Antioch. This appointment, as the event proved, was an

---

[26] The text is found in Frend, *op cit*, pp 366-68.

unhappy one, as for instance in 571 when Paul was in Constantinople, and when he was accused by other Monophysites of taking communion with the orthodox. About three years later the new Monophysite Patriarch of Alexandria, Peter, formally deposed Paul as Patriarch of Antioch. But not all the Antiochenes approved of Paul's deposition. Nonetheless those who did proceeded to choose another Patriarch, Peter of Callinicus, but as Paul was still alive and had been irregularly deposed, Antioch in fact now had two Monophysite Patriarchs. These unhappy events and the continuation of the dispute need not detain us here, although they were of great importance to Monophysite historians (John of Ephesus, *Eccl Hist*, I. 23–29, 41; II. 1-8; IV. 10–20, 33, 39–40, etc.: *Chr de Michel*, 2, X. xxii, xxvi).

Despite persecution and despite internal dissensions, the Monophysites in north-eastern Syria continued to consolidate their position and even to grow. Chalcedonianism tended to be found in the cities and towns, for their bishops were appointed with the approval of Constantinople, whereas the countryside was apt to be Monophysite (*Chr de Michel*, 2, X, xxii, xxv). One of the strengths of rural Monophysitism was that in regions where olive culture and dry farming were practised, the villages and the Monophysite monasteries were often linked together by economic interests.[27]

11. The Scriptures.

As has been noted in ch 2, sect 5, the early history of the Syriac Scriptures is obscure. It is also extremely complicated, partly because some aspects of it involve problems of textual criticism (as is illustrated by G. Zuntz, *Ancestry of the Harklean New Testament*, London, 1945), and partly because of the dearth of reliable or unambiguous information about many important aspects of the subject. In the present survey, therefore, no attempt will be made to deal with this topic exhaustively. What will be done is to offer a broad view of the subject as the present writer sees it, and leave the matter at that.

It is a simple fact, which is reflected in the dates of the early Peshitta manuscripts in the British Museum, that by the late fifth and the sixth centuries a Syriac version of the Scriptures had emerged, to be known as the Peshitta ("simple," "common;" in this context, "the Syrian Vulgate"). Despite the theological quarrels of the age, this version of the Bible was accepted by all shades of opinion in the Syriac Church. But when we look into this matter further and attempt to trace the history of the Peshitta, we are faced with numerous difficulties.

The Old Testament.

As we have noted earlier in ch 2, it is highly likely that a Syriac translation of the Old Testament was made available quite early in the history of

[27] Id, pp 333–34 and footnotes.

the Syriac Church, and that it first appeared either in Osrhoene or in Adiabene. We can refer to this as the Old Syriac OT. It was probably the work of various hands, some of whom may have been Jewish Christians. It seems to have been made from the current Septuagint, though the influence of a Palestinian Targum has been detected in some books. The Peshitta OT as we have it, appears to be the result of a series of improvements of this Old Syriac text. For instance, when Philoxenus, bishop of Mabbog, had the current text of the Scriptures revised in 505–8 by his chorepiscopus, Polycarp, the revision seemingly covered parts of the OT, and for the latter the Greek of the Septuagint was the guide. But Polycarp's work seems to have had little permanent effect upon the currently accepted text of the OT. A century later, Paul, bishop of Tella (Constantina), attempted in 617–18 a further revision of the OT, using Origen's massive Hexapla (housed in a library at Caesarea, Palestine), and turning Origen's fifth column (Origen's own revision of the text of the LXX) into Syriac, and producing the well-known Syro-Hexaplar. Although the latter is an invaluable tool for textual criticism, it does not appear to have had much influence upon the traditional OT text of the Peshitta. Probably the nine years which the distinguished scholar, Jacob, formerly bishop of Edessa (d 708), spent on revising the current OT text, with the help of the Greek texts at hand, and it is said with the occasional assistance of Jewish scholars, had more to do with putting the OT Peshitta into its permanent form than the labours of either Polycarp or Paul. It must strike the modern reader as curious that the Hebrew text of the OT seems to have played so little a part in these various revision efforts aimed at improving the Peshitta OT, though, oddly enough, originally the Peshitta OT confined itself to books recognized by the Jews, despite there being uncertainty about Chronicles, Ezra-Nehemiah, and Esther. Later, some of the apocryphal books found in the LXX were added. We do not know what criteria were used to establish a book's right to be included in the canon.

The New Testament.[28]

The Old Syriac NT survives only in two manuscripts of the Gospels, both incomplete, one known as the Sinaitic (fourth century) and the other as the Curetonian (fifth century). The statement in Eusebius about Hegesippus (second century ecclesiastical historian) making extracts from a Syriac document may be a reference to a Syriac Gospel, possibly what is called the Old Syriac (*Eccl Hist* IV. xxii. 8).

The very existence of Tatian's Diatessaron (ch 2, sect 8) points to the availability of four Gospels from which the Diastessaron could be made, and the Diatessaron itself must be understood as an attempt to simplify Christianity's primary sources. The present writer finds it impossible to maintain

---

[28] See A. Vööbus, *Studies in the History of the Gospel Text in Syriac*, CSCO 128, Subsidia 3, Louvain 1951; J. Kerschensteiner, *Der Altsyrische Paulustext*, CSCO 315, Subsidia 37, Louvain, 1970.

(as does A. Vööbus, *Studies*, as in note 27, pp 17-20) that the Gospel text available to Tatian's constituency before he produced the Diatessaron was the Gospel according to the Hebrews. Eusebius classes the Gospel according to the Hebrews among the disputed books (*Eccl Hist* III. xxv. 5: xxvii. 4: xxxix. 17; IV. xxii. 8). If we assume that Tatian produced his work initially for a Greek-using Church, then the Diatessaron would have been first issued in Greek either in Rome or in the Roman East (perhaps in Antioch). The Greek fragment of the Diatessaron found at Dura has been discussed earlier (ch 2, sect 8). If the Diatessaron first appeared in Greek, it turned out to be of limited interest in the western Church. It comes into Eusebius's narrative only in connection with his discussion of the Encratites and Tatian, although he concedes that it was still in use in his day (*Eccl Hist* IV. xxviii-xxix). Whatever its first language, the fact is that the Diatessaron had its widest use in the Syriac Church, and for at least two hundred years it served as the Gospel in many churches and monasteries. Its position in the Syriac community is suggested by the fact that Ephraim of Edessa wrote a commentary on it. While the extensive use of the Syriac Diatessaron is beyond doubt, it is incredible that in the third and fourth centuries there was no knowledge among Syriac-speaking Christians of those early Christian documents which were now known as the NT, or that all of these documents, including the four Gospels, were not becoming available in Syriac to the Oriental Church. In short it appears to be a reasonable hypothesis that the Old Syriac must at one time have embraced most if not all of the NT.

As the Syriac Church matured, and as its leaders became more aware of the prime position enjoyed by the Four Gospels in the western Church, and as the fifth century theological disputes made the eastern Church more conscious of the importance of Christianity's primary literary sources, the position of the Diatessaron began to deteriorate. In the fifth century Theodoret, bishop of Cyrrus (423-58), mounted a campaign against its use in his own diocese, and is said to have collected and destroyed 200 copies of it.[29] Theodoret's older contemporary, Rabbula of Edessa (bishop, 412-435), enjoins in his rules for the clergy, "The priests and deacons shall exercise due care that in all the churches a copy of the Four Gospels shall be (available) and is being read."[30] It is in keeping with this counsel that Rabbula is recorded to have destroyed 400 copies of the Diatessaron. It must, however, have taken time for a Gospel that had served many Syriac Christians for so long, to be completely replaced, and probably there was a transition period when the Diatessaron (the Gospel of the Mixed, *mḥalṭe*) and the Four Gospels (the Gospel of the Separated, *mpharshe*) were used alongside of one another.

[29] A. Vööbus, id p 41.
[30] A. Vööbus, *Documents*, p 47, rule 43.

Rabbula is reported to have translated the NT from Greek to Syriac. We may assume that the existing Old Syriac was available to him, and that his work was basically both a revision of that text and an attempt to reduce or eliminate the variations in the existing manuscripts. Probably his efforts constituted an important step in the directions of a standard NT, the text later to be known as the Peshitta. But it goes beyond both the known facts and the probabilities to suppose that the Peshitta owes its origin solely to Rabbula. A. Vööbus maintains that a British Museum manuscript (12150), dated 411, which contains a Syriac translation of Pseudo-Clement, and which uses various biblical quotations, shows that the revision of the Old Syriac began earlier than the time of Rabbula.[31] M. Black takes substantially this position. He says that "Rabbula's revision probably comes somewhere between attempts to revise the Old Syriac, such as we find in C (the Curetonian manuscript) and the final definitive Peshitta text which has reached us."[32]

As we have previously noted, Philoxenus, bishop of Mabbog, commissioned Polycarp to produce an improved version of the NT (505–08), and this Philoxenian version, which remained in use for a hundred years, was itself revised about 616 by Thomas of Ḥarḳel (Heraclea), also bishop of Mabbog. This Thomas in his youth had studied Greek at Qen-neshrin, and in the early seventh century he was driven from his see in the persecution of the Monophysites conducted by Domitian bishop of Melitene. He went to Egypt to the convent of the Antonians (observers of the rule of Saint Antony) near Alexandria, and it was here, inspired and encouraged by the Monophysite Patriarch, Athanasius, that he revised the Philoxenian NT.[33] The view of G. Zuntz is that the versions of the Syriac NT display "an increasing approximation to the Greek original" (*The Ancestry of the Harklean New Testament*, p 10). As a result of these various efforts, the NT Peshitta began to take on its classical form, and books which had not appeared in the earlier canon, 2 Peter, 2 and 3 John, Jude, and the Apocalypse, were now included in the Syriac Bible, probably because of the influence of the Greek NT. A. Vööbus claims that the Peshitta never completely pushed aside the Old Syriac, especially in the monasteries, at least down to the early Muslim centuries.[34]

Kenyon notes that there is in the British Museum a Peshitta manuscript of the Pentateuch (Add. 14,425) dated 464 A.D., and that it "has the distinction of being the oldest copy of the Bible in any language of which the exact date is known."[35]

---

[31] A. Vööbus, as in note 28 above, pp 50–52.

[32] "The New Testament Peshitta and its Predecessors," SNTSB, I, 1950, pp 51–62.

[33] *Chr de Michel* 2. X, xxv. For a careful study of Thomas's work, see G. Guntz, *The Ancestry of the Harklian New Testament*, Oxford, 1945.

[34] *Studies*, as in note 27, pp 98–106, 173.

[35] F. Kenyon, *Our Bible and the Ancient Manuscripts*, (revised A. W. Adams), London, 1958, p 135. See also W. H. P. Hatch, *An Album of Dated Syriac Manuscripts*, Boston 1946, plate IV, p 55; the MS does not contain the text of Leviticus.

12. Canon Law in the Western Syrian Church.

Since the Western Syrian Church was initially the child of the Greek Church, it has been generally assumed that its life was largely shaped by the canons of the Greeks. It has also been taken for granted that many of the Greek canons were translated into Syriac for the Syrian Christians, and that Syrian synods and even individual bishops issued *ad hoc* canons for the guidance of the faithful.

The inquiry into this subject must now take into consideration two recent publications by A. Vööbus: *Die syrische Kanonessammlungen* I–II (Louvain 1970), and *The Synodicon in the West Syrian Tradition* I–IV (Louvain 1975–76). For a brief discussion of these volumes, see Appendix 4.

Part Two
In the Parthian and Persian Worlds

I.
In Parthian Times (to 224 A.D.)

Chapter 6.
The Beginnings of Eastern Christianity

1. Cultural Background.

If we assume that the earliest Christian missionaries reaching Parthia came from Roman Syria (from Antioch or Edessa), they very soon would have perceived that they were working in a somewhat different cultural milieu from their home base. While Hellenism was only a kind of veneer over much of western Asia, in Mesopotamia and Persia the Hellenistic deposit left by Alexander the Great and the Seleucids was much thinner than in the West. It is probably fair to say that Greek culture in these eastern regions, even at the apex of its strength, remained a kind of cult for the scattered Greek cities and never greatly affected the mass of the people. As the European element in these cities diminished through intermarriages with the local inhabitants, the vitality of the original Hellenism was slowly sapped. This probably explains why Greeks in Babylonia contributed so little to the intellectual enrichment of the Hellenistic age. In this respect Seleucia on the Tigris seems to have been the most stimulating centre.[1] This decline in Hellenism is illustrated by Parthian coinage. The legends on the earliest Parthian coins are in Greek. In the time of Vologeses I (51–80 A.D.) Aramaic lettering appears, and in the second century A.D. Greek words are increasingly barbarous and then they become illegible.[2]

The lack of documentation makes it difficult to treat the subject of religion in Parthia satisfactorily,[3] but such evidence as we have indicates that the Parthian world exhibited a wide variety of gods and goddesses, often associated in the western provinces with Babylonian astrology. What could come out of all this is illustrated by the emergence in Babylonia in the early Christian centuries of the Mandaeans, a primitive fertility cult enriched in the course of time by borrowings from various religious traditions.

---

[1] T. Frank (ed), *An Economic Survey of Ancient Rome*, IV, Baltimore, 1938, p 169 and footnote 32.

[2] M. A. R. Colledge, *The Parthians*, London, 1967, pp 51. 74–5, 97, 170, 222–23.

[3] On religion in Parthia, see Colledge, *op cit*, pp 98–114.

One religion in Parthia which we know something about, or about which we can theorize with some confidence, is Zoroastrianism. Zoroaster was a prophet of ancient Iran, his dates being 628–551 B.C.[4] In the polytheistic society of his day he came to believe himself to be the spokesman for the god Ahura Mazda (whose symbol was the ever-burning fire), and his career is best explained as an effort to reform Iranian religion to bring it into line with the demands of Ahura Mazda as he conceived them. For any acceptable reconstruction of the prophet's teaching we have to depend basically upon the Gathas, poems traditionally credited to Zoroaster himself (found in the Yasna, 28–34, 43–51, 53).[5]

The early Achaemenid kings, and certainly this is true of Darius I, seem to have followed the main tenets of primitive Zoroastrianism, but the later members of the dynasty were more latitudinarian. The result was that Zoroaster's message was slowly modified in the course of time, and here the influence of the Magi, a fraternity of Median origin who exercised sacerdotal functions in Iran, was probably an important factor. It is suspected that the Magi, or some of them, in embracing the Prophet's teaching, were instrumental in combining with it older beliefs and practices. Some such hypothesis seems required to explain the differences between the early Gathas on the one hand, and the Achaemenid inscriptions, the Gatha of the Seven Chapters (Yasna 35–42), the comments of Herodotus on Persian religion (I. 131–32, 140), and the Avestan Hymn to Mithra,[6] on the other. It is noteworthy, especially in the light of later Sasanian practice, that the Achaemenids displayed a general tolerance of all forms of religion, as the benevolence extended to the Palestinian Jews attests (see the OT books of Ezra and Nehemiah).

We do not know what effect the fall of Achaemenid Persia in the fourth century B.C. had on the fortunes of Zoroastrianism. It may have been a very unsettling experience for the more devoted followers of the prophet. The rise of Parthia in the third century B.C. and its continuance in power thereafter must have allayed their fears. The Parthian rulers proved to be just as tolerant religiously as they were politically, and there was, to our knowledge, no religious persecution, as their treatment of the Mesopotamian Jews illustrates. Probably a faithful Zoroastrian minority, perhaps mostly Magi, continued to treasure what they believed were the essentials of the faith. Strabo's description of Persian religion and of the Magi of Cappadocia (*Geography* 15. 13–15, 20; 16. 2. 39) relates to the Parthian period, and it is clear from these passages that in Zoroastrian circles the ever-burning fire continued to be important in the ritual (Strabo notes that the Magi were

---

[4] R. C. Zaehner, *The Dawn and Twilight of Zoroastrianism*, London, 1961, p 33; R. N. Frye, *The Heritage of Persia*, London, 1962, p 29.

[5] For ET, see J. H. Moulton, *Early Zoroastrianism*, London, 1913, pp 343–90.

[6] I. Gershevitch, *The Avestan Hymn to Mithra*, Cambridge, 1959.

called *puraithoi*, "fire-kindlers"). In Isidorus's *Parthian Stations* there is an allusion in section 11 to Assak (east of Hecatompylos) "where Arsaces was first proclaimed king, and an everlasting fire is guarded there." Altars appear on some of the coins of the Parthian kings and their vassals.⁷ The first of the coins referred to in this foot-note (item jj) belongs to Vologeses I (51–80 A.D.), and its fire alter may be the first instance of such an object on an official coin issue. R. Ghirshman in plate 35 a of his *Iran* (Harmondsworth, 1954) shows a free-standing bas-relief at Behistun with a man putting something on an altar. This altar, like those on the coins, is usually considered to be a fire altar. The appearance of the altar motif on the coinage of Vologeses I strengthens the case for identifying this ruler with the Valakhsh mentioned in the *Denkart* (ninth century A.D.) as having begun the compilation of the Avesta (the scriptures of Zoroastrianism) and the *Zand* (commentary).⁸

Water, as one of the elements, was holy and not to be defiled by Zoroastrians. Hence Tiridates, son of Vologeses I, ruler-designate of Armenia and apparently a practising Zoroastrian (according to Dio he worshipped Mithras), went to Rome to be formally invested with his throne by Nero, travelling by land lest he pollute the water by a sea journey, although he is reported to have gone part way home by sea.⁹ The later Syriac tradition, as found in the *Doctrine of Addai*, refers to Zoroastrians in the country of the Assyrians as "the fire-worshippers and the adorers of water."¹⁰

Not all the Magi were faithful custodians of the Zoroastrian faith. Some of them adopted ancient astrological ideas and practices and claimed to possess occult knowledge. This was the case even as early as the fifth century B.C. (Herodotus VII. 37). Lucian of the second century A.D. probably reflects current ideas of what the Magi in Parthia were like when he makes one of his characters, Menippus, journey to the Orient, and on reaching Babylon, put himself under a Magus, Mithrobarzanes, who is able to take the Greek visitor on a tour of the nether world.¹¹

The other non-Christian religious group that appears within Parthia is the Jews,¹² whose settlements the Parthians found scattered throughout Babylonia when they took over this area from the Seleucids. The probable

---

⁷ Colledge, *op cit*, plate 6, jj, ll, nn; notes on pp 222–23. For a larger selection of Parthian coins, see A. U. Pope (ed), *A Survey of Persian Art*, VII, Oxford, reissued 1964–65, plates 140–44.

⁸ The relevant passage from the *Denkart* (412–15) is quoted by R. C. Zaehner, *op cit*, pp 175–77.

⁹ Dio LXII (LXIII), i. 1–7. 1a. On the refusal of Vologeses I to go to Rome, see LXII (LXIII), vii. 2.

¹⁰ *Ancient Syriac Documents*, ed W. Cureton, London, 1864, p. 16, ll 11–12.

¹¹ See H. W. Fowler and F. G. Fowler, *The Works of Lucian of Samosata*, Oxford, 1905, I, pp 156–67.

¹² See J. Neusner, *A History of the Jews in Babylonia: I. The Parthian Period* (Studia Postbiblica 9), 2nd ed rev, Leiden, 1969.

origin of these Jews cannot be dealt with here. The fact is that the Parthians recognized them as a separate group, religiously and culturally, and made no attempt to interfere with their internal life. The Jews, on their part, accepted the Parthians as their political masters and remained loyal to them until the Arsacid regime collapsed in the third century A.D.

The Parthian Jews lived for the most part in the larger urban settlements both in northern and southern Babylonia. Whether there was any sizable Jewish community in the vassal kingdom of Adiabene is doubtful. Josephus preserves an account of the conversion to Judaism of Queen Helena and her sons, Izates II and Monobazus II in the early first century A.D., but whether their example was followed by other citizens of Adiabene we do not know. We are also told that these conversions in the royal family were not well received either by the nobility or by the common people (*Ant* XX. 17–68, 75–6, 92–6).

The tension between the Jews and their Gentile neighbours, reflected in Josephus's narrative referred to above, appeared in more violent forms in Babylonia later in the first century, being partly encouraged by political instability within Parthia. It is Josephus who records the rise to power of two Jewish brothers from Nehardea, who for fifteen years (20–35 A.D.) exercised ruthless political power in Babylonia with the approval of Artabanus III (12–38), but who eventually lost both their power and their lives. The aftermath of their fall was a violent reaction to Jews in Babylonia. Some Jews went for refuge to Seleucia, but after a few years of peace there, violence erupted in which 50,000 Jews lost their lives. Ctesiphon, to which some fled, offered no improvement, and most found safety only in Nehardea and Nisibis (*Ant* XVIII. 314–79).

The scattered Jewish communities of Babylonia eventually recognized a titular head, the Resh Gelutha or Exilarch, but when this official was first accepted is uncertain, nor do we know how he was chosen.[13] R. Nathan's father is the first Exilarch that we can be sure about, and his date would appear to be in the first half of the second century A.D. The Exilarchate, which was basically an ethno-religious office, carried with it a certain amount of social and political prestige, and its holders were generally *persona grata* to the Parthian kings.

Various features of Jewish life in Babylonia are referred to in the literary sources (we exclude here the rabbinic material). Josephus, for instance, mentions Sabbath observance (*Ant* XVIII. 319, 354) as well as the annual payment of the temple tax. The latter was collected in two towns, Nehardea and Nisibis, and forwarded to Palestine with a caravan of pilgrims heading for one of the festivals in Jerusalem (*Ant* XVIII. 311–13). Bardaisan of Edessa (d 222) alludes to the circumcision of males, the abstinence from

---

[13] For a discussion of the Exilarchate in Parthian times, see J. Neusner, *op cit*, pp 50–58, 97–112.

idolatry, and the observance of the Sabbath (BLC, p 56, 11 22-5; p 58, 11 1-19).

Biblical and rabbinical studies were never as fully developed among Babylonian Jewry in Parthian times as they were back in the homeland. Nonetheless the foundations for scholarly traditions were laid in the Parthian period, and upon these foundations the work of the later Babylonian scholars (the Amoraim) rested. It is highly probable, for instance, that an Aramaic Targum of some of the Scriptures goes back to Parthian times, and this may be true also of parts of the Scriptures which were translated into the vernacular Aramaic. Further, some schools were in operation for the training of young men with a scholarly inclination. Hillel, who migrated to Palestine before 4 B.C., must have had his preliminary education in such a school. There was a limited two-way movement of scholars between "the land of Israel" and Babylonia. We know from the Mishnah that R. Akiba visited Nehardea before 132 A.D. (*Yebamoth* 16. 7). After the Hadrianic war (132-35) two of the disciples of R. Ishmael took refuge in Babylonia. One of them, R. Josiah, founded (or strengthened) a school at Huzal (near Nehardea). The other, R. Jonathan (cited once in the Mishnah, *Aboth* 4. 9), is also thought to have served in the school at Huzal. Other schools appear to have developed at Nehardea and Nisibis, and possibly elsewhere. Such evidence as there is suggests that the traditions in these schools were essentially of the same genre as was found in Palestine.[14]

Towards the end of the Parthian period, an important development in the homeland, the compilation of the Mishnah by the patriarch (Nasi) Judah c 200 A.D., was to have a far reaching effect upon Babylonian Jewry. When Judah ordained two Babylonians who had studied under him, Rav and Rabba b. Hana, to teach and decide certain legal cases outside of Palestine, and when these men returned to Babylonia and brought with them Judah's Mishnah, their return, as the event proved, was to inaugurate a new era in the life of the Parthian Jews. Although the ordination of Rav and R. Hana had seemingly to be validated by the Exilarch if they were to function within his jurisdiction, the latter, R. Hana, welcomed the adoption and encouraged the study of the Palestinian Mishnah.

2. The Early Church in Parthia.[15]

There is no reliable source for reconstructing the history of the early Church within Parthia. If we concede that Christianity reached Edessa and Nisibis in the late second century, we might expect that the Gospel would overflow the political boundary, cross the Tigris, and make its way into Adiabene, whose chief city was Arbela. We might also expect that the Parthian

---

[14] See J. Neusner, *op cit*, pp 122-77.
[15] See F. M. Fiey, *Jalons*, pp 1-75.

capital at Seleucia-Ctesiphon, which had been successfully reached by Roman forces under Trajan, Verus, and Septimius Severus, would have been an early target for Christian evangelists. But we have no trustworthy information about such hypothetical missionary efforts. The *Chronicle of Arbela*, first publicized by A. Mingana in 1907,[16] claims to offer an account of the see of Arbela down to the time of bishop Ḥenana (c 346), but for a number of reasons the *Chronicle* is suspect, especially for the Parthian period (pp 1-27 of the Syriac text).[17] For instance, its unsupported assumptions that Addai of Edessa extended his missionary work to Adiabene, that in the Parthian period the Christians were subject to persecutions by the civil authorities, and that the extension of the Church was aided by the performance of miracles, have greatly diminished the credibility of the *Chronicle*, and would appear to justify the present writer in ignoring its testimony. All that we can say with any degree of confidence is that Adiabene was on the periphery of the war zone between Parthia and Rome, and if Christianity somehow gained a foothold in this region, it would have faced fewer external difficulties in the late second and early third centuries than, let us say, Christians in Nisibis and Edessa.

It is Bardaisan of Edessa, writing before 222, who refers in his *Book of the Laws of Countries* to an extensive spread of Christianity of which otherwise we have no knowledge, and he mentions in particular that Christians were to be found in Parthia, Persia, Media and Ḥatra (BLC p 61). As this reference is meant to underline the distinctive mores of Christians, in contrast with the customs obtaining among other peoples, it may be partly rhetorical. It is, however, difficult to suppose that the comparison would have been made at all if there had not been in Bardaisan's time some actual dispersion, perhaps only a modest one, of Christianity into the areas mentioned.

The traditional founders of the Church in Parthia are Addai and Mari (cf SO, p 514, note 1; p 581, note 1). There is, however, no convincing evidence that Addai's mission ever extended beyond Osrhoene. This leaves us with Mari, supposedly a disciple of Addai. According to the *Acts of Mari*,[18] Mari came to the Parthian cities of Seleucia-Ctesiphon, and built a church in the district south of Ctesiphon and east of Seleucia known as Koke (Syr *kwk'*). J. M. Fiey maintains on the basis of geography (involving a change in the course of the Tigris river) that this occurred between 79 and

---

[16] *Sources syriaques* I, Leipzig, 1907, pp 1-75. For a German translation, see E. Sachau, "Die Chronik von Arbela," Abhdl, PAW 1915, Nr 6, pp 1-94.

[17] For a critical appraisal of Mingana's *Chronicle*, see F. M. Fiey, "Auteur et dâte de la Chronique d'Arbèles," *L'Orient Syrien*, XII, 1967, pp 265-302.

[18] *Acta Sancti Maris* in *Analecta Bollandiana*, 4, ed by J.-B. Abbeloos, Paris, 1885, pp 43-138.

[19] J. M. Fiey, "Topography of Al-Mada'in" in *Sumer* XXIII, 1967, pp 3-38; cf *Jalons*, pp 34-44.

116.¹⁹ The tradition about Mari and Fiey's proposed date for him are too involved to be discussed here except to say that there can be no objection to the historicity of Mari as the earliest Christian evangelist in Parthia, but if Mari is to be treated as Addai's follower, and if Addai is to be placed as earlier suggested (ch 2, sect 4) between 150 and 190, then Fiey's date for Mari is much too early. It is probable also that Mari would commence his work in the semi-Greek city of Seleucia rather than in Ctesiphon which at this time was essentially a Parthian military establishment.

II.
In Sasanian Times

Chapter 7.
The Cultural Surroundings of the Church

1. Zoroastrianism.

As we have earlier seen (ch 6), some form of Zoroastrianism was kept alive during the Parthian period, and one Parthian king, Vologeses I, appears in the Zoroastrian tradition as having had a share in the early stages of the compilation of the Avesta. It was Ardashir, the founder of the Sasanian dynasty, who built upon this foundation. Coming from Istakhr (near Persepolis) where a shrine to Anahita existed and where Ahura Mazda and Mithra were also venerated, he determined to strengthen the worship of Ahura Mazda (popularly known as Ohrmazd), and he in fact instituted a revival of Zoroastrianism. Like Vologeses of Parthia he is credited in the *Denkart* with having carried a step further the collection of Zoroastrian traditions, which eventually were to become the Avesta.[1] In these endeavours Ardashir is said to have had the help and counsel of one, Tansar, who was undoubtedly a Zoroastrian priest (*mobad*), and who may have become the high priest of the revitalized religion.

Ardashir probably knew little about other religious groups in his kingdom, and we suspect that his attitude towards them was one either of indifference or perhaps even of disdain. His son, Shapur I, also seems to have tolerated non-Zoroastrian religious traditions, at least for most of his reign, as is evidenced by his friendly attitude to Mani, and in his treatment of the captives (presumably mostly Christian) taken from Antioch in 256 and 260, and there is no evidence that either he or his father instituted any persecution of Persian Christians.

It was the high priest Kartir, who came into prominence near the end of the reign of Shapur I, who organized the Zoroastrianism which had been revived earlier in the century by Ardashir.[2] He established many new fire

[1] R. C. Zaehner, *The Dawn and Twilight of Zoroastrianism*, London, 1961, p 176.
[2] Kartir (Karter) is now known from four inscriptions. See R. N. Frye, *The Heritage of Persia*, London, 1962, pp 218-20, 286 note 31. Under Hormizd I (272-73) Kartir became "the *mobad* of Ahura Mazda," and in the reign of Varahran II (276-93), he was made head of religion, chief judge of the empire, etc. See also R. C. Zaehner, *op cit* p 186.

temples, rearranged the hierarchy, fought against heresy, and laid the basis for a greater influence of the Zoroastrian priests in Sasanian society, an influence that was to rival that of the nobles. It was also Kartir who gave Zoroastrianism a new dimension by turning it into a religion that would brook no rivals in Iran. In the inscription first published in 1940, Kartir claims to have attacked various non-Zoroastrian groups, such as Jews, Buddhists, Hindus, Nazoreans (a Christian sect or the Mandaeans?), Christians, MKTK (?), and Zandiks (possibly Manichaeans). This resulted in Zoroastrianism becoming an essentially intolerant religion. Although, as we shall see, from time to time certain Sasanian kings granted formal toleration to Christians in Persia, the fact remains that the Zoroastrian hierarchy remained consistenly opposed to all non-Zoroastrian religion, and whenever circumstances permitted, the Magi made things extremely unpleasant for the noncomformists.

An outstanding achievement of the Sasanian age was the final compilation of the Avesta. This enterprise, furthered by Ardashir and Shapur I, was more or less finished by Shapur II (309–79) who convoked a council which established the definitive text of the Avesta.[3] In the *Denkart* Khusru I (531–79) refers to the Avesta as a text that should be studied zealously.[4]

The impetus that led to the revival of Zoroastrianism in the third century was nationalistic in the sense that this Persian religion was associated with the recovery of the political power of Persia in western Asia. In the following centuries the Zoroastrian faith and Sasanian power went hand in hand. Each of these undoubtedly helped and strengthened the other, but the flaw in this partnership as far as Zoroastrianism was concerned was that the religious system was anchored to the state. When the latter collapsed, as it did under the advance of the Arabs in the seventh century, Zoroastrianism was left to fend for itself. For a while it lingered on, but it lacked the strength to go it alone, and it slowly withered in the land of its birth. It did survive in some districts, but it was Persian refugees fleeing to India who did the most to keep the ancient faith alive in the form of Parsiism.

2. Manichaeism.[5]

Mani's teachings have only a limited connection with our subject, but they do testify to the existence of some form of Christianity in the

---

[3] A. Christensen, *L'Iran sous les Sassanides*, Copenhagen, 2nd ed, 1944, pp 140–43.
[4] R. C. Zaehner, *op cit*, pp 176–77.
[5] For general discussions of Mani and Manichaeism, see F. C. Burkitt in *The Religion of the Manichees*, Cambridge, 1925, and in CAH XII (1939), pp 504–14; A. Christensen, *op cit*, pp 179–205; G. Widengren, *Mani und der Manichäismus*, Stuttgart, 1961 (ET, C. Kessler, London, 1965); L. J. R. Ort, *Mani*, Supplement to *Numen*, Altera Series, I, Leiden, 1967; A. Henrichs and L. Koenen, "Ein Griechischer Mani-Codex," *Zeitschrift für Papyrologie and Epigraphik*, V, 1970, pp 97–216.

environment in which Mani spent his formative years. They also illustrate the variety of religious ideas and practices with which Christians in Persia had to contend. Although some aspects of early Manichaeism are still under debate, there is considerable agreement on the basic points. It is a summary of the latter which is offered here.

Mani's life.

Mani was born in Seleucia-Ctesiphon c 216. His father, Patek, who had come from Hamadan, had some connection with the Arsacid family and his mother also was of noble lineage. The father had developed an interest in religion, and we surmise that Mani was influenced by this circumstance. What religious views Patek espoused is a matter of speculation, but in view of what his son later exhibited, we are bound to think of some form of Christianity, or of early Mandaeanism, or of some gnostic baptismal sect. At the age of twelve, the tradition goes, Mani had his first revelation from the Father of Greatness through an angel (probably the being called "the Twin Spirit"), and if this is true it suggests a youth, somewhat precocious, with a predilection for religious values. He must now have begun to be aware of himself as, in some sense to be fully understood later, the bearer of truth and the apostle of light. It was apparently not until 242, the year of Shapur I's coronation, that he felt moved through another revelation to preach his message publicly. Mani's father accepted his son's claims, as did other members of his family, which meant that Mani had influential social and political support, and this must explain how he was able subsequently to have three audiences with Shapur. The king seems to have been impressed with Mani's sincerity and allowed him to proclaim his views freely, although we may suspect that the Zoroastrian clergy resented this toleration.

We have few reliable data about Mani's career after 242. He is credited with power to cure the sick, including the demon-possessed, but to what extent this faculty was an important factor in the wide acceptance of his message is unknown. He was a zealous propagator of his views and he seems to have traveled extensively. He is said to have been in India (perhaps before 242), and if this is so, it could have given him contacts with Buddhism. Mani or his representatives went to the Roman world, first, it seems, to Egypt, and the teaching subsequently spread westwards in Africa, so that in the next century the famous Augustine was a Manichaean "hearer" from 376 to 384. Closer to home, Mani's letters to disciples or communities in Ctesiphon, Babylon, Mesene, Edessa and Susiana indicate the firm establishment of his followers in the western part of the Persian empire within his own lifetime.

The death of Shapur I removed Mani's most powerful supporter. Three years later, in the reign of Varahran I, his plans to visit Kushan were vetoed by the king whose estimate of Mani was quite different from that of his father. Mani was now seized, doubtless at the instigation of the Zoroastrian priests, and tried in court; the principal charge evidently was "Mani has taught against our law." He was found guilty and sent heavily shackled to prison where he died in 276. He had lived long enough, however, to leave behind him an organized and devoted body of adherents.

Mani's teaching.

Cosmology and metaphysics. Mani's portrayal of the nature of the world and of how things became the way they are can only be described as a bizarre myth. To contemporary Christians and Jews, whose understanding of creation was mostly derived from Israel's Scriptures, Mani's speculations must have seemed utterly whimsical. The probable antecedents of his medley of ideas cannot be dealt with here.

To begin with, there were two parts to Reality, the Kingdom of Light, where the chief actor is the Father of Greatness, and the Kingdom of Darkness. This dichotomy is sometimes represented as consisting of the Truth and the Lie, or of God and Matter. The troubles of the universe began when the Ruler of Darkness invaded the Kingdom of Light. To make a long and intricate story short, this invasion resulted eventually in the creation of the universe which in fact is a mixture of Light and Darkness. Even man displays in himself this intermingling of the two elements. Phase two in this myth shows the Father of Greatness taking steps to liberate the Light from the Darkness. One of his moves was the sending of the Redeemer, Jesus, into Judea, with a view to rescuing mankind by reclaiming the particles of Light within them. This Jesus was only human in appearance and is not to be confused with the son of the widow who was crucified (cf *Koran* IV. 155f).

It is evident that Mani espoused a theory of revelation, i.e., he held that the Father of Greatness from time to time has sent prophets and teachers to show mankind the right way to live so as to release the Light which each person harbours within himself. He mentions in particular, Buddha, Zoroaster, Hermes, Plato and Jesus. Mani appears to have considered that he belonged to this succession: he was the messenger of the Father of Greatness to Babylonia, and he was the last and greatest of these prophets.[6] His letters, at least those addressed to those within the Christian domain, usually begin, "Mani, the Apostle of Jesus Christ" to so and so.

Ethics. Basically, Mani's ethics demanded that people should live in such a way as to bring to an end the mixture of Light and Darkness which is in each individual. This ideal, if carried to its logical consequence, would involve all believers in a strict asceticism. Mani learned, however, to temper his demands to the human situation, and he ended by sponsoring a double standard for his followers. The lower morality was for the catechumens or "hearers," who led a normal domestic life. They were to keep the ten

---

[6] The substance of this paragraph, down to "these prophets," is frequently quoted by writers on Manichaeism, and goes back to *The Chronology of Ancient Nations* by Al-Biruni (d 1048); see L. J. R. Ort, *op cit*, p 102. The passage is believed to be a quotation from a book by Mani.

Manichaean commandments (no idolatry, lying, greed, slaughter of any living being, adultery, theft, etc.), and they must follow the group's rules about fasting, confession, repentance and prayer. They also had to prepare food for the "elect." The higher morality was for the "elect" or "righteous" (there were four categories of these), who were to keep the ten commandments, and also to abstain from wine, meat, marriage, the possession of property, etc.

Eschatology. It is difficult to offer a clear and consistent account of Mani's eschatology. Seemingly the long process of separating the Light particles from the Darkness will one day end because it will have gone as far as it can go. References to a last judgment suggest that at some juncture most of the remaining Light (Good) will be separated from the Darkness (Evil). There are also references to Jesus having a temporary reign here on earth. When this period is concluded, the earth will be set on fire and this fire will burn out most of the residue of the unrescued Light particles; this cosmic bonfire will last 1468 years. At the end of this conflagration, the residue, a mass of burning filth, will be compacted and sealed off by a wall. Thus the realm of Darkness will be forever separated from the realm of Light. In all this there is no suggestion of a cyclic theory of the universe, whereby the contest between Light and Darkness will be repeated *ad infinitum*.

Organization and worship. There seems to have been a head of the Manichees, a kind of successor to Mani himself, and below him were 12 magistrates, 72 bishops and 360 priests, though we know little about any of these groups. Then come the "elect" and below them the "hearers." Each of the categories displayed a distinctive dress, except te "hearers." It is possible that, as in Mithraism, appropriate ceremonies marked the passage from one category to another. Of cultic practices we can speak only in the most general terms. As Mani laid great stress on the written word, it is probable that readings from his writings played some part in worship.[7] It is also evident that preaching, hymn-singing and prayer were integral parts of the liturgy.[8] We know that there was an annual Bema festival which commemorated the suffering and death of Mani, and that on this occasion an empty seat (Syr *bym'*; Gk *bema*) symbolized his presence.

3. Judaism.[9]

The end of Parthian rule in Babylonia and the advent of the Sasanians was more than a change of political overlord for the Babylonian Jews. "Fire

---

[7] On works by Mani, nearly all of which were in Syriac, see L. J. R. Ort, *op cit*, pp 20–22, 106–17; G. Widengren, *op cit* (ET), pp 76–81.

[8] L. J. R. Ort, *op cit*, pp 97, 109, 112–17, 156; G. Widengren, *op cit*, pp 83–94.

[9] G. Widengren, "The Status of the Jews in the Sassanian Empire" in *Iranica Antiqua*, I, 1961, pp 117–62. The most recent study of this subject is found in J. Neusner, *A History of the Jews in Babylonia*, II–V (Studia Post-biblica 11–12, 14–15), Leiden, 1966–70.

worship," known under the Parthians, now became a religion actively supported by the new rulers, and while there is no evidence that Ardashir suppressed non-Persian cults, the Babylonian Jews no longer enjoyed the rather cosy relationship which in recent years they had had with the Arsacids. They now appear to have had to pay a poll tax as did other minority groups (Tal *Nedarim* 62 b). The exilarchate survived but its powers were restricted. Some synagogues were destroyed (Tal *Yoma* 10 a), but this may have been due to local fanatics and may not have reflected Sasanian policy. Some Jewish practices may have had to be altered so as to conform with Zoroastrian views, as for instance the location of the Hanukkah lamp (Tal *Shabbath* 45 a). But the Jews, who were a self-governing religious community, accepted political domination by the Persians and by and large they were left to themselves. Jewish courts of law, mostly concerned with relatively minor matters, appear to have continued to function provided that Persian law, administered in Persian courts, was followed in all major issues.

Apparently there was no change in this policy in the reign of Shapur II (309–79) who, while he persecuted Christians (largely for political reasons), seems to have left Jews alone.[10] It was not until the fifth century in the reigns of Yazdagird II (439–57) and Peroz (459–84) that the Jews were subjected to severe persecution, which entailed the death of an Exilarch and of various rabbis. Jewish courts and schools appear to have been closed, and even practices which affected the Jewish laity, such as Sabbath observance, were made illicit.[11] From the limited evidence available, it seems probable that either in the time of Kavad (488–531) or in the reign of Khusro I (531–79) Judaism became once more a tolerated faith. If the Jews supported Varahran Chobin's unsuccessful bid for the Persian throne (590–91), this may have led to further Jewish troubles and to the extinction of the exilarchate. J. Neusner's conclusion is that there was no exilarch from 590 to 640.[12]

One of the reasons for the Sasanian government being obliged to have some workable policy towards Babylonian Jewry was the sheer size of the Jewish community. It is impossible to produce reliable population statistics for this period, but such evidence as there is leads to J. Neusner's conclusion that there may have been 860,000 Jews in Sasanian Babylonia.[13] This figure seems extraordinarily large, especially in view of the very modest numbers of Jews deported to Babylonia by Nebuchadrezzar in the sixth century B.C., and can only be accounted for by resistance to assimilation despite intermarriages, unusual fecundity, and considerable proselytization.

The most distinctive group in Babylonian Jewry were the rabbis. These men, educated in the various academies which were now available, devoted

---

[10] So J. Neusner, *op cit*, IV, pp 20, 35–39, 55–56, 239.
[11] For a discussion of these persecutions, see J. Neusner, *op cit*, V, pp 60–72.
[12] J. Neusner, *op cit*, II, pp 241-50.
[13] J. Neusner, *op cit*, II, pp 124–27.

themselves to the task of interpreting the Law (Torah) in accordance with the traditions laid down in the Mishnah brought to Babylonia from Palestine in the early third century. Their goal was to transform the whole of Jewish life so that it would conform to the Torah. In so large and scattered a constituency their success must have varied. We know that in the somewhat isolated Jewish community at Dura Europus, the local synagogue was decorated by murals which orthodox rabbis would have viewed with horror,[14] and they must have reacted similarly to the mosaic floors in synagogues at Sura and Nehardea.[15] Jews in commercial centres like Maḥoza and Mesene were long known for their disregard of rabbinical rules.

The abiding literary monument to the rabbis of this age is the Babylonian Talmud. This is basically a commentary on the Palestinian Mishnah, although only thirty-six and a half tractates of the Mishanh's sixty-three are dealt with, and as such it sets forth legal principles and relates the details of various legal actions. In this process, however, it becomes almost encyclopaedic, for it embraces theology, moral and natural science, medicine, astronomy, legend, folk-lore, etc. It was destined, as the event proved, to shape the thought, ideals and actions of orthodox Judaism from that day to this.

There is considerable difference of opinion among Jewish writers and sources about how, when and why the Talmud reached its definitive form. A tradition generally accepted is that R. Ashi, head of the Sura school, or latterly of the school at Mata Meḥasia (d 427), was the leading figure in the initial effort to organize the growing mass of rabbinical material,[16] and that a later head of the Sura school, R. Rabina II bar Huna, brought the initial effort of R. Ashi to a conclusion c 500. What other rabbis contributed to this vast editorial endeavour need not concern us here. It is theorized that unfulfilled Messianic expectations (some thought the Messiah would come in 468)[17] and the persecutions in the fifth century, may have been factors in the decision to organize and safeguard the achievements of the academies, and so to produce the Talmud.

There is no evidence that even small numbers of Jews ever turned to Zoroastrianism and became "fire-worshippers." On the other hand, the facts that Jews and Christians lived under a common political master, that they were sometimes found in the same neighbourhood, and that they shared a common Scripture which Christians called the OT, facilitated the movement of some Jews into the Christian community. This would most likely have taken place when individuals were impatient with rabbinical opinions or in

---

[14] *The Excavations at Dura-Europos*, Final Report VIII, Part I, *The Synagogue* by C. H. Kraeling and others, New Haven 1956; the Decorations, pp 34–254.
[15] J. Neusner, *op cit*, II, p 78.
[16] J. Neusner, *op cit*, V, pp 135–46.
[17] J. Neusner, *op cit*, V pp 65–72.

areas where rabbinical influence was weak. Such Jewish conversions to Christianity, which to the best of our knowledge were never very numerous, did nothing to improve relations between Jews and Christians. The attitudes of both groups towards one another remained much as they had been in the first century (as in *Acts* in the NT), being characterized by mutual bitterness and hostility. We note that Aphraates of the fourth century felt obliged in his treatise XVII to reply to Jews "who blaspheme the people gathered among the Gentiles." Christians, speaking generally, tended to group Jews with heretics and pagans as being opposed to orthodox Christianity (SO: p 364 re canon 20 of the Synod of 554; p 417 re canon 25 of the Synod of 585; p 457 re the Synod of 596). In the *Chronique de Séert*, PO 4— covering the years 250 to 422, Jews are described as the friends of Satan, XXVII, p 297. Such attitudes on the part of Christians towards Jews were apt from time to time to create tensions between the two communities.

Occasionally there were formal discussions between Christians and Jews (cf Aphraates' reference in his treatise XXI to his conversation with a Jewish scholar), but these meetings tended to develop into extended arguments regarding the proper interpretation of the OT. The record of one such colloquy in Syria (near Emesa), which allegedly occurred in the eighth century is found in a Syriac text entitled "The Disputation of Sergius the Stylite against a Jew."[18] While the date of this document takes us beyond the period covered in the present volume, it undoubtedly illustrates what easily could have taken place in Sasanian Persia. It is suspected by some that the dialogue of Sergius in its present form may be a literary forgery, although such a view need not rule out the possibility of there being an actual discussion with a Jew behind the text. The dialogue, as we have it, is quite inconclusive. Near the end of the discussion the Jew says, "I am amazed how there are among you some Christians who associate with us in the synagogue, and who bring offerings, and at the time of the Passover, send unleavened bread."[19]

4. Mazdakism.[20]

It was in the latter part of the period under review that Persia was turmoiled by the Mazdakite movement. Its founder, Mazdak, was a social revolutionary who may have been influenced by Manichaeism. In a society which had fairly rigid class distinctions and in which the lot of the peasants was utterly wretched, he preached equality in the distribution of property

---

[18] Ed and tr by A. P. Hayman, CSCO 338, 339, Scriptores Syri, 152, 153, Louvain 1973.

[19] For a somewhat discursive study of Christian-Jewish relations in the Syriac Church, see S. Kazan, "Isaac of Antioch's Homily against the Jews" in OC 45 (1961), pp 30–53; 46 (1962), pp 87–98; 47 (1963), pp 89–97; 49 (1965), pp 57–78. For another voice on the same subject, see M. Albert, Jacques de Saroug, *Homélies contre les Juifs*, PO 38.1, 1976.

[20] A. Christensen, *op cit*, pp 316–62.

(including the possession of wives and concubines), and a life marked by non-violence. These views and practices constitute a form of communism, and they appear to have met with widespread endorsement. Even the king, Kavad I (488–531), championed Mazdak's cause, perhaps hoping to use it as a lever against the power of the nobility, but this in the end only led to his own temporary deposition. When he regained the throne (499), he was much cooler to Mazdak's ideas, which in the meanwhile had instigated uprisings marked by various excesses. A public disputation held in 528–29 in which the leading Mazdakites participated, ended up with Mazdak and his supporters being murdered. When Khusro I (531–79) succeeded his father, he determined to stamp the revolutionaries out, and thousands of them were seized and put to death, and those who survived were driven underground. Whatever else it shows, the Mazdak movement points to an underlying hostility among peasants and lower-class townspeople to the social and economic system of the Sasanian empire.

Chapter 8.
The Church in the Third and Fourth Centuries

The Church we are about to examine was built on the foundations laid in the Parthian era, but our knowledge of its early years is very defective. We can deduce from the Synod records from 410 on (*Synodicon Orientale*) some basic facts about the geographical distribution of the episcopal sees, but the history of these sees prior to 410 is for the most part not known. We have to assume that behind this growth are the devoted labours of countless unknown Christians.

The Persian Church was clearly indebted to the Greek Church in many ways. As in the West, certain ascetic tendencies were a feature of Persian Christianity almost from the start, and eventually these were to manifest themselves in organized monasticism (see ch 11, sect 6). The episcopal structure of Church government, also inherited from the West, was accepted, although the control over the monasteries by the bishops was often a vexatious matter. Similarly the liturgy appears to have been modelled on Western practice (see Appendix 3). The theology of the Orientals, while biblically centered, was clearly derivative, being taken over entirely from the Greek Church. The same observation can be made of many of the canons adopted in the East. The one non-western factor which adversely affected the life of the Persian Christians was the attitude of the Magi. The latter were Christianity's implacable foes, and whenever they could put sufficient pressure upon the king or the local authorities, then the Christians were subject to persecution. The Church under the Sasanians was therefore never supported by the state; it was always on its own, and to some extent always on the defensive.

1. In the Third Century.[1]

Toleration and Persecution.

The Persian Church appears to have grown slowly but steadily, probably on a congregational basis. As there is no evidence of large numbers of Jews turning to Christianity, most of the converts must have come from the ranks of either pagans or Zoroastrians. Some augmentation of the numbers of Christians also came, as we shall see, from prisoners of war from the Roman West. With the growth of the Church, the episcopal structure

---

[1] See M.-L. Chaumont, "Les Sassanides et la christianisation de l'Empire iranien au IIIe siècle de notre ère," *Revue de l'Histoire des Religions*, 165 (1964), pp 165-202.

gradually established itself, though the tensions and quarrels reflected in the proceedings of later Synods (as evidenced in the *Synodicon Orientale*), indicate that the discipline of an organized religious community was not easy for some Persians to accept.

As we have observed in ch 7, both Ardashir I and his son Shapur I seem to have been tolerant towards non-Zoroastrians. This is illustrated in Shapur's case by his allowing captives taken from Roman Syria to practise such religion as they wished in their new surroundings in Persia. This toleration did not preclude the imposition on Christians, Jews, and other minorities of a special personal or head-tax (Tal *Nedarim* 62b). Unhappily the increased influence of the high priest Kartir (ch 7, sect 1) brought about a change in the official posture towards Christians as Shapur I's reign drew to a close. With the accession of Hormizd I (272-73) and of Varahran II (276-93), Kartir's power reached its zenith, and we know from his inscriptions that this extremely powerful person, as the leading champion of Zoroastrianism, was unalterably opposed to other religions. We infer from one of these inscriptions that Christians were persecuted, but the particulars are not known, The *Chronique de Séert* records that the Magi persecuted the Christians without distinction, that one, Qariba bar Hanania, a Christian of Aramaean origin, was killed at this time, possibly being the first Persian martyr, and that Qandira, the Christian wife of Varahran II, was also a victim (PO 4, ix, pp 238-39). But the Manichees were in fact a greater threat to Zoroastrianism than the Christians, and they seem to have suffered most from Kartir's measures. Chaumont, following the *Chronique de Séert* (reference as above) claims that this wave of persecution ended about 291 when Varahran II was constrained by various circumstances to restore religious peace to his kingdom.

It is possible that either the Magi's opposition to Christian burial customs, or the persecution of Christians unleashed by Kartir, had something to do with the construction of about sixty tombs cut into a coral bank on the island of Kharge (near Bushire and opposite Bahrain) in the Persian Gulf. These structures which show "some affinities to Ardashir's buildings at Firuzabad," display vestiges of Syriac inscriptions on vertical columns, and are thought to belong to the third century.[2] We can theorize that Christians on the mainland, perhaps from Rev Ardashir, chose to bury their dead in a spot where fanatical Zoroastrian priests would be unlikely to disturb them.

The third century, on the whole, except for the years when Kartir's influence was at its peak, was a period of peace for the Church, and Christians were therefore able to strengthen themselves for the trials that lay ahead of them in the next century.

---

[2] E. E. Herzfeld, *Archaeological History of Iran*, London, 1935, pp 103-4; plates xviii and xix.

Prisoners of War from the West.

Shapur I's penetration of Roman Syria and his two captures of Antioch (256, 260), as well as his defeat of Valerian in 260, seem to have brought an unexpected boon to the Church in Persia. On these occasions the Persian king sent back to his own kingdom large numbers of captives and settled them in various centres. According to line 16 of the inscription KZ (Frye, p 213) they were placed in Fars, Parthia, Khuzistan and elsewhere. This is substantially what is attested by the *Chronique de Séert* (PO 4, pp 221-22) which claims that the exiles were put in Iraq, Susiana and Persis, and it mentions specifically certain cities (Sod Sapor in Mesene, Sapor in Persis, Marw Habor on the Tigris, and Gundishapur in Khuzistan).[3] The settlement of Syrian prisoners, many of whom were probably Christians, in Persis, the stronghold of Zoroastrianism, was an extraordinary move, and may reflect Shapur's impatience with the Zoroastrian hierarchy. The *Chronique* further states that the people involved were assigned lands to cultivate and houses to dwell in. Provision would have to be made for housing, feeding and employing such numbers of people, but we may suspect that the *Chronique* is romancing in its account of the benevolence extended to the Syrian prisoners. While some may have been treated better than others, we would expect most of them to become part of the Persian labour force which could be drawn upon by wealthy land-owners or by those in charge of government construction projects; the great dam at Shustar, for instance, was reputedly built by Roman prisoners. To leave the third century and glance briefly at the fourth, when Shapur II captured Singara in 360 he followed the same pattern as Shapur I, and settled his numerous captives in Persia. The prisoners taken later at Bezabde presumably met the same fate. These probably included the local bishop who had tried unsuccessfully to bring an end to the fighting (Ammianus Marcellinus XX. 6. 1-8; 7. 1-15).

We know almost nothing about such prisoners of war, nor do we know whether physical fitness to undertake the arduous trek to Persia was even considered. We can theorize that their numbers included Christians, Jews and pagans, and that some were Greek-speaking and others Syriac-speaking. The Christians, as aliens in a strange land, may very well have attempted to make contacts with local Christians and to associate with them insofar as their status and limited freedom permitted. Among the prisoners of 256 from Antioch there was one, Demetrianus, the bishop of the city, and while he died within a year or so, he seems to have done much to make Beth Lapaṭ an important see in the Persian Church. It would appear, therefore, that the prisoners of war helped to strengthen the Christian cause in Persia. It is of interest that the *Chronique de Séert* refers to the building of monasteries and churches in the third century, and it also reports that there

---

[3] Cf W. B. Henning, "The Great Inscription of Shapur I," BSOS 9, 1937-38, pp 823-49.

were two churches in Rev Ardashir in Persis, in one of which Greek was used in the liturgy, and in the other Syriac (PO 4, II, p 222).

2. In the Fourth Century.

Apart from the writings of Aphraates, we have very little first-hand information about the Persian Church in the fourth century. What we do know about in some detail is the persecutions to which Christians were subjected by both Shapur II and Varahran IV, and which were sufficiently dreadful to reach the ears of the western Church, as the references to them in Sozomen (II. 9-14) indicate.

Aphraates (or Aphrahat).

Our knowledge of Aphraates comes from 23 treatises, mostly hortatory discourses, which he wrote between 337 and 345. The Syriac text, with a Latin translation, of 22 of these treatises (also known as "demonstrations") is found in PS I, columns 1-1051. An English translation of 8 of them is available in *Nicene and Post Nicene Fathers* XIII, pp 35-412. Twenty-two of these writings are a kind of acrostic, each beginning with a different letter of the alphabet; 10 were composed in 337 and the remainder in 344. A twenty-third was written in 345. On the dates of composition see V.5, XXII, 25, XXIII. 69.

Aphraates describes himself as "a man sprung from Adam, and fashioned by the hands of God, a disciple of the Holy Scriptures." In some circles he was apparently known as Jacob, but a commoner designation was "the Persian sage."[4] If this title suggests that he was a Persian won over to Christianity, it is curious that there are no allusions in his treatises to Zoroastrian beliefs. Judging from his expert use of the OT, he is just as likely to have come into the Church from a Jewish family in Persia living away from the centres of rabbinical tradition in Mesopotamia.

Aphraates was a monk (cf XVIII on "Virginity"), and probably a bishop, for some of his words would be most appropriate in the mouth of a bishop (cf X on "Pastors"). As treatise XIV is directed principally to the bishops, clergy, etc. of the church in Seleucia-Ctesiphon, it may be presumed that Aphraates' status in the Church permitted him to speak to such a group. It has been conjectured that he was abbot of the monastery of Mar Mattai near Mosul.

Aphraates displays a very simple Christian faith, firmly centered in the Scriptures (of which he shows considerable knowledge), and oblivious of the theological problems which the Greek Church was facing in his time. There is a passing reference in III.9 to Valentinus, Mani, and Marcion, but their teachings do not seem to have been an issue in the Church as Aphraates

---

[4] As, for example, in the list of Mar Abd Jeshua (1298), Part IV, found in G. P. Badger, *The Nestorians and Their Rituals*, 2 vols, London, 1852, 2, p 369. On Aphraates as a Persian name (Frahata), see F. Justi, *Iranische Namenbuch*, Marburg, 1895, pp 101-2.

knew it. Most strange, in the light of his known dates, is the absence of any allusion to Arius and the Council of Nicaea. We can only conclude that the community in which Aphraates moved was somewhat secluded, with few contacts with the Church in the Roman world.

In his treatise on "Persecution" (XXI), dated 345, Aphraates says, "I have written unto you . . . that those who today are persecuted for the sake of the persecuted Jesus may be comforted," and he adds, after recounting the persecutions of earlier saints, "also in our days these things happened to us." While there is no elucidation of these references, there can be little doubt in view of the date of the treatise, that it is the persecution initiated by Shapur II that Aphraates has in mind.

A notable feature of the treatises is their interest in Jews and Jewish practices, and we might conclude from this that the Christians for whom Aphraates was writing lived in communities in which Jews, like the Christians, were a prominent minority group. Thus we have XI (circumcision), XII (Passover), XIII (Sabbath), XV (divers meats), XIX (the dispersion of Israel). XVII (Christ the Son of God) is a reply to Jews "who blaspheme the people gathered from among the Gentiles," and who claim that "God has no son." Some of this material is recapitulated in XXII.25. It is difficult to determine the purpose of these particular treatises. Some may have been useful in persuading Jews to enter the Church. Others may have been intended to guard Jewish Christians from slipping back into Jewish ways. This may have been a real danger, for the evidence indicates that Shapur's persecution of nonconformists did not extend to the Synagogue.

The reference in XXI 1–3 to a discussion with a Jewish scholar raises the question of the extent to which Aphraates was indebted to rabbinical teachings. L. Ginsburg,[5] F. Gavin[6] and others argue that he was greatly influenced by them, whereas J. Neusner[7] takes the contrary view. The present writer is inclined to side with Neusner. Most of Aphraates' opinions and methods of biblical exegesis appear to rest on Christian traditions that go back to the first century. This position does not rule out the possibility that on certain specific points, Jewish influence may be detected.

Many of Aphraates' Christian convictions are presented in his first treatise ("Of Faith"). His basic position is a familiar one: "Our Lord Jesus Christ is the foundation of all our faith" (2); "Take heed what is needed for the service of Christ . . . pure fasting, . . . pure prayer . . . love, meekness, virginity. . . holiness" (4). The citation of a number of biblical characters who acted by reason of their faith (14–16) is strongly reminiscent of Heb. 11. In 19 we have what may be called Aphraates' credo: "Now this is faith: when a man believes in God, the Lord of all, who made the heavens and the

---

[5] *Jewish Encyclopaedia*, New York 1901, i, pp 663–64.
[6] *Aphraates and the Jews*, New York, 1922 (1966).
[7] *Aphrahat and Judaism*, (Studia Post Biblica XIX), Leiden, 1971.

earth, and the seas and all that is in them; and he made Adam in his image; and he gave the law to Moses; he sent of his Spirit upon the prophets. He sent moreover his Christ into the world. Furthermore, that a man should believe in the resurrection of the dead; and should furthermore also believe in the sacrament of baptism. This is the faith of the Church of God."[8] In view of the reference to baptism, the absence of any allusion to Holy Communion is noteworthy.

Some of Aphraates' views on particular topics may be noted:

The treatise "Of Wars" (V), written in 337 and seemingly on the verge of an outbreak of war, illustrates the way the book of Daniel could be interpreted in the light of contemporary history.

The treatise "Of Monks" (VI) is addressed to monks that love virginity and with its high moral tone is almost sermonic. Very sensibly it concedes that if a monk desires that a woman, bound by a vow of celibacy, should dwell with him, it would be better for both parties to marry and live openly together.

The treatise on "The Resurrection of the Dead" (VIII) has to be taken in conjunction with what is said on the subject in VI. Aphraates' position is that man consists of a body and an animal spirit. When one is baptized he receives the Spirit of Christ. When he dies this Spirit goes back to Christ, but the body and the animal spirit go to the grave where they commence a long sleep which continues until the Last Day. When the resurrection occurs, the Spirit of Christ will again be conjoined to the body and its animal spirit, "and the animal spirit shall be swallowed up in the heavenly Spirit, and the whole man shall become spiritual" (VI. 14). Aphraates contends, against those who say that the resurrected will have a heavenly body, that the resurrection means initially the resurrection of the body laid in the earth: "In the day of the resurrection, your body shall arise in its entirety" (VIII. 25).

It is interesting to observe that near the end of treatise XXII, Aphraates affirms, "Whatsoever is written in these chapters was not written according to the thought of one man, . . . but according to the thought of all the Church."

Aphraates writes lucidly, earnestly and at times eloquently. His biblically-centered Christian faith is free from any Greek influence, and his thought, therefore, is not marked by theological hair-splittings. His use of the Scriptures, which are treated as historical documents, is comparatively free of allegory, and within the limits of his age, he can argue quite logically from Holy Writ. That his good qualities were not more widely recognized and emulated was a loss to the Syriac Church.

Constantine the Great and Shapur II.

The relations between Shapur II (309-79) and Constantine were, if not cordial, sufficiently friendly to maintain peaceful relations between them.

---

[8] J. Gwynn's translation in *Nicene and Post Nicene Fathers*, 13, p 352.

According to Eusebius (*Life of Constantine* IV. 8-13; cf Sozomen II. 15), the Persian king sent an embassy to Constantine with a view to forming an alliance between the two powers, but nothing came of this. The same source gives us the text of a letter which Constantine sent to Shapur. It was evidently prompted by Constantine's learning that there were many Christians in Persia, and in it the emperor prays that both Shapur and his Christian subjects may enjoy abundant prosperity. He commends the Christians to Shapur's protection, "for there is nothing in their religion of a reprehensible nature" (Sozomen), and hopes that the Persian King will cherish them with his wonted humanity and kindness. Neither Constantine nor Eusebius lived long enough to see the shattering of this hope.

Constantine's declared interest in the Christians in Persia may have done the Persian Church more harm than good, for Shapur's advisers could point out that the Christians in their midst had a champion in the Roman world, and that the loyalty of such subjects to the Sasanian throne was in question. This argument lost none of its force when it was realized that most of the Persian churches were in the western part of the kingdom, in those very districts likely to become the theatre of war between Persia and Rome.

Persecution.[9]

It was not until after Constantine's death (337) that Shapur II began a persecution of the Church which lasted for most of his reign.[10] This change from the policy followed by Ardashir I and for most of his life by Shapur I can be explained by the growing political influence of the Magi, by Christianity's change of status in the Roman world, and by the suspicion that the Christians of Persia were now bound to be more friendly disposed towards the Roman emperors. The persecution started in Seleucia in 340 with an order to arrest Simeon bar Ṣabbaʿe, bishop of that city (apparently he was assumed to be the head of the Christians in Persia), and to release him only when he agreed to collect for the king in Beth Aramaye a double poll-tax from the monks and double taxes from all the Christians "who share the sentiments of Caesar, our enemy" (*Chr de Séert*, PO 4, XXVII, p 300). Simeon refused to meet these conditions and was decapitated in April 341. Then the king instituted a general persecution of all Christians, but appalled by the deaths and violence which ensued (church buildings also suffered), he modified his earlier order and had the persecution henceforth apply principally to the Christian clergy. In actual fact the severity of the anti-Christian measures varied considerably from one locality to another and

---

[9] Accounts of the persecution are found in the *Chronique de Séert*, PO 4, xxiii, pp 287-89; xxvii, pp 296-305; Sozomen II. 9-14; Labourt, pp 43-82; A. Vööbus, HASO I, pp 234-58; J. M. Fiey, *Jalons*, pp 45-65, 85-99.

[10] The death of Constantine may have had nothing to do with the commencement of the persecution. What probably made Shapur wait until after 337 to act against the Christians, were his own political troubles (cf Christensen, pp 234-35).

seems to have depended upon the whims of the local authorities. Beth Garmai and Adiabene, by reason of their greater Christian population, appear to have suffered most. Accused persons were imprisoned, frequently for some months; torture was often used, and sometimes prisoners were interrogated by the king himself before finally being put to death. Among the better known martyrs were Usthazanes, a prominent member of the king's palace staff, Pusices a leading artisan of the king, Shahdost and Barbashmin successors in turn of Simeon in the see of Seleucia-Ctesiphon, Miles, bishop of Susa, and so on. In the capital 120 members of the clergy were imprisoned for six months and then executed. The *Chronique de Séert* (PO 4, XXIII, pp 288–89) asserts that there was a temporary suspension of the persecution during the reign of the Roman emperor Jovian (363–64). If we assume with M. J. Higgins (see note 11) that Qayuma occupied the see of Seleucia 372/3 to 379/80, this suggests that the persecution ended about seven years before Shapur's death in 379. If so, it appears to have been vigorously continued both by Ardashir II (379–83) and by Varahran IV (388–99). Sozomen claims that in the persecutions of the fourth century 16,000 Christians were known to have perished (II. 14). Whatever the figure, it was a time of great trial for the Church. Labourt concludes his account of the persecution with these words: "the persecution . . . was inferior neither in duration nor in intensity to that which the Churches of the Roman world had undergone. It is the great honour of the Persian Christians to have sustained such a dreadful storm without foundering." (p 82).

The Bishops of Seleucia-Ctesiphon.[11]

At the beginning of the fourth century, one, Papa, was bishop of Seleucia. Presumably he had been consecrated by one of the western prelates, probably the archbishop of Antioch. He had suffered for his faith in the time of Varahran II but had survived (*Chr de Séert*, PO 4, IX, p 238). Being in the Persian capital and with communications with Antioch severely restricted especially in time of war, Papa was fully aware of the need for a strongly centralized and autonomous Persian Church, and he became the leader of a movement aiming at this goal. But his actions appeared to many of his colleagues to be arrogant and over-bearing, and at a synod held in 315 he was deposed. Papa, however, appealed to Antioch, the deposition was annulled and Papa was reinstated in his office. Mar Simeon was made his archdeacon with the right to succeed Papa when the latter died (cf SO, pp 289–92). The *Chronique de Séert* claims that it was Simeon who represented Papa at the Council of Nicaea in 325 (PO 4, XVIII, p 277). Papa died 326/7, and Simeon bar Ṣabbaʿe became bishop of Seleucia.[12] He

---

[11] M. J. Higgins, "Chronology of the Fourth Century Metropolitans of Seleucia-Ctesiphon," in *Traditio* 9, 1953, pp 45–99.

[12] *Chr de Séert*, PO 4, xxvii, pp 296–305.

was an early victim of Shapur's persecution, being martyred in 341 (or with M. J. Higgins, in 344-45). His archdeacon, Shahdost, succeeded him, but he was arrested and put to death within a year (*Chr de Séert*, PO 4, XXIX, pp 309-11). Barbashmin, the next bishop, was also seized and beheaded (c 346-47). We are not surprised in view of the mortality rate of its incumbents, that the see of Seleucia was vacant for a number of years. Higgins claims that the post was occupied during the closing part of Shapur II's reign, and it is here that he places Qayuma (372/3 to 379/80), possibly preceded by Tomarsa (364/5 to 372/3). After Qayuma's death, Seleucia had no bishop for about twenty years.

Nisibis.

In the peace which the emperor Jovian concluded with Shapur II in 363, the territorial gains in northern Mesopotamia won from Nerseh by the peace terms of 298, reverted to Persia (on the events of 363, see Ammianus Marcellinus XXV. 5-9). This meant that the city of Nisibis came once more under Sasanian control. Nisibis was never recovered by Constantinople, and until it fell to the Arabs in 640-41, it was a leading city in the western part of the Persian kingdom. One reason for its importance was that by the treaty of 298 between Diocletian and Narses, it was specified that Nisibis should be the only official market for trade exchanges between the two empires (see ch 1, sect 2). We suspect that as a trading mart its population was somewhat of an ethnic hodge-podge. Whether the whole populace (which included the famous Christian Ephraim) was forced to leave the city when the Persians took it over in 363, as Ammianus Marcellinus implies, or only Roman citizens, is uncertain. In any case trade must have quickly renewed the city's normal life and Christianity soon re-established itself. We know from the proceedings of the Synod of Mar Isaac that in 410 Nisibis was the seat of a metropolitan bishop. For a recent treatment of Nisibis in Persian times, see J. M. Fiey, *Nisibe*, pp 21-66 (CSCO 388, Subsidia 54, Louvain 1977).

Chapter 9.
The Church in the Fifth Century

It appears that it was early in the Catholicate of Timothy I (780–823) that the collection of material pertaining to the Nestorian Synods, known to us as the *Synodicon Orientale* (hereafter SO; edited and translated by J. B. Chabot), was put together. This work chronicles the acts of thirteen Synods from 410 to 775, although only eleven of these fall within the chronological limits of the present volume. It is probable that there were gatherings of Persian bishops prior to 410, but the persecutions of the fourth century made all such assemblies clandestine and even dangerous, and such records as they left did not find a place in the *Synodicon Orientale*. Much of the history of the Church in Persia after 410 is in fact presented to us through this *Synodicon*.

1. The Synod of Mar Isaac (410).

The account of Mar Isaac's Synod, which is said to be the first Synod held in the country of the Persians (SO, p 262), leaves some questions unanswered, and we are obliged in such instances to resort to conjectural reconstructions of what actually happened. Mar Isaac appears to have been elected bishop of Seleucia about 399, and by this time the incumbent of the see of Seleucia was *de facto* the leading bishop of the Persian Church. Once, in the preface to the Synod's proceedings, he is referred to as the Patriarch (SO, p 253), but this title at this date is an anachronism, and its appearance here supports the view that SO in places shows signs of an editorial hand. The commoner titles for Mar Isaac are Catholicos and archbishop of all the Orient, though he is also designated as "the great metropolitan, the Catholicos of Seleucia and Ctesiphon, the one who occupies the see of Koke." Issac was one of the two principals at this Synod, the other being Marutha, bishop of Maiperqaṭ. As we have earlier seen (ch 5, sect 1), Marutha came to the Persian court twice as ambassador from Constantinople, and as one who was *persona grata* to Yazdagird I, he seems to have prevailed upon the king (a) to end the persecution of the Church, (b) to recognize Isaac as the duly elected head of the Christians in Persia, (c) to order (does Syr *pqd* here mean "authorize"?) the reconstruction of churches destroyed in the recent persecution, and to free Christians still in prison, and (d) to allow Christian clergy to move about freely within the kingdom. The prayer which all the churches are to offer for the peace and tranquility of the kings and governors of Persia (SO, pp 258, 262) is doubtless a sincere response to Yazdagird's actions.

The other aspect of Marutha's work relates to the calling of the Synod. We have here to assume that prior to coming to Persia, Marutha held conversations with the bishops of Syria, one result of which was that he was furnished with a letter, signed by the bishops of Antioch, Aleppo, Edessa, Tella and Amid, which urged the Church in the Orient to adopt the rules and canons of the western Church. This letter, when read in a Persian translation to Yazdagird, was favourably received by him, and, surprisingly, it was the king who ordered the bishops of the Persian Church to assemble in the capital and hear what the western bishops had written. Forty bishops are said to have been involved, although only thirty-eight signatures appear at the end of the record.

The first session of the Synod was held in the great church in Seleucia-Ctesiphon on January 6, 410, but how many later sessions there were we do not know. Apparently the king was kept informed of the Synod's actions. Early in the course of the meetings, the king sent two representatives to the assembly to announce formally the end of the persecution of Christians, to confirm Isaac as the head of all the Christians of the Orient, and to promise state support for policies recommended by Marutha and Isaac.

The Synod's subsequent actions were threefold. First, it adopted the Nicene Creed as the creed of the Persian Church. The text of this document is given in SO (pp 262–63), and it is clear that this followed the original Nicene Creed, not the somewhat expanded later version commonly known as the Nicene Creed, but more accurately as the Niceno-Constantinopolitan Creed.[1] Second, it agreed that the principal Christian festivals were to be celebrated at the same time in both the West and the Orient. Third, the Synod adopted or established twenty-one canons dealing with the life and discipline of the Church. It is clear both from the account of the meeting of the Synod and from the canons (especially canon 21), that prior to 410 there had been internal troubles in the Church. The Synod's expectation was that its decisions would bring peace and unity to the Christian community.

The canons of the Synod of 410, which are summarized below, as well as the canons approved by later Synods, are presented principally to illustrate the day-to-day problems of the Persian Church. The relation of the various collections of Persian canons to one another, and their relation to the canons of the Greek Church, are matters of considerable interest and importance, but to explore them would take us beyond the purpose of the present volume.[2]

1 and 11. The qualifications and election of a bishop. After his consecration in his own city, he must go to the capital to be confirmed by the Catholicos.

2. The place of eunuchs in the Church.

---

[1] For the text of the earliest Nicene Creed, see A. C. McGiffert, *A History of Christian Thought*, 1, New York, 1932, pp 262–63.

[2] SO, pp 259–60, note 3.

3 and 4. Concubinage and dishonest gain (usury) among the clergy.

5. Divination, amulets, incantations, etc. (We know from the magic bowls published by Pognon, Montgomery, Gordon, and others, how widespread the use of incantations was in the Euphrates-Tigris area at this time.)

6. Biennial Synods.

7. Hospices associated with churches.

8. The behaviour of the clergy with respect to secular feasts and funerary banquets.

9. Procedure at the Sunday services.

10. Metropolitan bishops, each of whom should possess a copy of these canons. Chabot suggests that this canon marks the end of the decisions taken at the first session of the Synod (SO, p 266, note 1).

12. The honour and obedience due to the Catholicos.

13. The ministry, the services, the sacrifice (Holy Communion), and the feasts are to follow the rules practised in the West, which the bishops Isaac and Marutha have taught us. The oblation is to be offered on an altar in a church, and not as hitherto in the houses of believers.

14. There is to be only one chorepiscopus for each bishop.

15. The duties of the archdeacon (the bishop's chief assistant).

16. The requirements for ordination. Even a sub-deacon must be able to recite the Psalms by heart.

17. This is not really a canon, but a compact to observe all these regulations. Anyone not doing so will be subject to the wrath of God.

18–21. The precedence, dignity and duties of the metropolitans. Canon 21 supplies the details of the ecclesiastical divisions:

The first see is that of Seleucia-Ctesiphon, whose bishop is the Catholicos. The latter is the head of all the metropolitans and bishops. The bishop of Kashkar serves as his auxiliary;

The bishop of Beth Lapaṭ is the metropolitan of the province of Beth Houzaye (Khuzistan or Susiana);

The bishop of Nisibis is the metropolitan of the province of Beth 'Arbaye;

The bishop of Pherat is the metropolitan of the province of Mesene (Maishan);

The bishop of Arbela is the metropolitan of the province of Hedayab (Adiabene);

The bishop of Karka (Karka of Beth Selok) is the metropolitan of the province of Beth Garmai.

The names of the metropolitans and of the bishops and their sees are then given. At the time of the Synod there was no recognized incumbent to serve as the metropolitan of Beth Lapaṭ.

At the end of this catalogue there are references to bishops in more distant places—in Persis, on the islands of the Persian Gulf, in Media, in Upper Media, and even in Khurasan.

The account of Mar Isaac's Synod concludes with the signatures of those present at the sessions. Mar Issac and Marutha head the list, and are followed by four metropolitans and thirty-two bishops. Why a city such as Rima should have two bishops is not clear.

The proceedings of the Synod of 410 give us our earliest comprehensive picture of the extent and organization of the Persian Church. When we consider the mostly unfavourable environment in which Christianity had to operate, we cannot but admire the faith and tenacity of all those who in the course of two centuries brought the Christian cause in Sasanian Persia to the stage reflected in the Synod of Mar Isaac.

2. The Synod of Mar Yahbalaha I (420).

Mar Isaac was succeeded as Catholicos by Mar Ahai, abbot of the monastery at Dair Qoni, and he in turn c 415-16 by Mar Yahbalaha who was also from the same monastery. About 417-18 the latter was sent by Yazdagird on an embassy to Constantinople, and two years later Acacius, bishop of Amid, came to Persia on a mission from Theodosius II. It was in 420, while Acacius was in Persia and when he and Yahbalaha were with Yazdagird in Beth-Ardashir (Seleucia), that ten of the Persian bishops and their clergy gathered in the capital and petitioned Yahbalaha (that Acacius was included as an addressee may have been merely a courtesy) about the canons to be recognized in the Persian Chruch. This petition and what followed from it can hardly be classified as constituting a meeting of a Synod, but they are treated as such SO (pp 276-84).

The petitioners noted the divisions and discords within the Church (some of which may have arisen during Yahbalaha's absence in Constantinople), and requested, in order to cope with this situation, that the canons of the Western Church, particularly those endorsed by the Councils of Ancyra, Neocaesarea of Cappadocia, Gangra, Antioch and Laodicea (in Phrygia) be made operative in the Persian Church. It would appear that the canons accepted by the Synod of 410 were largely ignored. Whether Acacius had suggested the use of the Greek canons we do not know. It was further requested that each of the bishops be given a copy of the aforementioned canons. Although the wholesale acceptance of the western rules must have been of doubtful value to the Oriental Church, the Catholicos acceded to the request and agreed to give to each of the petitioners the texts of the laws in question. He made the point, however, that these are to supplement, not supplant, the canons adopted in 410.

The proceedings of this so-called Synod are signed by Mar Yahbalaha, Acacius, the metropolitans of Beth Lapaṭ and Nisibis, and eight other bishops. The opening paragraph of the record credits the Catholicos with authority over twenty-eight sees, one of which, Abrashahr, is as far east as Khurasan.

3. The Synod of Mar Dadjesus (424).

Dadjesus, who was elected Catholicos c 421-22, came to his post amid troubled times in the Church. His immediate successor, Marabokt or Pharabokt, had caused a schism among the Christians and had been removed from office, a circumstance which created difficulties for his successor. The dissidents seem to have laid charges against the new Catholicos, which resulted in the latter's imprisonment. From this plight Dadjesus was delivered by "a faithful messenger," who may have been Acacius, bishop of Amid (if we can assume that he was still in Persia on behalf of Theodosius II). But Dadjesus did not like the milieu in which he found himself, and he wished to resign from office. The *Synodicon* suggests that he may actually have left his work. This was the *raison d'être* of the Synod which met at Markabta of the Arabs in 424, and to which thirty-six bishops in addition to the Catholicos came. The site of Markabta has not been identified. Chabot suggests (SO, p 676) that it may be an error for Mabrakta which is near Seleucia-Ctesiphon.

The Synod opened with a plea from the assembled bishops (their spokesman is unnamed) that Dadjesus should return to his see and take up anew his duties as head of the Church of God. The Catholicos, in reply, referred to the difficulties with recalcitrant bishops, eleven of whom are named, and some of whom had been censured in times past. They have turned for help to powerful pagans, claiming that they have been treated unjustly, and they have shown themselves unwilling to accept the authority and discipline of the Catholicos. Moreover they have accused Dadjesus of various misdeameanours, and even of ignorance of the Scriptures.

Agapit, bishop of Beth Lapat, was the next to speak. He read the canons (perhaps only some of them) which the Greek Church had sent to the Orient (see the Synods of 410 and 420), He also cited the role which the western bishops had played in the preceding century in restoring Papa to the see of Seleucia. But, he argued, whereas in the past the western fathers had come to our assistance, the time has now come for the Persian Church to look to itself to right its wrongs through its own Catholicos. Hence he insisted that the high authority of the Catholicos must be recognized. Agapit ended his peroration with a plea to Dadjesus to return and take up again the government of the Church.

Hosea, bishop of Nisibis, then spoke briefly, endorsing what Agapit had said. The bishops, presumably through a representative, added their plea to those of Agapit and Hosea, being somewhat more explicit regarding the treatment of the rebellious bishops, and agreeing that the Oriental Church cannot complain regarding its head before the western prelates: the Catholicos can be judged by Christ alone. Dadjesus responded to these expressions of loyalty by agreeing to return to his post. He continued in office until his death in 457.

The signatories on the proceedings of the Synod of 424 are the Catholicos, five archbishops, and thirty-one bishops. The latter include bishops from Merv, Herat, Segestan, Abrashahr, Rai, Ispahan (Isfahan), Shushtar, and Istakhr. Clearly the Persian Church had moved into central and eastern Persia, into regions that were predominantly Zoroastrian.

It is manifest from the Synods of 410, 420 and 424 that two fundamental features of the Oriental Church were now fully established. One was that the Nicene Creed would be its primary theological document (apart from the Scriptures), and the other was that Persian Christians were in every respect independent of the Church in the Byzantine world, and their Catholicos was answerable to God alone.

4. Persecution.

The Synod of Mar Isaac (410) seemed to herald an era of toleration for the Persian Church. But as matters turned out, the freedom extended to the Christians was short-lived, for even Yazdagird I had to maintain good relations with the nobility as well as with the Zoroastrian hierarchy. The intemperate zeal of some Christians, the adherence of government officials to Christianity, and the growth of the Church in regions heretofore largely Zoroastrian, all helped to create a climate in which some persecution of Christians was almost inevitable.

Yazdagird I seems to have instituted limited repressive measures against the Church towards the end of his reign, although Socrates (VII. 18) denies this. The immediate cause of his action was the unrestrained fervour of a bishop ('Abda) in Hormizdardashir, who destroyed a Zoroastrian fire-temple next to his church. The bishop refused to reconstruct the pagan structure, although he was warned that if he did not do so, all the Christians would suffer, and he was executed. A similar story is told of Narsai from Beth Raziqaye in Media, who would not rebuild a fire-temple he had damaged, and whose subsequent execution was a public spectacle. The persecution thus begun was continued by Yazdagird's son, Varahran V (421–39), and is described with many of the unpleasant details in Theodoret V. 39 (cf *Chr de Michel*, 2, VIII. iii pp 15–16). Three of the better known martyrs at this time were Hormizdas, Suene, and Benjamin, the first two being from the Persian nobility. Early in Varahran's reign, a war broke out between Persia and Byzantium (Socrates VII. xviii), and when peace was finally arranged, one of its conditions was that liberty was guaranteed to Christians in Persia. This, however, was only a temporary respite for the Church, for Yazdagird II (439–57) and Peroz (459–84) revived the policy of persecution, the former being credited with a massacre lasting several days in 446 outside of Karka of Beth Selok. The number said to have perished is given as 153,000, which seems an incredible figure. According to the *Chr de Séert*, PO, 7, viii, pp 112–13, the future Catholicos, Acacius, was imprisoned for a while by

Peroz. The last year of Peroz (484) was marked by his murder of the Catholicos Babowai. The latter, originally from Tella, was a convert from Zoroastrianism, and had succeeded Dadjesus as Catholicos in 457. For some reason, possibly because he had abandoned his ancestral faith, he was imprisoned for two (or seven) years, and was released only when Peroz concluded a peace treaty with the emperor Zeno in 464. Twenty years later Babowai was again in serious trouble. A letter which he had sent to Zeno, and in which he had referred to the "accursed kingdom" in which Persian Christians had to live, was intercepted and read to Peroz. The king was understandably furious at the Catholicos, and decreed his immediate death (484).[3]

It is evident from the known facts and what appear to be reliable traditions that the fifth century was a time of serious external trouble for the Persian Church. When we consider that at the same time this Church had many problems connected with its own inner life, we can well understand why the *Synodicon Orientale* records no Synods of the Church between 424 and 486.

5. Nestorianism.

The fifth century is notable in the history of the Persian Church because the theological controversies of this century which troubled the western Church, now became important issues in the Orient. Persian Christians whose religious views hitherto had been based on the Nicene Creed found themselves involved in the same theological disputes as their brethren in the Greek Church. The first of these conflicts to be dealt with here is Nestorianism (see ch 3, sect 9).

Although Nestorius was condemned at the Council of Ephesus (431) and his views at the Council of Chalcedon (451), his supporters continued to be prominent in Syria. Ibas, bishop of Edessa (see ch 5, sect 4) was one of these. He had been a teacher in the Edessan School before he became bishop of Edessa in 439, and he continued some of his teaching duties at the School after his elevation to the episcopate. He was one of the translators of the works of Theodore of Mopsuestia and other Greek writers into Syriac. His moderate support of Nestorius's teaching caused him to be deposed by the Robber Council of Ephesus in 449, but the Council of Chalcedon two years later reinstated him (Evagrius II. 18). After the death of Ibas in 457, the growing strength of Monophysitism in Syria (see ch 5, sect 10) made it possible for one, Nonnus, a Monophysite, to be made bishop of Edessa (457-71), and he in turn was succeeded in this see by another Monophysite, Cyrus. This strong Monophysite influence in Edessa created tension between

---

[3] This is a simplified presentation of a somewhat perplexing incident. See Labourt, note 6, pp 142-43; *Chr de Séert*, PO 7, pp 101-2.

the School and the local clergy, and resulted as we have earlier seen (ch 5 sect 7) in the closing of the School by order of the emperor Zeno in 489.

During its one hundred or so years of life, the School of Edessa had been the only institution available to the Christians in Persia for the training of their clergy, and therefore many of the School's students were from Persia. With the rise of Nestorius, and with the Edessan School tending to support him, Persian students at the School were given a sympathetic exposure to Nestorius's views, and when they returned to Persia, their attitude towards the Nestorian cause was apt to be favourable. One such former student at the School was Barṣauma, who became bishop of Nisibis after 457. It was probably after 471, when Cyrus took over the see of Edessa, that most of the Persians in the School, both teachers and students, began to move back to Persia, a movement completed eighteen years later when the School was closed.

Many of the Persian Christians who had studied at Edessa and who could be labelled Nestorians (and who were therefore opponents of Monophysitism), now came into prominence in the Persian Church, and through their influence this Church acquired its strong Nestorian bent. The principal names to be cited in this connection are Acacius, a teacher in the School at Seleucia, who was to become Catholicos 485–495/6; Ma'na of Beth Ardashir (Rew-Ardashir), Joḥannan of Karka of Beth Selok, Barṣauma of Nisibis, Paul of Karka of Ledan, Pusai of Shushtar, Abraham of Madai, and Narseh, a teacher in the School at Nisibis. All of these clergy except Narseh attended the Synod of 486 (SO, pp 299–301, 306–7; cf Labourt, pp 132–33).

If we henceforth speak of the Christians in Persia as Nestorians, this term should not be thought of in a pejorative sense. Theologically they were Chalcedonians (supporters of the Council of Chalcedon), except that they did not accept that Council's condemnation of Nestorius. Their Monophysite opponents, who habitually speak of themselves as the "orthodox," refer to the Nestorians as the followers of Nestorius, or as Diophysites or as Chalcedonians. From the Monophysite point of view, there was no substantial difference between the Nestorians and those who accepted the Council of Chalcedon.

6. The School of Nisibis: Its Early Years.[4]

While the date of the actual founding of the School of Nisibis is not known, it is clear that it must bear some relation to Narseh's departure from Edessa (c 471) and to the suppression of the Edessan School in 489. Whatever the date may be, the School of Nisibis was in fact the continuation of the one at Edessa and the heir of its scholastic traditions.

---

[4] Barḥadbeshabba, *Cause de la Fondation des Écoles*, ed A. Scher, PO 4, (1908) pp 317–404; J. B. Chabot, "L'école de Nisibe, son histoire, ses statuts," JA, ser IX, tome 8, Paris 1896, pp 43–93; A. Vööbus, *Statutes of the School of Nisibis* (PETSE, 12), Stockholm, 1961/62. A. Vööbus, *History of the School of Nisibis*, CSCO 266, Subsidia 26, Louvain, 1965.

When Narseh[5] left Edessa he headed eastwards and came to Nisibis which had been in Persian hands for over a century. Here he found a small school established by one, Simeon, and being offered its headship, he decided to accept it. Barṣauma, the bishop of the city and a graduate of Edessa, became interested in Narseh's work, and the two men gave thought to the project of setting up a Nestorian School in Nisibis as a replacement for the one in Edessa which was now in difficulties. The bishop's interest and support were of basic importance, for a site had to be purchased and buildings erected. Narseh, on the other hand, could supply the practical skills of an experienced teacher and administrator. The matter was proceeded with, the existing school of Simeon becoming a part of the new establishment and its pupils forming the nucleus of the enlarged student body. The School got off to a splended start, with Narseh at its head and with some of his fellow-workers from Edessa joining him as teachers. Narseh was a great asset to the new foundation. Since boyhood he had shown extraordinary talents as a student, and as a mature man he was renowned for his piety, his learning and his poetic talents. In addition to all this, he brought to his new work a varied experience both in the monastery in Kephar Mari and in the School of Edessa. He held office until c 503.

Barṣauma and Narseh cooperated in drawing up a set of regulations governing the School's corporate life and the conduct of its individual members. These rules are not extant. It seems likely, however, that the gist of them was included in the second group of statutes promulgated in 496,[6] when Hosea was bishop of Nisibis and when Narseh was still head of the School. Presumably new circumstances as well as experience made some revision of the original rules imperative. Most of the regulations conclude with a reference to the penalties for disregarding them. Expulsion from the School and even from Nisibis was a common punishment for the more serious offences.

The administration of the School was headed by the director (Syr *rbn* "our master"), chosen from the teachers of the School. He was always the chief instructor and he exercised supervision over all the teaching. His chief assistant was the steward or dean (Syr *rb byt'*), who attended to the details of the School's administration, serving as a dean of students and a steward of the School's property (canons 1, 2, and 22). In some circumstances the steward was assisted by a small council from the staff of the School.

Almost nothing is said in the statutes about the courses of study available. Apparently to meet the needs of students of different backgrounds basic training was given in reading, writing and grammar (cf canons 8 and 20). The teacher of these subjects was the scribe (Syr *spr'*). One of Narseh's disciples, Joseph Huzaya (i.e., of Khuzistan), became an expert in Syriac

---

[5] On Narseh, see *Chr de Séert*, PO 7, ix, pp 114–15.
[6] These have been published by A. Vööbus (*Statutes* as in note 4), pp 73–85.

grammar and wrote the first treatise on this subject that we know of. The teachng of reading involved the correct recitation of the contents of the liturgy, and this in turn led to an interest in music and liturgical chanting.

Little is known about the place of secular subjects in the curriculum. The great emphasis in the School was upon biblical studies, which were pursued in the tradition of the School of Edessa, and therefore rested on the teachings of Theodore of Mopsuestia. Chabot suggests that the three-year course covered the Scriptures in this order: the Pauline Epistles and the Pentateuch; the Psalms and the Prophets; the rest of the NT. In this area the primary aim was to study the Scriptures in their historical and literal sense, and to veer away from the use of allegory in order to discover some hidden spiritual truth in the written word. Our sources tell us nothing about theological studies other than those in the biblical field. Presumably there was some instruction available in the tenets of Nestorianism as well as in the history of the Church. In Abraham's time (director from c 510 on) considerable interest was shown in polemics (Nestorians versus Monophysites, Jews, and Magi). The School was of course strictly for those of the Nestorian persuasion.

A good many of the rules relate to the internal discipline of the institution. It is clear from these that the young men attending the School were not markedly different from youth the world over, particularly when living in an educational establishment. The School was a modified monastery in that students lived on the premises and were required to remain celibate (canon 3). They were not required to surrender their private property, as the references to lending denars at interest and to making a will indicate (canons 6 and 17). They did not occupy single cells but rooms that could accommodate several persons (canon 10). One source states that students had to look after their own meals, the School attending to the needs only of the disabled and the very poor (cf canon 11). A student's life was a rigorous one. While in the School he was up at cockcrow, and spent the day reading, hearing lectures, copying manuscripts and practising the recitation of the liturgy (cf canons 8 and 9). He was normally not allowed to indulge in gainful employment during the academic term but he could do so from August to October, when the School suspended its activities (canon 5), but even during these three months a student was under some degree of supervision. At a later date there was a change in the School's time-table, with the year being broken into two terms related to agricultural activities, one following the grain harvest and the other the fruit harvest. One thing the School was disinclined to permit was the visiting of the Byzantine world, which was allowed only under special circumstances (canon 4).

7. Monophysitism.

While Monophysitism had been condemned at the Council of Chalcedon (451), it continued to be a disturbing factor in the life of the western Church, and the accession of the emperor Zeno in 474, whose Henoticon was issued in 482, gave heart to the Monophysites (cf ch 3, sect 9; ch 5, sect 10). In Syria most of the monasteries appear to have been either supporters of or sympathizers with the Monophysite cause.

While the evidence is very scanty, we have to assume that in the years following Chalcedon, Monophysitism began to percolate into the Persian Church, perhaps at first mostly through the monasteries. In the Edessan School during the time of Ibas as bishop of Edessa (c 435–57) there were Persians who were opposed to the School's Nestorian sympathies, among them being Papa of Beth Lapaṭ, Philoxenus of Taḥal (later, bishop of Mabbog), his brother Addai, Barhadbeshabba of Qardu, and Benjamin of Beth Aramaye.[7] These men, and probably others, must have seen to it that the Monophysite claims were made known to Persian Christians. Barṣauma, who became bishop of Nisibis c 459, found that the Monophysites were strong in his diocese, and when king Peroz, with whom he was on good terms, gave him some civil responsibilities in connection with the western frontier and placed troops at his disposal, he decided with the compliance of his fellow bishops, and seemingly with the tacit approval of Peroz, to use force in suppressing the Monophysites. Undoubtedly some blood was shed, but the figure of Bar Hebraeus (over 7,700 killed) seems inflated.[8] In a letter to the Catholicos Acacius (485–95/6), Barṣauma refers to the troubles in Nisibis (thought to be with Monophysites, although they are not specifically named), and he urges Acacius to excommunicate the persons involved and threaten to denounce them to the king if they do not come to their senses (SO, p 536). At this time, with Zeno and later Anastasius (both at heart Monophysites) reigning in Constantinople (474–518), it could be argued by the Nestorians that they, the Nestorians, were more likely to be loyal to the Persian king than the Monophysites whose main support lay in the Byzantine world.

8. The Synods of 484 and 486.

Barṣauma and the Synod of 484.

Barṣauma, born early in the century in Qardu, studied at Edessa where he became an ardent Nestorian. He probably left the Edessan School at the death of Ibas (457), and went to Persia where c 459 the Catholicos Babowai (457–84/6) designated him metropolitan bishop of Nisibis. Barṣauma, who was in some respects a strong character, was not always able to accept superior authority, and his irascibility did not make things easy for him. He is said to have married after the Synod of 484. His rather abject expressions of contrition for wrongs done to Babowai and his successor Acacius only excite our pity. He died c 491–96.

[7] Labourt, pp 132–33.
[8] Labourt, p 136.

In 484 Barṣauma called together quite uncanonically a group of bishops at Beth Lapaṭ. All those present were discontented with the rule of Babowai and they formulated various charges and reproaches against him (SO, pp 308-9). They may even have pronounced his deposition. Soon after this, but for another reason, Peroz, as we have earlier seen (sect 4 above), put the Catholicos to death. In letters addressed to the new Catholicos, Acacius, Barṣauma completely annuls all that was done and said against Babowai at Beth Lapaṭ (SO, pp 531-39).

The Synod of Mar Acacius (486).

This Synod which seems to have been preceded by an earlier one at Beth 'Edrai (SO, p 300, note 2), was held at Seleucia in the second year of the reign of Valash (484-88) under the guidance of the Catholicos, Mar Acacius. The record of proceedings (SO pp 299-307) is signed by Acacius, three metropolitans, and twenty-one bishops, the signatures of four of the latter being by their deputies. Barṣauma of Nisibis explains in a letter to Acacius why he cannot be present (SO, pp 532-34). Acacius and five of the bishops were among those who had left the School of Edessa after the death of Ibas, the bishop of the city.

The Synod is recorded as having adopted the following canons:

1. After noting the presence in the Church of those who teach heretical doctrines (thus fulfilling I Tim 4:1-3), the true faith as regards the Incarnation is described as holding two natures (Syr *kyn'*), divine and human, the two natures maintaining their separate identities but united in one person (Syr *prṣwp'*). It would seem from this that the heresy in question was Monophysitism (for a contrary opinion, see Fiey, *Jalons*, p 119).

2. We can infer from the preface to this canon that there were in Beth Aramaye a number of extreme ascetics who were inculcating practices and teaching doctrines contrary to accepted usage and faith. The canon concedes that such ascetics may be sincere in their profession, but insists that they live in isolated places. They must not enter towns or villages where there are bishops, priests or deacons, nor must they administer the sacrifices. Those who go into monasteries are to be under the jurisdiction of bishops, priests or periodeutes. Penalties are set down for those who disregard, or for those who help anyone to disregard, these injunctions.

3. In the preamble in which the NT references to marriage are utilized and in which the opinions of Zoroastrians with respect to Christian conduct are obviously in mind, it is enjoined that bishops must not put obstacles in the way of marriage within their dioceses. When we come to the text of the canon, it is prescribed (a) that bishops can bestow ordination for the diaconate only on married men, and it is implied, following I Tim 3:1-5, that bishops, too, should be married; (b) that those who voluntarily choose not to marry, must live in a monastery in purity and continence; (c) that a bishop cannot oppose the wish of an unmarried priest to marry, or if a priest

is widowed, to marry again. In short, the choice for Christian clerics is either the perfection of celibacy, or marriage adorned by the procreation of children. Penalties are set forth for those who disregard these rules.

9. The Synod of Mar Babai (497).

Babai, of a Persian family (his father was in the civil service) and a married man, succeeded Acacius as Catholicos in 497. Curiously, he is not mentioned in the records of the Synod of 486 as filling any position in the Church at that time. He is said to have been the disciple of Mare of Taḥal. Apart from his holding of a Synod in 497 we know little about him as a Catholicos. The *Chronique de Séert* summarizes a short dissertation on the resurrection of the dead which he delivered before king Zamasp (PO 7. xv. pp 129-30). His closing years in office were contemporaneous with Persia's renewal of the war with Constantinople, a war which was in full swing at the time of his death (502/3).

As the background for the Synod of 497, we must keep in mind, first, the continued quarrelsomeness of Barṣauma of Nisibis, now a very old man. Starting in the fourth year of king Kavad I (492), Barṣauma had renewed his dispute with the equally old Catholicos, Acacius. The main points at issue were the primacy of the see of Seleucia, and the propriety of holding Synods every two years. The issues were such that both parties resorted to anathematizing each other. While both the principals died before the Synod of 497 met, their sharp differences left the Church in a weakened condition. A second matter which must have been in the thoughts of many Christians at this time was Mazdakism which was currently being propagated throughout the land (see ch 7, sect 4). Mazdak advocated not only the community of goods but the community of women; the latter ran counter both to Zoroastrian and to Christian practice. To what extent Mazdak's views on marriage were a factor in 497 in leading the Synod to reaffirm the Church's stand on marriage, we do not know.

The Synod of Mar Babai was held in Seleucia-Ctesiphon in the second year of Zamasp, the king who in his short term in office (496-98) seems to have been friendly disposed to the Church. He was especially interested in encouraging the Christian clergy to marry. Indeed the *Synodicon Orientale* states that the king actually ordered a Synod to be held with a view to clarifying the matter of clerical marriage (p 312). The Synod's chief decisions were:

To state publicly that any Christian cleric, from the Catholicos ("patriarch" appears in SO, p 312, l 8) down, can openly contract a marriage. This was basically a reiteration of the position on clerical marriage known to be the view of Barṣauma, and taken by the Synod of Mar Acacius in 486.

To abrogate both the anathemas issued by Mar Acacius against Barṣauma and his partisans, and the anathemas issued by Barṣauma against

Mar Acacius and his partisans, except that those who were deservedly anathematized (this is not elaborated) are to remain under the ban.

To continue, in accordance with the usage of the Church, to acknowledge as Catholicos the bishop of Seleucia. At the moment the holder of this office is Mar Babai. Anyone opposed to his primacy will separate himself from communion with those who accept the headship of Mar Babai.

To reaffirm that the bishops of a metropolitan province ought to meet in assembly twice a year.

To modify an earlier canon which required a meeting of all the bishops of the whole Church every two years; the revised canon stipulates that such a meeting is to be held every four years in the month of Tishri, unless some emergency demands an earlier meeting. All the bishops must attend such a Synod, but if a bishop cannot come he should send in his place one of his clergy, provided with his written consent. If a bishop absents himself for an unsatisfactory reason, he will be forbidden to exercise his ministry until he comes to the Catholicos and consents to what the assembly did.

To attempt to settle the troubles centering in Papa, bishop of Beth Lapaṭ, and Yazdad, bishop of Rew Ardashir. Apparently both clerics had refused to attend Mar Babai's Synod. They are given a year to think things over. If they finally agree to subscribe to the actions of the Synod, well and good. But if Papa does not do so, an earlier anathema against him by a synod of bishops will stand, and if Yazdad does not submit, he will be deprived of his episcopal status. The record does not state whether the real issue as regards these two bishops was their Christology. It is usually assumed that they harboured Monophysite views.

To accept as a legitimate bishop any one who was properly chosen as bishop during the period commencing in 492 (the time of the quarrel between Barṣauma and Acacius), but anyone not properly chosen and who therefore degrades the episcopacy, will be rejected by members of the Synod.

The proceedings of the Synod are signed by Mar Babai, seven metropolitans and thirty-one bishops, in some cases the signing being done by an approved proxy. Actually the *Synodicon* gives three episcopal lists of those present at the Synod (pp 310, 311, and 315-17).

Chapter 10.
The Church in the Sixth and Early Seventh Centuries to 608/9

1. The Catholicos Shila (505–23) and the Subsequent Duality in the Catholicate.

Shila, who had been the archdeacon of Mar Babai (he signed the proceedings of the Synod of 497 on the latter's behalf), succeeded Mar Babai in 505 as Catholicos. Originally from Seleucia, he was a married man with at least one daughter, and although he is said to have been incredibly avaricious, he directed the Church with wisdom and firmness. He seems to have sensed the need for Christians to keep aloof from the controversy centering in Mazdak, a policy which doubtless contributed to the external peace which the Church enjoyed in Kavad's time (488–531). It is reported that a theological debate took place in Ḥira (sometime after 518) between Shila and the Monophysites from Syria exiled by Justin I, who had taken refuge in the Arab city.

Shila, who died in 523, had designated his son-in-law, Elisha, a medical doctor, as his successor, but this nomination was not endorsed by many of the bishops, who put forward another candidate, Narseh, a skilled writer from Khuzistan. Each of these persons was now elevated to the Catholicate by his partisans (quite an irregular proceeding), and so the Church had a dual head. Since each Catholicos consecrated such bishops as were needful and as these appointees were frequently in the same see, a destructive schism developed in the Church. Although Narseh died c 535, the surviving Catholicos was not accepted by the rival group, and the confusion in the Church continued.

It was in the period of the "duality" that Khusro I (Chosroes, 531–79) came to the Persian throne.[1] Commonly recognized as the greatest of the Sasanian kings (hence "Anosharvan," "of the immortal soul"), he instituted various social, economic, and military reforms. Court procedure became grander than ever before, but alongside more superficial interests, Khusro encouraged the pursuit of learning. It is less to his credit that in 540 he broke the "endless peace" made with Justinian in 532, and renewed the war with Constantinople by raiding Syria. Finally, after three truces had expired, a treaty was agreed upon in 562. But this was broken in 572 by the

---

[1] For a good account of Khusro, see Christensen, ch 8, pp 363–440.

emperor Justin II, and it was not until the time of Tiberius II (578–82) that peace was once more established. It was in these wars with Byzantium that Khusro's forces obtained hordes of prisoners, mostly from Syria, who were sent to Persia to begin a new life there. Another result of Khusro's wars was that anti-Christian feelings were again aroused in Persia, and there was some persecution of Christians by the Magi. This persecution was not as extensive as in Shapur I's time, being directed mostly against Persians, and especially members of the nobility, who had turned to Christianity. This explains why Mar Aba, the Catholicos, was a prime target for the Magi, and why the saintly Christian woman, Shirin of Karka of Beth Selokh, the daughter of Zoroastrian parents, was arrested and put to death in Seleucia in February, 559.

Elisha's moral conduct and arbitrary judgments continued to vex the bishops, so the latter deposed him in 539, and chose as Catholicos, one, Paul the archdeacon in the see of Hormizdardashir (another source says of Seleucia). Paul's case was strengthened by his enjoying the favour of Khusro. Unfortunately he was an old man and he died within a year after his appointment. He was succeeded by Mar Aba in 540.

2. The Synod of Mar Aba I (544).

Mar Aba I[2] was an exceptionally able man. Born into a Zoroastrian family, he became a Christian, being baptized at Ḥira. He was a student at Nisibis and from there he proceeded to Edessa where he received some instruction in Greek. He subsequently travelled in the Byzantine world, though the extent of his journeys is uncertain. Chabot thinks that he went only to Constantinople. In any event he returned to Nisibis where he became a distinguished teacher in its School. When Paul died he was the bishops' choice as Catholicos. This was a dangerous role for a former Zoroastrian to fill. It was also a demanding task for the Church was still suffering from the effects of the years of the "duality."

It was in Mar Aba's time that another lot of war prisoners from the West reached Persia (Procopius, *Wars* II, 13. 1–6; 14. 1–4), and presumably many of them eventually were integrated into the Christian community of Persia. It is thought that the Monophysites profited more from this infusion of fresh blood than did the Nestorians.

It was also during Mar Aba's Catholicate, c 542-45/6, that Persia and the Byzantine world experienced one of their worst visitations of the bubonic plague which periodically afflicted these areas. The *Chronique de Séert* gives us one Oriental account of this terrible calamity (PO 7, XXXII, pp 182–86); for Procopius's version, see *Wars* II. xxii–xxiii.

In the *Synodicon Orientale* (pp 318-51) Mar Aba is credited with summoning a Synod in 544 (four years after his elevation to the Catholicate),

---

[2] On Mar Aba, see *Chr de Séert*, PO 7, XVIII, pp 154-70.

but this record appears to be in some disorder. We know, for instance, that in 544 the Catholicos was actually under house arrest in Azerbaijan. We cannot attempt here to suggest ways of righting this confusion, and we shall content ourselves with commenting on the various documents which purport to be the records of the Synod.

The first is an account of the visit, begun in February 540, by the Catholicos and some clergy to various cities, and of the actions taken to settle disputes regarding bishoprics in Peroz-Shabur, Kashkar, Maishan, Hormizd-Ardashir, Rew-Ardashir, Shushtar, and Beth Lapaṭ. At the last named city, they had much trouble with one, Abraham, son of Audmihr, who, failing to live up to his earlier professions of penitence, had to be deprived of all his religious functions and excommunicated. The record of this peregrination is signed at Beth Lapaṭ by Mar Aba, two metropolitans, eight bishops and various priests and other witnesses.

The second document (third in SO) is a communication from Mar Aba to the metropolitans, the bishops, and the whole Christian Church of the Orient. After an opening homily on the primary importance of the fear of God, the Catholicos proceeds to outline the purpose of true marriage and to list the various relatives whom a Christian may not marry.

The third document (fourth in SO) is a letter from the Catholicos to the faithful in Segestan and is a reply to a letter which he had received from them. He explains how the "duality" in the Church occurred, and how both he and his predecessor Paul have attempted to deal with it. He then proceeds to the regularization of the episcopal situation in Segestan, involving two men, Yzedaphrid and Sergius. The letter is signed by Mar Aba, two metropolitans, and eight bishops.

The fourth document (fifth in SO) is a letter from Mar Aba addressed to the metropolitans and bishops, insisting on obedience to superiors within the Church, and commenting on the situation in Beth Lapaṭ and Nisibis, places which Mar Aba was unable to visit on his earlier tour of the sees (cf, however, the reference to what seems to be a visit to Beth Lapaṭ in the first document, SO p 324). It is reaffirmed that nowhere in the Church can a metropolitan or a bishop be ordained or installed without the authorization of the Catholicos. This is signed by Mar Aba, four metropolitans and thirteen bishops.

The fifth document (second in SO, where it is placed in the appendix, pp 550–53) is a letter dated October 540 from the Catholicos to the whole Church, and is in fact a statement of the orthodox faith. About Christ we may note that "Christ is not an ordinary man, nor God stripped of the garment of humanity wherein he is revealed, but Christ is God and man, that is to say the humanity is anointed with the divinity which anointed him."

The sixth document (it is placed in the appendix is SO, pp 553–55) is a fragment of a letter from Mar Aba, and it deals with the choice of his successor. At least three metropolitans are to be summoned, as well as three bishops from each province, and they will choose a man and appoint him to the church of Koke (the patriarchal see in Seleucia). The letter may also have dealt with the choice of metropolitans. It is signed by Mar Aba and three bishops, but the list of signatories is clearly incomplete.

The last item in the record is described as the Canons of Mar Aba (SO, pp 555–61). These may have been approved by the Synod of 544.[3] Some of the laws are manifestly adopted from the Council of Nicaea and from various other Councils of the Greek Church, as well as from the Synod of Mar Isaac (410). They are summarized below.

1. The difference between a village priest and a city priest.

2. If a priest, deacon or urban clerk leaves his district to go elsewhere, he cannot exercise his ecclesiastical function in his new territory. If his bishop calls him back and he does not come, he will be deprived of his status in the Church.

3–5. Liturgical niceties involving priests, deacons, and sub-deacons.

6. Exorcism can be practised only with the permission of the bishop.

9. Meat-eating is approved.

10–11. On avoiding relations with heretics, including praying with them.

12. On excluding rapists from the Church.

13. An archdeacon must remain in the province, and a bishop in the city, to which they were appointed.

14. On priests and deacons, and the correct procedure in receiving communion.

16. On a woman who married two brothers (in succession).

17. Women may not cut their hair.

18. There is to be only one bishop in a town or city.

20. Voluntary eunuchs cannot be received into the Church.

24. Clerics when invited by the faithful to funerary or secular feasts, are to eat moderately.

25. On Sunday the Gospel and "the other books" are to be read; the word of God should be preached until the third or fourth hour; then the sacrifice is to be offered.

27. A priest or deacon under a bishop's interdiction is not to be received by another bishop.

29–31. A priest, a deacon or a sub-deacon, absent without excuse from the church when divine service is on, will be deprived of his office.

33. Thirty years is the minimum age for ordination to the priesthood.

35. Gifts for the church ought to be entrusted to a faithful lay steward.

36. A sub-deacon, to qualify for ordination, must be able to recite the Psalms by heart.

37. On the selection of a bishop after the death of an incumbent bishop.

---

[3] Labourt (p 187, note 2) questions the authenticity of these canons.

38. Those contracting consanguineous marriages (these are described in detail) are to be censured and excommunicated (cf the second document, a letter from Mar Aba, referred to earlier).

39. Appeals against censure.

40. Our interpretation of the Nicene Creed is the one proposed by Theodore, the bishop of Mopsuestia.

The twelve years of Mar Aba's Catholicate illustrate the difficulties which Christians had in an environment in which the Zoroastrian leaders were consistently hostile to them. The Catholicos was called before a council of the Magi c 541–42, but he refused to change the Church's canons regarding marriage, nor would he abandon the proselytization practices of Christians, and he was therefore committed to detention in a village in Azerbaijan. Here he remained for seven years but he was allowed limited freedom so that he carried on many of his duties as Catholicos and saw those who could make the journey to where he was. About the year 548 an unsuccessful attempt on his life by an excommunicated Christian, persuaded Mar Aba to flee from the village in which he was kept, and he came to Seleucia and presented himself unexpectedly to the court. Despite the anger of the Magi, the king spared Mar Aba's life and put him in prison, and when the court moved about, so did Mar Aba. The Catholicos played a part in suppressing a revolt against the king begun by one, Anoshazad a Christian, in Beth Lapaṭ, by counselling the local Christians not to support the rebel and for his services the king freed Mar Aba. But he lived only till 552. Another account is that he remained in prison and there died. He is said to have been given a magnificent public funeral in the Persian capital.

According to sources cited by Wright (pp 19–20), Mar Aba translated the whole of the OT into Syriac (presumably from the Septuagint) and perhaps also the NT. But what effect this work had on the current text of the Scriptures used by the Nestorians is not clear.

3. The Synod of Mar Joseph (554).

Joseph,[4] after training in medicine in the Byzantine world, returned to Nisibis, possibly his home, and became a monk. One tradition states that he successfully treated Khusro for an illness, which may explain why in May 552 the king nominated him as Catholicos in succession to Mar Aba. Apparently the metropolitans and bishops had congregated in Seleucia to accept the king's nomination and formally to elect the new Catholicos, but Joseph after his election adjourned the clerics, claiming that the circumstances were unfavourable for a Synod. In 553 he again postponed the assembly. We can only conjecture about the true reasons for these postponements, but the fact that the canons later passed by the Synod of 554

---

[4] On Joseph, see *Chr de Séert*, PO 7, XXXII, pp 176–81.

(SO, pp 355–65) refer to outside (non-Christian) influence in Church affairs (canons 1, 4, and 9), suggests that the Catholicos at first was uncertain about the method of dealing with this problem.

We do not know whether Joseph had any reliable information about what was going on in Constantinople in 553. If he had, he would be aware that in that year a General Council (the Fifth) of the Western Church was held in the Byzantine capital, and that it condemned, on the insistence of the emperor Justinian (who was anxious to conciliate the Monophysites in his empire), the Three Chapters (see ch 3, sect 9). As one of these Chapters was "the person and works of Theodore of Mopsuestia," and as canon 40 of Mar Aba's Synod, as we have earlier noted, committed the Persian Church to the acceptance of the teaching of Theodore, it would appear that as long as both parties adhered to their stated positions, there was little likelihood of a genuine fraternity between the Byzantine Christians and the Nestorian Christians in Persia.

The long awaited Synod was finally called to meet in Seleucia in January 554 (SO, pp 352–67). It commenced its work by making a solemn profession of the orthodox faith; this was patently directed against the Monophysites. It next proceeded to draw up twenty-three canons, most of which are referred to in what follows.

1. On priests remaining in their own parishes; on clerics using the influence of non-Christian laity to improve their position in the Church.

3. On bishops who, with non-Christian support, make ordinations outside of their own dioceses.

4. On improper procedure in the election of a bishop.

5. A reference to the 15th canon Nicaea regarding a bishop who leaves his see for another one.

6. Bishops must obey what their fellow bishops prescribe in their assembly.

7. The metropolitan bishops and the Catholicos ought to act with the advice of the episcopal community. If there is something urgent and there is no time to call everyone, at least three bishops should be consulted.

8. Priests and the superiors of convents must not abandon their places of residence and go somewhere else, without the consent of their bishop.

9. On priests guilty of iniquities (not described) and accused of the same both by Church people and by outsiders.

10. On priests, deacons and clerks who have taken pagan wives; the danger of Magian punishment in such a situation; sacerdotal rights cannot be exercised by these men.

11. The property of churches and monasteries can be disposed of only with the consent of the communities concerned.

12. On clergy and laity who, because of their faults, have been deprived of their sacerdotal functions or of the right to receive the sacrament.

13. On the behaviour of laity in the Synods of the Church.

14. What is to be done in the event of the death of the Catholicos amid troubled times, and how his successor is to be chosen.

15. The Catholicos ought not to take the title Patriarch until he receives the imposition of hands by the metropolitans; a metropolitan bishop ought not to be entitled metropolitan until he has been instituted by the Patriarch.

16. Each bishop is subject to the metropolitan and the bishops of the province in which he works.

17. On a layman or cleric who commits fornication.

18. On the situation in which the establishment of a new episcopal see is felt to be desirable.

20. The sacrament is to be given in new churches and monasteries only with the consent of the bishop, and only on certain days of the week. The rest of the time communion is to be available only in the principal (i.e., the old) church.

21. When the Patriarch dies, the bishop of Kashkar shall convoke a Synod in the capital to choose his successor. We should note that the part which the reigning Persian king in fact has in the choice of a new Catholicos is ignored (cf also canon 14 above).

22. The canons of Mar Aba are to be carefully observed.

23. On appeals against censure or interdiction.

The record is signed by Mar Joseph, four metropolitans[5] and thirteen bishops. Others (one metropolitan and sixteen bishops) approved of the proceedings by letter. The metropolitans of Beth Garmai and Pherat of Maishan were late in arriving but they have also approved.

The last recorded act of the Synod (SO, p 367) was to rank the metropolitans in the following order:

Beth Huzaye (Khuzistan)
Nisibis
Pherat of Maishan
Hedayab (Adiabene)
Beth Garmai
Rew Ardashir
Merw.

We do not know in what ways the threat of further hostilities between Persia and Constantinople affected the Persian Church in Joseph's time. As we have earlier seen, the war between the two empires had been renewed by Khusro I in 540, and it was only after three truces had expired that peace was finally agreed upon in 562. Our information about the peace negotiations comes from Menander Protector. After giving us the various

---

[5] One of these is the metropolitan of Maḥoze-Ḥedata, whose name is QLDYN', which may be a Syriac form of Claudius or Claudianus. Possibly this individual or his father was originally a prisoner of war from Syria. The reference to Maḥoze-Ḥedata as a metropolitan see is strange, for the capital of the ecclesiastical province of Fars (Persis) was Rew-Ardashir.

clauses of the truce (which was to last for fifty years), we read in P. N. Ure's translation:

> When all had been decided and put into force, separate consideration was given to the question of Christians in Persia, and it was agreed that they should build churches and hold services freely. . . . The Christians . . . agreed that they would by no means venture to convert Magians to our belief. And it was further enacted that in the matter of the dead, the Christians should have permission to bury them in graves as is customary among us.[6]

We can only speculate about the person or persons in the Byzantine delegation who brought up the question of Christians in Persia. While it is improbable that the Catholicos was involved in any way in the peace conference, we can well imagine that when he learned what had been agreed upon with respect to Christians in Persia, he made it widely known in the Christian community. He may, however, not have been entirely happy about the Church giving up its right to proselytize Zoroastrians.

Joseph turned out to be a very despotic Catholicos. He refused to hear the complaints of the bishops, and he was accused of theft, blasphemy and sacrilege. Finally a delegation of Christian notables headed by one, Moses (or Narseh), a medical doctor of Nisibis, took the matter to Khusro, who consented to the deposition of the Catholicos, although the date of this is uncertain (probably between 564 and 567). Joseph died two years after his removal from office.

4. The Synod of Mar Ezekiel (576).

We do not know why at least three years elapsed after the deposition of Joseph before Ezekiel, with the approval of Khusro, became Catholicos. During this interval, Mari, bishop of Kashkar, directed the affairs of the Church. Regarding Ezekiel's earlier life, one source relates that he had been a baker of Mar Aba, then he became his disciple, and under his tutelage he had entered the priesthood and was eventually made bishop of Zabe. This appointment must have occurred after 544, for in the latter year Mihrnarseh was bishop of Zabe. In 572, about three years after his accession, Ezekiel accompanied Khusro as far as Nisibis, which was then being besieged by the Byzantines under Justin II. Khusro relieved the city, and Ezekiel, it appears, then returned to Seleucia. Ezekiel's Catholicate witnessed the death of Khusro I in 579 and the accession of Hormizd IV, the latter proving to be friendly to the Christians. The Catholicos during his term of office had two unhappy conditions to face. The first affected all the people of Persia, Christian and non-Christian, viz., the plague which once more and for about ten years desolated the population, and which called forth special prayers in the churches, one such being "the rogation (or petition) of the Ninevites,"

---

[6] P. N. Ure, *Justinian and His Age*, Harmondsworth, 1951, p 99.

a three-day fast, three weeks before Lent, which is still observed in the Nestorian Church. The second reason for Ezekiel's anxiety was undoubtedly the growth of the Monophysites. Jacob Baradaeus, of whom we have spoken earlier (ch 5, sect 10), died in Ezekiel's time (578), but not before he had revitalized Monophysitism in the Byzantine world, and this was to stimulate somewhat indirectly the Monophysites within Persia. Ezekiel, who is said to have been very despotic, became blind in his last years and died in 581.

The only Synod which Ezekiel held met in February 576, six years after his accession (SO, pp 368–89). It was attended by three metropolitans and twenty-seven bishops, while four other bishops who were not present indicated their approval of what was done. The preamble to the Synod's canons refers to the schisms, troubles, and quarrels in the Church, most of which, thanks to Ezekiel, are now over (this seems unduly optimistic). It then proceeds with an outline of the true Christian faith, and concludes with a condemnation of Mani, Marcion, Bardaisan and other heretics. The main body of the proceedings is taken up with the thirty-nine canons which were adopted. These are summarized below.

1. The Messalians ("praying ones," a pietistic sect with heretical views, who originated in the Syriac Church in the fourth century) are condemned, and provision is made for those of them who repent.[7]

4. On Christian behaviour in a bereavement.

5. On those who have rebelled against Church discipline and now wish to return to the Church.

6. On those under an interdict, and those who allege that they have been interdicted unjustly.

7. On illegitimate marriages.

8. On those, whether clergy or laity, who ravish the wives of other men.

9. On household servants compelled by their master or mistress to engage in fornication.

10. On gifts offered to churches or convents by prostitutes.

11. On gifts bequeathed by Christians to a church, convent or hospice, or to the poor, or to some particular person, and regarding slaves who either are to be given their liberty, or are to be allotted to churches, convents, etc; if these bequests are not faithfully carried out by the heirs of the deceased, the heirs are to be censured and anathematized until they execute the provisions of the will.

12. On slaves who can be received into the clergy only if they are properly manumitted by their masters.

13. On the maintenance of the proper orders within the Church, and the recognition of the rights of each order—bishops, metropolitans, and Patriarch.

---

[7] On this sect in the Greek Church, see Theodoret, *Eccl Hist* IV. xi; in the Syriac Church, see *Bk of Gov*, 2, pp 91–92, note 3. On the whole movement, see A. Vööbus, HASO II, pp 127–39.

14. Since the Patriarch is "the father of the principality," and all in ecclesiastical authority receive their power from him, it is fitting that his name be proclaimed when the liturgy is recited in all the churches.

15. Every four years there is to be a Synod before Lent. When the Patriarch calls this meeting, all concerned will come promptly. Those who fail to do so will be censured.

16. The bishops of a province are to assemble under their metropolitan once a year in September. Absentees will be censured.

17. On the importance of metropolitans, bishops and priests living blameless lives, free from all jealousy, hatred, anger and enmity.

18. and 19. On the ordination of a bishop.

20. Priesthood cannot be procured from a metropolitan or bishop either by gifts or by money.

21. Priests must not accept gifts.

22. No metropolitan or bishop can perform an ordination in, or give an order relative to the administration of, the diocese of a colleague, without the consent of the Patriarch.

23. What is to be done when a metropolitan or a bishop dies. Evidently lay people are to have a voice in the choice of the new appointee.

26. The records of goods bought for churches, monasteries and hospices must be kept in the archives of the church.

27. Gifts and tithes for churches, monasteries and hospices are to be under the jurisdiction of the bishop and are to be administered according to his order.

28. A somewhat obscure canon. The meaning seems to be that an ordinand must meet the usual conditions for ordination.

29. On property belonging to churches and monasteries, which clergy and laymen ought to know about, so that in the event of the death of the bishop, ecclesiastical property can be identified and separated from the private property of the bishop. The latter may leave his own property to whomsoever he wishes.

30. Bishops should not give church property to their families, but should use it for the maintenance of the clergy, the poor, and the pilgrims.

31. Complaints against a bishop or other cleric should be made known to the metropolitan, and if this does not resolve the matter, it should be brought before the Patriarch.

33. On factions who, on the death of a bishop, attempt to advance the claim of someone to the succession, when in fact he is unworthy of the office.

34. On certain men who for lack of education or because of their unworthiness, have not been admitted to clerical orders, and who have sought help from the laity or from pagans.

35. If a monastery is built, some revenues must be assigned by the builder for its maintenance before it is consecrated. Apart from the

housekeeping requirements, everything connected with a monastery is under the jurisdiction of the bishop.

36. Clergy are not to act as attorneys or stewards for the laity or for pagans.

37. Christians are not to allow their daughters to study pagan music.

38. Priests who live in the town or city where the bishop resides, have precedence over those who live in the country districts of the diocese.

39. This rather obscure canon appears to establish an order of precedence in the hierarchy, so that all the first places in the Synod are not occupied by bishops of the province of which the Patriarch, as a metropolitan bishop, is the head.

5. The Synod of Mar Jesusyahb I (585).

Jesusyahb was from Beth 'Arbaye and had studied at the School of Nisibis under Abraham its director. He was subsequently made bishop of Arzon, and is reported, while in this see, to have supplied the Persian king Hormizd IV (579-90) with intelligence reports on Byzantine troop movements in the border area. As Hormizd showed himself very tolerant in religious matters and well-disposed to his Christian subjects (thus incurring the ill will of the Magi), he had no reason to oppose the Church's election in 582 of Jesusyahb as the new Catholicos, and in fact some suspect that he himself may have nominated the bishop of Arzon to the Patriarchate. Whether, as some traditions have it, the Catholicos was sent by Hormizd as an envoy to the emperor Maurice (582-602) is doubtful.

The Catholicos had serious troubles to contend with in the Christian community, particularly with the claims of the Monophysites and with the views of Ḥenana, the celebrated teacher at Nisibis. But he also had the political situation within Persia to face. He lost a good friend when Hormizd was dethroned in 590 and later killed, but his efforts to keep the Church out of the ensuing struggle for power did the Catholicos very little good. The general, Varahran Chobin, who had hoped to succeed Hormizd, had at first some success, but the aristocracy who had rid themselves of the king, thought it best to proclaim his son, Khusro II, as his successor. But the new king had limited military resources, and in desperation he fled to Circesium and from there he sought assistance from Maurice of Constantinople. The Byzantine emperor espoused Khusro's cause and placed some forces at his disposal. Maurice's actions may not have been entirely disinterested for he may have hoped, by interference of this sort, to weaken the Persian kingdom. In any event the Byzantine support made it possible for Khusro to assert himself as the legitimate heir to the Persian throne. In all these political developments the Catholicos tried to maintain an impartial position, and he therefore offered no help to Khusro in initiating the negotiations with Maurice. Khusro, perhaps naturally, resented the studied neutrality of the Catholicos, and the latter, sensing that trouble was in store for him, went to Ḥira whose Arab prince, Nu'man, had recently received Christian baptism. It was while he was in Ḥira that Mar Jesusyahb took ill and died in 594/5.

It was not until 585 that Mar Jesusyahb summoned his first Synod (SO, pp 390-455). It set itself two tasks, to define the true faith, and to produce canons for the guidance of the Church.

The first canon is, in effect, the desiderated profession of faith (SO, pp 393-98). It offers an exposition of the Creed of Constantinople,[8] with some slight changes in the Creed's text. Chabot says that it is "the most explicit (exposition of this Creed) preserved in Nestorian documents" (SO, p 393, note 5).

What follows is a summary of canons 2-31.

2. A defense of the books and doctrines of Theodore of Mopsuestia. Those who are opposed to Theodore are to be excommunicated.

3. On the advantages of laws for mankind, and particularly those found in the Scriptures.

4. On the honour due from disciples and children to teachers and parents.

5. The conduct of the clergy of the Church should correspond to the sublimity of their ministry.

6. On the stealing by clerics and laity of property belonging to churches, monasteries, hospices and episcopal residences, and the means to be taken to cope with this evil.

7. On heirs who violate the stated wishes of the deceased with respect to what is to be given to churches, convents, hospices, schools or episcopal residences, or with respect to the manumission of slaves.

8. Those who are clothed in a religious habit, and wish to practise chastity and poverty, should live in their parents' home, or with clergy in a church, or with monks in a monastery. If they propose to study outside their diocese, they should have a letter of recommendation from their bishop. This canon may have the Messalians especially in view. It is further stated that such a person is not permitted to walk about with a woman, or live with her in a monastery or cell. The rule is that women must not cohabit with men in a monastery for men, nor men in a convent for women, though emergency visits of no longer than a day (or a night) are provided for.

9. It is not permitted to religious women to live in isolation; on the contrary, at least four or five of them should live in a convent. Like all Christians they should not forsake the church assemblies on Sundays or on the feasts.

---

[8] Properly the Nicaeno-Constantinopolitan Creed. For the Greek text, see SO, p 394, note 3, and for ET of the Greek, see A. C. McGiffert, *A History of Christian Thought*, 1, New York, 1932, p 273.

10. On churches and monasteries which have been allowed to fall into ruin, and which should be rebuilt.

12. On avoiding ostentatiousness in giving offerings to churches and convents; it is prescribed that donations and alms should first be given to local churches, and afterwards, if the donors so desire, to churches or convents in other places.

15–16. Neither ordinary Christians nor those in the ministry should take interest on loans.

17–18. On those who have been interdicted and anathematized.

19. On the functions and responsibilities of an archdeacon.

20. One suitable person is to be designated, with the consent of the bishop, to administer the business affairs of each church, monastery and hospice.

21. On uncharitable conduct by Christians, especially when directed against their chiefs (the clergy?).

22. Bishops must ensure, preferably through a trustworthy layman, that property left to orphans is properly administered until the children come of age.

23. The clergy are not to become involved as voluntary advocates in legal matters that do not concern them nor have relations with a woman repudiated by her husband.

24. A wife has a right to her dowry after her husband's death, even though this is not mentioned in his will.

25. Christians are not to participate in the festivals of Jews, heretics or pagans, nor accept anything sent to them from these festivals.

27. Marriages between Nestorians and heretical Christians are forbidden unless the former are allowed to practise their own faith. The altars of the orthodox must not be used by heretics, nor must the orthodox receive from them either consecrated bread or gifts.

29. On the ecclesiastical hierarchy; the procedure to be observed in the election of a Patriarch; the rules to be observed in imposing an interdict or an anathema. It is assumed that there are four Patriarchs in the Western Church, and one in the Orient.

30. Synods called by a metropolitan or by the Patriarch must be attended by those concerned. In the present instance (Synod of 585), Simeon the metropolitan of Nisibis, and Gregory, the metropolitan of Rew-Ardashir, who have not appeared, will be interdicted unless they come in penitence to the Patriarch within this year.

31. Each one present at the Synod is to have a copy of these canons and is to read them once a year in the assembly of his diocese.

The proceedings of the Synod are signed by the Catholicos, two metropolitans (three others by proxy), and twenty bishops (two others by proxy). Five others, including one metropolitan, have given their concurrence in writing.

The record of the Synod includes at the end two extraneous documents. The first comprises some canons which Mar Jesusyahb drew up for James, bishop of the Isle of Darai, in reply to various questions (SO, pp 424–51). What is stated constitutes the teaching of the Patriarch, as a master to a disciple, and is not to be considered as the decrees of the Synod.

On how a priest should commence his duties at the altar;
When should the priest who celebrates take communion?
On giving communion to a priest;
on quarrels within a church;
on secret sins;
on a priest anathematizing himself;
on taking an oath;
on taking interest or usury;
on how the goods of an intestate Christian should be dealt with;
on the non-fulfilment of vows and promises of gifts to local churches and monasteries;
on a priest ceding his rank in the hierarchy to an inferior;
on an allegorical treatment of the parable of the talents in Matt 25:14–30 (it is found to refer to deacons, priests and bishops);
on the Lord's Day (the first day of the week);
on taking a sterile wife.

The second of these documents is a statement of the orthodox faith composed by Mar Jesusyahb (SO, pp 451–55). It is essentially an elaboration and defense of the doctrine of the Trinity, with passing references to various heretics, including Eutyches, Apollinarius, Photinus, Paul of Samosata, and Severus of Antioch.

It will be noticed from the Synod's canons, particularly those numbered 7, 22 and 24, that some matters falling within the purview of what westerners call "civil law" are seemingly under the control of the Church. This suggests that by the sixth century the Christians in Persia, like the Babylonian Jews, had become in some respects an independent community, responsible for their own interior discipline. In matters related to "criminal law," Persian law doubtless continued to be the only operative law.

6. The Synod of Mar Sabarjesus I (596).

Sabarjesus was originally from Perozabad in Beth Garmai. He became a monk and then studied at Nisibis under Abraham the director. His earlier ascetic practices were continued and intensified after leaving the School, and he also carried on proselytizing very actively, but in Beth Garmai this resulted in the opposition of the Magi and in his temporary internment in Karka of Beth Selok. On the death of Saba, bishop of Lashom (a signatory of Mar Ezekiel's Synod of 576), Sabarjesus, despite his protests, was elevated to his see. He continued his ascetic way of life and was widely regarded as an exemplry saint. Apparently it was the order of Khusro II which made him the successor of Jesusyahb I in 596 (after a vacancy of 1–2 years), and it was in this year that he held a Synod. When Khusro renewed the war with Constantinople in 604, the Catholicos accompanied the Persian army. But age and infirmities obliged him to return to Nisibis, where he died in the summer of 604, while Dara was being besieged by the Persians. His body was buried in Beth Garmai in the convent of which he had earlier been a member.

The record of the Synod of 596 (SO, pp 456–61) does not bear the signatures of those present, although the Catholicos and some unnamed metropolitans and bishops are referred to in the text. The first topic dealt with is various heretical views, such as those which affirm that it is in the nature of man to sin (which may be a form of Pelagianism), or that man was created immortal, or that the teachings of Theodore of Mopsuestia should be rejected. This leads to the Synod's reaffirmation of the faith as set forth by the Council of Nicea. Various unacceptable opinions are castigated such as are held by pagans and Jews, and by those who deny that both divinity and humanity were found in Christ. The views of Theodore of Mopsuestia are again cited as the paragon of orthodoxy (this in contrast with the teaching of Henana of the School of Nisibis, although the latter's name is not mentioned).

Two practical issues are next dealt with. One relates to friars and sisters who live close to one another, whose conduct is reprehensible and who need instruction and correction. The other concerns the liturgy. Some clerics have disregarded canonical usage and have instituted unwarranted changes in the liturgy, two of which are cited. If those responsible for these alterations do not correct this situation, both they and those who tolerate the changes will be forbidden to share in the sacramental life of the Church.

A copy of the Synod's recorded actions is to be sent to the absentee metropolitans and bishops. If any one of them opposes the decisions taken or the views expressed, he will be anathematized until he accepts them.

The record of the Synod has two documents appended to it (SO, pp 461–70), neither of which appears to be directly related to the proceedings of the Synod. That they have been included here may reflect the continuing interest of the Catholicos in the ascetic life. The first, dated in 598, is a pact and convention, and concerns the monks of three monasteries, the New Monastery, the monastery of Bar Qaiṭi, and a third unnamed one nearby. All three are located in the mountains around Singar. After a somewhat long theological premise, it is agreed that we (presumably the monks concerned) should apply ourselves to prayer (i.e., to the various offices of the liturgy) and to fasting. We should not go outside of our convents or cells, except of necessity and only with the permission of the superior, by whom also we are authorized to go into the villages. On Sundays and fast days we assemble together in the convent for the liturgy and the public reading of the Scriptures, after which we return to our cells or our monasteries. Those who will not conform to these arrangements are to be appropriately punished. The document is signed by four bishops located in Beth Garmai.

The second of these supplementary documents (SO, pp 465-70) is a letter from the Catholicos addressed to the superiors of the convents mentioned in the aforementioned pact. The Patriarch has learned of troubles in the monasteries, but these have not diminished his recognition of the benefits of the monastic life. However, the latter must be lived in obedience to the superior, and this some of the brothers have not been doing. There is possibly here an oblique reference to Messalian influences among the monks. Furthermore, the three monasteries in question are under the jurisdiction of the Catholicos, and must not be interfered with either by a metropolitan or by neighbouring bishops.

7. The Synod of Mar Gregory I (605).

Gregory I[9] was from Pherat and he had become a teacher of the Scriptures in the School at Seleucia. After Sabarjesus I died in 604, Khusro II ordered the bishops to come to the capital to choose his successor, and the record states that those who had to travel from distant places were to come by the royal post at the expense of the king. Once they were assembled, the king indicated to the bishops both the sort of a person the Catholicos should be and the one he wished to be chosen. If the bishops had another name in mind, such as Gregory of Kashkar, bishop of Nisibis, they felt obliged to elect the king's nominee, Mar Gregory of Pherat. It is thought by some that Monophysite sympathizers, such as Queen Shirin and Gabriel, the court physician, had urged Khusro to favour Gregory from Pherat.

After his election the new Catholicos addressed the assembly. The account of the latter's decisions (SO, pp 471-79) does not follow the pattern of presenting to the Church a series of canons. To begin with, Mar Gregory reaffirmed the Church's adhesion to the Councils of Nicaea and Constantinople, and reiterated the view (against the Monophysite position) that the two natures of Christ, the human and the divine, are united in one person. The Catholicos noted the existence in the Church of certain schismatic ideas, often due to a perversion of the true sense of the Scripture. As a sure guide to the latter, the faithful turn to the commentaries and other writings of Theodore of Mopsuestia. Anyone not recognizing the authority of Theodore, or calumniating him, is to be anathematized.

Clergy and sisters, unattached to ecclesiastical institutions, and moving about in the villages, often cause problems. All such clerics should be in a church, convent, school, or an isolated congregation of monks. An unmarried woman, not employed in the local church, should belong to a convent of

---

[9] CF *Bk of Gov*, 2, I, xxv, pp 85-88.

sisters. But attachment to a monastery does not solve all the Church's difficulties, for it is noted that often monks attack or reject the canons of the Church, and neglect certain "proclamations" in the liturgy.

The local bishop is required to take appropriate action in cases where the custodians of gifts, intended by the donors for the maintenance of monasteries, have diverted some or all of these donations to their own use.

The last matter brought before the Synod relates to bishops who disobey the canons and ordain priests improperly.

The proceedings are signed by the Patriarch, three metropolitans, and twenty-six bishops.

Mar Gregory I did not live up to his earlier promise, and the king seems to have lost confidence in him. He proved to be a very avaricious person, and when he died 608/9, the crown confiscated his personal wealth. More tragic for the Church at this particular time, Khusro opposed the election of a successor, and for the next twenty years, until 628, the Nestorians had no Catholicos.

As the Synod of 605 is the last of Nestorian Synods to be considered in the present volume (the next one in the *Synodicon Orientale* is that of Mar George in 676), we note below the geographical distribution of some of the sees whose incumbents signed the Synod record of 605. This will suggest the extent of the Nestorian Church on the eve of the Muslim era.

Three metropolitan sees are named: Maishan (Mesene), Lower Babylonia; Adiabene, east of the Tigris and north of the Little Zab river; Beth Garmai, east of the Tigris, and between the Little Zab and the Diyala rivers. No metropolitan is mentioned for Beth Huzaye (Khuzistan), although bishops sign from Karka of Ledan (north of Susa), Hormizd-Ardashir (modern Ahwaz on the Karun river), Shushtar, and Shush (modern Sous or Susa). Nor is there a metropolitan named for Beth 'Arbaye, northern Mesopotamia between Mosul, the Tigris, and the Khabur river. Bishops appear for Holwan (cf *ḥlḥ* in II Kgs 17:6) and Beth Madaye, both of which may designate sees in Media. To the north-west of Media is Azerbaijan (east of lake Urmia), which also has a bishop, as does Qardu (Syr *qrdw*), the country of the Kurds. Although the location of some sees is unknown (Syr *brḥys, tḥl*), it is noteworthy that unlike the situation reflected in the signatories of the proceedings of the Synod of 424 (SO, p 285), there are no bishops from Merv, Herat, Segestan, Abrashahr, Rai, Ispahan, or Istakhr. Whether this means that in the early seventh century the Nestorian cause had declined or even disappeared in central and eastern Iran is not clear.

8. Monophysitism.

While Persian Monophysitism took a beating from Barṣauma, it had sufficient resilience to weather the storm. When Papa returned from Edessa and became bishop of Beth Lapaṭ, he proved to be a strong protagonist of Monophysitism, although he turned up at the Synod of Acacius in 486 and signed its record. It was apparently immediately after this that he was deposed from his see. The Synod of Babai (497) left open the possibility of the anathema against him being lifted. This Synod also dealt with Yazdad, bishop of Rewardashir, who had shown the same predilection for Monophysitism; he too must adhere to the orthodox faith or be deposed. This active opposition to Monophysitism by the Nestorians is further illustrated by the plea of the Persian delegates to the Monophysite council held at Dvin in eastern Armenia in 506. They brought tales of oppression at the hands of the Chalcedonians, and asked for help from their co-religionists.[10]

In the late fifth century, Simeon of Beth Arsham,[11] who may have been orthodox to begin with but who presently adopted Monophysitism, became one of the best known apostles of the Monophysite cause in Persia. We know little of his personal life except that he spent his early life at Ḥira, which suggests that he was a native of that region. Some locate Beth Arsham near Seleucia. He subsequently travelled widely in Persia and engaged so effectively in disputes with Nestorians, Marcionites, Manichees and others, that he came to be known as "the Persian disputant." One of these debates was held in Persian Armenia, at which the Catholicos Babai (497–502/3) was present (there were five Monophysite bishops on hand).[12] Simeon was present as a priest at the Monophysite conference in Armenia in 506. It was subsequent to this that c 510 he was made an itinerant bishop for the Monophysite cause. He is reported to have taken part in a theological debate between 518 and 523 at Ḥira, when the Nestorian position was defended by Shila the Nestorian Patriarch.[13] As we have earlier noted (ch 9, sect 7), the suspicion that the Monophysites were friends of Constantinople sometimes landed them in trouble. Simeon himself is said to have been imprisoned for seven years, being released only by the intervention of an Ethiopian delegation then visiting the Persian court. He made three visits to Constantinople, the last to get such support for the Monophysite cause as he could from the empress Theodora. He died in the Byzantine capital c 533.

The policy of the emperor Justin I (518–27) of suppressing Monophysitism in the Byzantine world, which doubtless sent some exiles and Monophysite sympathizers to north-west Persia, may have been a factor in the growth of Monophysitism in the Persian Church. A contemporary of Simeon of Beth Arsham was John, bishop of Tella. While most of his missionary work for Monophysitism was done within Roman Syria, he seems to have stimulated the Monophysite cause in north-west Persia, particularly in Adiabene. He died in 538 after a year's imprisonment near Antioch.

---

[10] Frend, p 313; Fiey, *Jalons*, pp 123–25.
[11] See *Chr de Michel* 2, IX. ix, pp 165–67; Fiey, *Jalons*, p 120.
[12] *Chr de Michel* 2, p 166; Fiey, *Jalons*, p 120.
[13] Fiey, *Jalons*, p 122.

Further invigoration of the Monophysite party in Persia came as a by-product of the work of Jacob Baradaeus in the Byzantine West (see ch 5, sect 10). In Jacob's time one, Ahudemmeh,[14] born at Balad in Beth 'Arbaye, was the Nestorian bishop of Nineveh, and as such had signed the record of the Synod of Mar Joseph in 554. Evidently soon after this he was won over to the Monophysite camp, but we know nothing of the circumstances of this conversion. Five years later, in 559, Jacob Baradaeus made him Monophysite bishop of Beth 'Arbaye and metropolitan bishop of the Orient. Fiey notes that in another source, Ahudemmeh was made bishop of Beth 'Arbaye c 540 by the Armenian Catholicos Christopher (Jalons, p 128). His see was evidently Tagrit, though Fiey doubts this (Jalons, p 131). He became specially active in proselytizing the semi-nomadic Arab tribes in northern Mesopotamia, and he even won some of them over to the ascetic life. John of Ephesus records (*Eccl Hist* I. vi. 20, pp 417-20) that Khusro I (531-79), who is credited with a personal interest in religious matters, arranged in response to accusations (unspecified) directed against the Monophysites by the Nestorians, to have the two Christian parties confront one another in his presence. Ahudemmeh was the chief Monophysite spokesman on this occasion. The Persian king was so favourably impressed with the presentation by the Monophysites that he ordered the Nestorians henceforth to leave them alone to build such churches and monasteries as they pleased. Ahudemmeh's stature in the Monophysite community was considerably heightened by this confrontation, but whether, as John of Ephesus claims, he was made Monophysite Catholicos as a result of it seems uncertain. Ahudemmeh, like Jacob Baradaeus, was a tireless worker for Monophysitism, but his zeal was ultimately his undoing. In 573 he converted a son of the royal family to Christianity, an action which brought about his imprisonment in that year, and his death two years later. The progress of Monophysitism is illustrated by the fact that its adherents had a church in Seleucia before 575 and a "new church" there in 580. Yet, oddly enough, in Ezekiel's Synod of 576, while other dangerous movements in the Church are condemned, no mention is made of the Monophysites. It is presumably a sign of the times that nine years later, in 585, the second canon of Jesusyahb's Synod, held in that year, defends the teaching of Theodore of Mopsuestia and anathematizes all those opposed to it.

Qamjesus, priest of the Jacobite church in Seleucia, was not appointed as Ahudemmeh's successor until 579, and under him Tagrit continued to be a strong Monophysite centre. The next holder of this position as *de facto* head of the Persian Monophysites was Samuel whose dates are 614-24. Another very active place in the life of Persian Monophysitism was the great monastery of Mar Mattai, north-east of Mosul.

---

[14] See F. Nau, *Histoire de Mar Ahoudemmeh*, PO 3, pp 7-51.

A figure of considerable importance now looms up in the Monophysite community, viz Marutha,[15] who was born c 565 in a village near Balad, north of Mosul. His Monophysite parents were concerned with their son's studies and directed him to the facilities available in the monasteries of Mar Samuel and of Nardas; his sojourn in the latter convent evidently qualified him to be an interpreter of the Scriptures. In the period of peace between Persia and Constantinople (after 593), Marutha went to the Byzantine world where he spent about ten years, 593–603, mostly in a monastery near Callinicus, and latterly in the cells around Edessa and then in the monastery of Beth Reqoum. The outbreak of war between Byzantium and Persia made it prudent for him to return to his homeland. While in Beth Reqoum he had refused to become a Monophysite bishop, and now in 605 he came to the monastery of Mar Mattai where he taught for about ten years. In addition he did considerable missionary work all along the Tigris valley. Taking a cue from the Nestorians he was also active in establishing schools for the young. Later he transferred his teaching activity to a monastery in the capital founded by Queen Shirin. It was at this time that he again refused to be named a bishop. The queen was a Monophysite, and her protection, as well as the influence of a court physician, Gabriel, a Monophysite from Singar, were a great boon to the Monophysite cause at this juncture.

But the war with Byzantium was changing Khusro's attitude to Christianity, and both Nestorians and Monophysites now realized that they were out of the king's favour. Furthermore the death of doctor Gabriel deprived the Monophysites of a powerful friend. Marutha found it expedient to remove himself from public view and he retired to a suitable spot near 'Aqula (west of the Euphrates and south of later Baghdad), and he remained here until the death of Khusro in 628.

Although Monophysitism never dominated the Church in Persia down to the mid-seventh century, its adherents were sufficiently numerous to constitute a serious and persistent threat to the Nestorian community. We can infer this from the statements of faith found in the records of the Nestorian Synods. The Synods of 554, 585, 596 and 605 all have theological affirmations that are obviously intended to counter the views of the Monophysites (SO, pp 355, 393–98, 457–59, 473–75).

---

[15] See F. Nau, *Histoire de Marouta*, PO 3, pp 52–96.

Chapter 11.
The Seventh Century to 643 A.D.

1. The Later Years of the School of Nisibis.

The third director of the School of Nisibis was Abraham of Beth Rabban, who may have been a nephew of Narseh the first director. He took office sometime after 510, and remained at the School probably until c 569. He was a very successful teacher as well as an extensive writer on the OT, though none of his writings has come down to us. He was also renowned for his asceticism. Under the early years of his leadership the School grew immensely, one source reporting that the number of students exceeded one thousand. This necessitated a considerable expansion of the School's physical facilities, which included the building for the first time of a hospice. Abraham also improved the lot of the teachers, buying a farm for the School and arranging that its income should be used for stipends for the staff.

It is curious that the era of Abraham's directorship, which at first witnessed an expansion in the School, also displayed in its later years a sharp decline in the institution's life and strength. The nature of the problem which beset the School is not perfectly clear, although the personality of the director may have had something to do with it. Moves within the Western Church to heal its divisions, as for instance the emperor Justinian's conference of 532 in which Greek orthodox and Monophysites participated, and at which Paul a teacher at Nisibis was present, do not seem to have been favourably looked upon by Abraham, an attitude which doubtless increased tension within the School. But the most serious blow to the School was an external one. In the sixth century Khusro I authorized a fresh persecution of Christians. This involved, among other measures, the exile of the Catholicos, Mar Aba, to Azerbaijan, and the closing of the School of Nisibis for two years, 540–41. The School was reopened c 542, but in some respects it was never quite the same again. Its student body had dispersed, some going to the School at Seleucia. What happened to Abraham the director at this time of crisis we do not know, but it is usually assumed that he remained in office until c 569.

A new, and in some respects a more tragic, epoch in the School's life is associated with Ḥenana of Adiabene, who after a period as one of the teachers, became director c 570–71. He brought to this office his great gifts as an instructor, especially in the exegesis of the Scriptures, and it is said that in his time, the number of students in the School once more greatly increased, rising to eight hundred. Partly due to this influx, the rules of the School, now almost a hundred years old, were revised in 590 and ratified in 602.[1] The following matters were important enough to find mention in the revised canons: the duties of the curator of the hospice (apparently there had been dissatisfaction with one curator); compulsory residence in the School for students if accommodation is available; the study habits of students; the safeguarding of books in the library; the appearance of students' dress and hair; participation by students in the social activities of the town; begging from townspeople; relations with women; the teaching of boys in the town; attendance at vigils; the sheltering of war captives or fugitive slaves. The reference to a body of students studying medicine leaves many questions unanswered, although it is clear that theological and medical students were kept apart (canons 19 and 20).

Ḥenana, however, was a controversial figure, and he was inevitably drawn into theological disputations. In particular he became impatient with the School's traditional espousal of Theodore of Mopsuestia, and he made clear his own strong preference for John Chrysostom, and for an allegorical approach to the Scriptures such as Origen had sponsored. Further, his theological understanding of the person of Christ was considered to be dangerously near, if not identical with, that of the Monophysites. All who were concerned with the welfare of the Nestorian Church were naturally disturbed by Ḥenana's views. One of the first expressions of this discontent was the founding by one, Elisha, of another School, Beth Sahde, in or near Nisibis as a rival to the one directed by Ḥenana. Elijah, metropolitan bishop of Nisibis, gave his blessing to this new foundation, and Abimelek, head of a School in Balad, was named its director.

The next phase in Ḥenana's directorship leads to his repudiation by the Nestorian Church. The Catholicos, Jesusyahb I, had his work condemned in 585, and a Synod convened by the Catholicos Sabarjesus I in 596, condemned and anathematized all who reject the teachings of Theodore of Mopsuestia. The same action was taken in 605 by the Synod held by Gregory I. But Ḥenana was temporarily rescued by the Persian court, where two Monophysite physicians, Gabriel and Mar Aba, proved to be his supporters. Gregory, the Catholicos, was ordered by Khusro to leave Nisibis. But Ḥenana was also a loser in these ecclesiastical politics, for it was clear that he had been kept in office through the influence of Monophysites in high places.

We come now to the last act in this drama centering in Ḥenana. Since the director's opponents could not oust him from office, they decided to abandon the School. About three hundred of them, including students and most of the teachers, departed en masse from the School, and at the gate of

---

[1] For the text of Ḥenana's canons, see A. Vööbus, *The Statutes of the School of Nisibis*, pp 91–102.

the city, concluded their prayers and went their several ways. This occurred shortly after Gregory the Catholicos had been ordered from the city. Some of those who thus left the School went to the monastery of Mar Abraham in Mount Izla, others to a new School in Balad, and others returned to Nisibis itself to strengthen the School of Beth Sahde. As for Ḥenana, he was left with a few teachers and some students, one source giving the total as twenty persons. So the School carried on, but in a greatly weakened condition. Ḥenana himself passed from the scene between 609 and 612, although his supporters lived on to vex the orthodox. Nestorians and Monophysites continued to battle in the Church, but in this struggle the School of Nisibis played only a very minor part. In truth, the School's heyday was over, both as a teaching centre and as a stimulus to scholarly writing, and from now on it was merely one of a number of educational centres of the Nestorian Church, the most important of which had now become the School at Seleucia.

2. The School of Seleucia.

Acacius of Beth Aramaye, who studied at Edessa, left that School after the death of Ibas (457), and is reported to have become a teacher in Seleucia. He was thus engaged until he became Catholicos in 485. It is probable, however, that his teaching in the capital was not done in an established institution. Anything that we can call the School of Seleucia is not firmly attested until the sixth century, when, sometime after 540, the new Patriarch, Mar Aba, is credited with founding a School in the city. In 585 one, Job, was the director of the institution and was sufficiently prominent to be a runner-up for the Catholicate at the time of the death of Ezekiel (581). A little later Gregory of Pherat taught the Scriptures at Seleucia until he became Catholicos in 605. We can infer from all this that there was a recognized Nestorian School in Seleucia, but of its history and internal arrangements we know very little. Despite the attraction which the location in the Sasanian capital must have exercised, it appears to have been a modest establishment, and as long as the School of Nisibis flourished, it remained somewhat in the latter's shadow. When, however, Nisibis declined, the School of Seleucia gained in prominence.

3. The Nestorian Church during the Reign of Khusro II (591-628).

The Christians in Persia benefitted from Khusro's friendship with the emperor Maurice, for it made the king more receptive to the view of his Christian wives, Shirin and Marie, that Christians should be tolerated. This, initially, became Khusro's policy, though the proviso that no proselytizing was to be carried out meant that converts to Christianity from Zoroastrianism, especially if they were from the upper classes, might be severely penalized. It is probably in this early part of his reign that we must place Khusro's building, probably at queen Shirin's request, of a church at

Halaḥ (Ḥolwan) in honour of St. Sergius (a fourth century martyr).[2] It may be doubted, however, if Khusro was ever entirely free from his animus, as a Zoroastrian, to Christianity, and this feeling may have been strengthened by Mar Jesusyahb I's strict neutrality both in the struggle that Khusro had in 590-91 with the usurper Varahran Chobin, and in the king's appeal to Maurice of Constantinople for assistance in regaining his throne. The king's reservations about Christians, nonetheless, did not prevent him from encouraging the Nestorians to hold a Synod in 605 to select a successor to the late Catholicos, Sabarjesus I.

Whatever benevolence Khusro had towards the Church in the early years of his reign seems to have been slowly dissipated by the renewal of hostilities with Constantinople in the spring of 604. Persia, a Zoroastrian state, was once more in confrontation with a Christian state, which meant that Christians in Persia were again in a delicate situation. When Heraclius came on the scene, and especially after his first serious campaign against Khusro began in 621, the Persian king's tolerance of Christians seems to have rapidly declined. Not only did he continue to refuse the Nestorians permission to elect a successor to Gregory I who had died 608-9, a refusal which he must have known would damage the Church[3] (we may detect in this policy the influence of his Monophysite physician, Gabriel), but we now have evidence of Christians being persecuted. For instance, sometime after 605 Nathaniel, bishop of Shiarzur (a signatory of the record of the Synod of 605), drove out of town a Zoroastrian fanatic who had destroyed the local church, and when the culprit complained to Khusro, the bishop was imprisoned for six years and then put to death.[4] At the same time one, Jesusabran of Beth Garmai, a converted Zoroastrian, was put in prison where he remained for fifteen years, at the end of which confinement he was taken to the capital with many other Christians from Beth Garmai and executed.[5] An outstanding martyr of this period was Yazdin, a member of a wealthy Christian family from Karka of Beth Selok. He had been made receiver-general for Persia, and for some years he exercised much influence at the court, but he was also a very zealous Nestorian. During Heraclius's invasion of Persia, he fell out of favour with Khusro, and he was seized and put to death and his considerable personal fortune was confiscated.[6] Monophysites suffered as well as Nestorians, as we know from the fact that Marutha, the distinguished Monophysite teacher in the Mar Mattai monastery and latterly in a monastery in Seleucia, had to flee to a grotto near 'Aqula where he stayed until the death of Khusro.[7]

[2] *Bk of Gov*, 2, I, xxiii, pp 80-82.
[3] *Bk of Gov*, 2, I, xxvi, pp 89-90.
[4] Labourt, p 224.
[5] Labourt, p 234, note 1.
[6] *Bk of Gov*, 2, I, xxiii, note 4, p 81: xxxv, note 1, p 113.
[7] Labourt, p 234.

In 612 there was a gathering of the Nestorian bishops of Persia at Seleucia, though the names of those present are not recorded. While some details of the assembly are obscure, it appears that its primary objective was to obtain permission from Khusro to elect a Catholicos, the Church now having been without one since 608/9.[8] But Gabriel, the court physician, and Queen Shirin, both of whom were Monophysites, contrived to obstruct the bishops' purpose by persuading the king to demand from the clerics a confession of their faith and satisfactory answers to certain questions. The confession of faith which they produced has come down to us, with a prologue marked by unctuous servility towards the king, and an epilogue claiming that the orthodox (Nestorian) faith is the only true Christian faith in Persia.[9] The questions, possibly phrased by Gabriel and other Monophysite leaders, concerned whether Christ had one nature and one person, whether God suffered in the flesh, whether the holy Virgin was the Mother of God or the Mother of a man, whether God is a quaternity or a trinity, and whether anyone before Nestorius taught that Christ had two natures and two persons. To each of these questions we are given the answers of the Nestorians.[10] To what extent Khusro would really understand what went on in this assembly we do not know. Perhaps he was not there at all, or if he was present at the beginning, he may not have stayed to the end. His armed forces at the time were fighting in Syria, and it is possible that the king had more important things to do at this juncture than to listen to a theological disputation between Christians. In any case he made no response to what had been presented, and his policy of not sanctioning the election of a new Nestorian Catholicos remained unchanged. It was subsequent to these events that the monk George, a well-born Persian who had converted to Christianity, and who had been at the above assembly and is thought to have assisted in drawing up the confession of faith referred to above, was seized and after eight months in prison put to death. His only offence, apart from being a convert from Zoroastrian, that we know of was that he had protested the handing over by Gabriel of the cloister of St. Sergius, hitherto under Nestorian control, to the Monophysites.

Since the appointment of a Catholicos now seemed to be out of the question, the Nestorian clergy had to make such arrangements as they could for the government of the Church. Basically each metropolitan took the responsibility for his own province. For instance, in the south in the city of Seleucia, the archdeacon Mar Abba, "a man imbued with both virtue and wisdom" directed the affairs of that area. In the north, Babai of Beth 'Ainata, a monk who was abbot of the great monastery of Abraham at Izla, was made inspector of monasteries by the metropolitans of Adiabene, Nisibis

[8] SO, pp 585–86.
[9] SO, pp 580–85.
[10] SO, pp 586–98. For a Monophysite view of this confrontation, see *Chr de Michel*, 2, IX. xxx, p 251; X. xvi, p 339.

and Karka (or Beth Garmai). Babai travelled about extensively, combatting various heretical views, and both by his presence and his writings, ensuring that the official Nestorian orthodoxy was adhered to, at least in the monasteries.[11]

Apart from the Monophysites who offered a permanent challenge to Nestorian views, various other dissidents continued to plague the Nestorians. One of these groups was the Messalians, the subject of canon 1 of Ezekiel's Synod of 576. The same sect were probably responsible for the unrest in the monasteries in and around Singar. We have earlier noted that two documents, dated 598, attached to the record of the Synod of Sabarjesus (596) pertain to these disturbances.[12] Another troublesome party was the Henanians, followers of Henana, former head of the Nisibis School. One of their main positions was opposition to the views of Theodore of Mopsuestia. Thus in the record of the Synod of Sabarjesus we find that all those rejecting the teaching of Theodore are to be anathematized (SO, p 459).

For a little light on the concerns and problems of a Nestorian bishop in the first quarter of the seventh century, we turn to a contemporary source, the letters of Jesusyahb III (later the Catholicos). Jesusyahb was made bishop of Nineveh-Mosul in 620, a post which he held until 628 when he became archbishop of Hazza (near Arbela) and Mosul. A number of letters which he wrote during his eight years as bishop have come down to us and have been published by P. Scott-Moncrieff.[13] Some of these are summarized below, being referred to by the numbers used in the Scott-Moncrieff edition.

3. To the most holy monk, Henanjesus, written amid great difficulties (not elaborated) which have come upon the Church, so that "the root of Christianity has begun to become dry." This decline has several causes: the dearth of priests, the death of a leader (an unidentified bishop?), the negligence of the protectors (prominent laymen?) of the Church, and most of all the coming of "that Magus" (a local Zoroastrian dignitary or a veiled reference to Khusro II), the persecutor of "the fear of God," who in fact caused many to fall away from their Christian faith. The troubles of the Church are also the subject of letters 23, 36 and 41.

5. To Sabhrewai, seemingly a convert from Zoroastrianism, and apparently an answer to a letter which described the sufferings of Persian converts to Christianity.

11. To one, Paul, who had been elected head of a monastery (unnamed). The new abbot is given various bits of advice about the course of conduct he should pursue.

---

[11] *Bk of Gov* 2, I. xxvii, pp 90–92; xxix, pp 97–100. On Babai's writings, see Wright, p 168, Baumstark, pp 137–39.

[12] SO, pp 461–70.

[13] *TheBook of Consolations*, London, 1904. Other letters of Jesusyahb III are edited and translated by R. Duval, CSCO, Series II, 64, 1904.

13. To the Patriarch, Mar Jesusyahb II, dealing with the fact that he, the bishop of Mosul, had fled from his diocese when the war was raging between Persia and Constantinople. No details are given of the military struggle, but we know that Heraclius's successful campaigns against Persia, begun in 621, led in 627 to a sweeping Byzantine victory near Mosul. That the bishop of Mosul, supposedly of some private means and a special target in a time of political unrest, should have fled under these circumstances is not difficult to understand on purely human considerations, but as a shepherd of a Christian flock, his action could be judged reprehensible.

From the title of the letter we may infer that the bishop had been censured for abandoning his people. The main text is an attempt by him to justify his action. He says that he had stayed at his post for some time ("an example of patience"), but finally he had felt compelled to leave, and that he had written to the Catholicos (this must have been done after 628), explaining why he acted as he had. The letter ends with various flattering remarks about the Catholicos.

16. To the monks of Beth 'Abe with reference to the selection of a new abbot. The bishop strongly urges the election of one, Mar John, an old monk who had been forty years in this monastery. The letter is of interest, as is number 24, for it illustrates the efforts of bishops to control the monasteries in their dioceses. We may infer from letter 17 that the monks in this case did not follow the bishop's recommendation.

18. A long epistle to one, Yazdeshabhor, seemingly an educated Persian layman, who is addressed as a "lover of God." The bishop writes in answer to an inquiry about the duality of persons in Christ.

32. To the Patriarch (this must therefore be dated in or after 628), informing him that five letters which he sent to the writer have not been received. This illustrates the communication problem which the Church had to face.

38. To the Catholicos about two monks, Shamjesus and Narseh, who were improperly consecrated as bishops, and who compounded this evil by consecrating a virtually unknown man to the bishopric of Azerbaijan.

39. To a priest, Moses, whose locale is not stated. The bishop has learned both from Moses and from others of a scarcity of food in the priest's district, and he describes the measures he has taken to relieve this distress. That such periods of want were endemic in Mesopotamia is suggested by letter 45 which records a famine in Nisibis and the gift of grain sent to that city's assistance.

41. A long letter to the honourable Mar Yazdannan who is a Christian layman, but who had developed some animus towards the Christian priesthood, and whose interest in the welfare of the Church seems to have waned. As the faithful are suffering everywhere because of government action, the bishop asks him about the grounds of his difference with the priests, and urges him to maintain his faith and to exercise his influence for the protection of the Church.

42. A long letter to Mar Gabriel, the metropolitan bishop, the burden of which is that the Jacobites have now built their first church in Mosul. The Jacobites who are "a nest of Satan," are the subject of another letter (47) to the same bishop.

43. To the clergy and believers in Balad, whose letter the bishop has just received. In this reply to it, the bishop's exhortation for unity and peace suggests that party feelings in Balad were very strong.

We are reminded by two of Jesusyahb's letters (42 and 47) that in the seventh century tension between Nestorian and Jacobite was a permanent feature of Christianity in Persia. An embarrassing loss to the Nestorians, sometime after 628, was the defection of Sahdona, bishop of Mahoze of Arewan, to the Jacobite camp. Sahdona defended his apostasy in a work entitled "The Fictitiousness of Faith." In a letter to the church in Mahoze of Arewan, Jesusyahb III wrote a long criticism of the apology, Budge's translation of which is reproduced in Scott-Moncrieff, *The Book of Consolations*, pp xii-xx.

4. Jesusyahb II (628–643).

When Kavad II became king in 628, he gave the Christians of his realm complete liberty, which resulted in the Nestorian bishops assembling at Seleucia to elect a Catholicos. Their first choice was Babai, abbot of the monastery of Abraham at Izla, who had in recent years rendered such outstanding service to the Church when there was no Patriarch. But Babai refused the honour with its heavy responsibilities, preferring to spend his remaining years in his monastery. So the bishops chose one of their own number, Jesusyahb II, bishop of Balad. Incidentally, the last bishop of Balad recorded in the *Synodicon Orientale* is one, Yedigird, who attended the Synod of Joseph in 554. Jesusyahb was a native of Gedala, a village of Beth 'Arbaye, who had studied at Nisibis. But he had left the School when the controversy centering in Ḥenana was at its height, and had actually written a treatise against Ḥenana's views. Budge claims that at one time he was head of the monastery at Izla.[14] He was subsequently appointed to the see of Balad, and now, although he was a married man, he was given the highest office in the Nestorian Church. Subsequent to his election he and a group of bishops accompanied Babai from Seleucia to the convent at Izla as a gesture of appreciation for what he had done for the Church during the reign of Khusro II.[15]

During the short reign of Queen Boran (629–30), the Catholicos led a party of Nestorian clerics to a previously arranged meeting with the Byzantine emperor, Heraclius, in Aleppo.[16] The purpose of this small

---

[14] *Bk of Gov* 2, note 3 on p 61.
[15] *Bk of Gov* 2, I. xxxv, pp 115–16.
[16] *Bk of Gov* 2, II. iv. pp 123–27, and note 2, pp 125–26.

gathering is not clear. If it was initiated by the Queen, it may have been intended as a formal announcement to Heraclius of her accession to the Persian throne, or it may simply have been a friendly gesture to Heraclius who was in Syria at this time (summer of 630). Whatever its primary purpose, it became the occasion for a theological dialogue between Heraclius and the Catholicos, in which the former was convinced of the orthodoxy (from the Greek point of view) of the Persians, so that the king and Catholicos were able to share together in Holy Communion. Nothing very tangible came of this meeting, except that when Jesusyahb returned home, he was met with strong criticism from those who were convinced that when in Aleppo he had not stood up stoutly enough in defence of Nestorianism.

Two incidents emerging from the Aleppo meeting deserve a brief comment. One relates to Sahdona, a member of the Persian delegation, later to become bishop of Mahoze of Arewan. While in Syria, Sahdona visited a monastery in Apamea and held a long conversation with one of the monks, the result of which undermined Sahdona's Nestorian beliefs. When he returned to Persia he developed, as we have seen in the previous section, into a full-blown Monophysite, and he eventually had to be expelled from the Nestorian Church.[17] Another occurrence stemming from the Nestorians' visit to Aleppo, shows us Jesusyahb III, the archbishop of Hazza and Mosul (the future Catholicos) in a rather peculiar light. This cleric who was a member of the Nestorian group that had interviewed Heraclius, was in Antioch for a few days on the way back to Persia, and in one of the churches of the city he saw a white marble casket said to contain relics of the blessed apostles and reputed to be the cause of miracles. The upshot of it all was that Jesusyahb, after appropriate prayer, stole the casket and brought it back to Persia with him and placed it in the monastery of Beth 'Abe.[18]

Living where and when he did, it was inevitable that the Catholicos should have to confront the expansion of the Arabs beyond their traditional homeland. He would realize that the fall of Ḥira (635), the battle of Qadisiyah (637) and the Arab entry into Ctesiphon (637) were major disasters for the Persian regime. As the months passed it would have become evident to him that the Arab attacks were more than a gigantic razzia, for along with the fighting and the plundering, a new religious creed was being propagated. The world that the Catholicos had known was in fact falling apart, an impression strengthened by the bits of news filtering through from Syria and Palestine: the battle of the Yarmuk river (636), and the fall of both Antioch and Jerusalem in 638 told the same tale. There was nothing to

---

[17] On Sahdona's abandonment of the Nestorian faith, see *Bk of Gov* 2, II. vi, pp 128–30. For the Syriac text of letters, written by Mar Jesusyahb III, which relate to Sahdona, see id pp 132–47.

[18] *Bk of Gov* 2, II. v, pp 127–28.

be done by the Catholicos and his Church but wait for whatever might emerge from this series of political disasters. It is doubtful if, at this stage in the expansion of Islam, the Christians of Persia were treated differently from those in the Byzantine world. We are told that when Khalid, the great Arab leader, stood before Damascus in September 635, he announced, "In the name of God, the compassionate, the merciful, this is what Khalid would grant to the inhabitants of Damascus if he enters therein: he promises to give them security for their lives, property, and churches. Their city shall not be demolished neither shall any Moslem be quartered in their houses. Thereunto we give to them the pact of God and the protection of his prophet. . . . So long as they pay the poll tax, nothing but good shall befall them."[19] Presumably this same general policy would have been applied to the cities of Persia and to the Persian Christians. The Persian campaign was under the direction of Saʻd ibn-abi-Waqqaṣ, one of Mohammed's "Companions," and it would be he with whom all agreements would be made. It is probable that the Catholicos entered into some understanding with Saʻd, but the conditions of such an agreement, given by Bar Hebraeus, may belong in part to a later period.[20] It is also possible that agreements made by the local Arab commander had to be confirmed by the Caliph, which may explain how the names of Abu Bakr and/or ʻUmar are connected with the tradition. Any hope Jesusyahb II may have secretly cherished of Persia regaining political power in western Asia was snuffed out in 641 when the last great battle between the Persians and the Arabs was fought at Nihawand, near Hamadan, a battle which resulted in an overwhelming defeat for what was left of Yazdagird's army.

We infer from Thomas of Marga that Jesusyahb II had a more than ordinary interest in the education of the young. He is credited by Thomas with attempting to establish a school close to the monastery of Izla. But his plan was frustrated by the opposition of the monks, and the Catholicos had to settle for a school in his native village.[21] We suspect that he may have built other schools as well. On schools which the Nestorians commonly established to propagate their teaching, see *Histoire de Marouta* in PO 3, pp 65–66. The Catholicos is also credited with a number of writings, including a commentary on the Psalms.[22] He died about 643. He was succeeded in the Catholicate by Mar Emmeh, who held office for about four years, and he in turn was succeeded by Jesusyahb III, who died between 657 and 660.

---

[19] Quoted from P. K. Hitti, *History of the Arabs*, London, 1937, p 150.
[20] These conditions are quoted by Budge in *Bk of Gov* 2, note 2 on pp 125–26; cf Labourt, pp 245–46.
[21] *Bk of Gov* 2, II. vii–x, pp 131–32, 147–53.
[22] Wright, p 170; Baumstark, p 196.

5. Monophysitism (after 628).

The Monophysites, like the Nestorians, enjoyed the freedom extended to Christians by Kavad II, and they proceeded to reorganize themselves for a future unclouded by Zoroastrian persecution. The recent struggles between the Byzantines and the Persians had resulted, in its early stages, in large numbers of prisoners from Syria being sent to Persia. We know, for instance, that when Dara was taken in 606, the bulk of its population was transferred to Persia. When Sahrbaraz captured Antioch in 611, the same thing took place. When Jerusalem fell in 614, 35,000 prisoners, who included many craftsmen, were taken first to Damascus and then to Persia (cf *Chr de Michel* 2, XI. 1, pp 400–401). Most of these prisoners would be Christian, and probably the majority of the Christians, at least from Syria, would be Monophysites, which meant that the Monophysite constituency in Persia would be strengthened numerically.

The first step in the renewal of Monophysitism was taken by Athanasius, the Jacobite patriarch of Antioch. The latter had sent his assistant John to Persia, presumably to take his compliments to Kavad II. John, on his return to Syria, prevailed upon some of the Monophysite bishops to accompany him, doubtless to plan their strategy for the future. The party which went to Antioch in 629 comprised Christopher, the abbot of the Mar Mattai monastery, four bishops and three monks, one of the latter being Marutha (on Marutha see ch 10, sect 8). One aim of the delegation was to have Athanasius ordain the monks as bishops, but Athanasius refused to do this, and the Persian bishops had to act independently. They therefore not only ordained Marutha, but made him grand metropolitan of Tagrit and gave him authority over all the orthodox (Monophysite) Church of the Orient. They even empowered him to nominate the head of the Mar Mattai monastery.[23] Marutha was in fact the Patriarch of the Jacobite Christians in Persia. The title for the holder of this office at a later date was to be Maphrian (Syr *mpryn*'). According to Bar Hebraeus (quoted by F. Nau, *Histoire de Marouta*, pp 57–58) Marutha had to begin with twelve bishops under him, but this number may be inflated and may reflect later usage. The sees are given as Beth 'Arbaye, Shiggar, Ma'alta, Arzun, Gomel, Beth Ramman, Karmeh, Gozarta of Qardu, Beth Nuhadra, Perozshapur, Shiarzur, the Arab Taglibetes (banu Taglib).[24] Marutha is said to have ordained at a later date bishops for Segestan, Herat and Azerbaijan. The location of these bishoprics give us a fair idea of the extent of Monophysitism in Persia in the early seventh century. Thus it was that the Monophysites settled down to life under a more tolerant political regime. Like the Nestorians, little did they know in 629–30 of the epoch-making changes that lay just ahead. But events soon caught up with them, and when the Muslim forces

---

[23] For the letter of Athanasius to the monks of Mar Mattai, see *Chr de Michel* 2, XL. v, pp 414–17.

[24] Cf the list of bishoprics in J. M. Fiey, *Jalons*, pp 141–42.

advanced up the Tigris river, it was Marutha who had the citadel of Tagrit opened to them to save the city from the calamity of a siege. Marutha died in 649 and was succeeded as Jacobite Patriarch in Persia by Denḥa, the author of the history of Marutha which F. Nau has edited.

6. Asceticism and Monasticism in Parthia and Persia.[25]

In treating this subject historically, we must go back briefly to the second century, for it seems probable that some forms of Christian asceticism had penetrated Parthia at this time. Tatian, for instance, who is said to have returned to the east (possibly Adiabene) c 172, and who had become an apostle of encratite views, probably made some converts east of the Tigris. Though it is of interest that in that part of the *Chronicle of Arbela* which covers the Parthian period (down to bishop Hiran, 225-58; pp 1-31 of the Syriac text), there are no references to any form of asceticism, nor to the uncleanness which most ascetics attached to marriage. On pp 45-6 of the Syriac text of this *Chronicle*, there is an allusion to one, Jacob, living in the early fourth century near the Persian-Roman border, who was a solitary saint, renowned for his prayers, vigils and fastings. The one fourth century ascetic figure of whom we have considerable knowledge is Aphraates (see ch 8, sect 2). His treatise on monks (6) and on virginity (18), and his listing of virginity with fasting, prayer, love, meekness and holiness as prime requisites for the service of Christ (1.4) illustrates how well-rooted this type of Christianity was in Persia at this time. As late as the Synod of Acacius (486) the Church was having trouble controlling extreme ascetics (canon 2). From canon 3 we may infer that the bishops still had to contend for the view that while celibacy was the more perfect path for Christians to take, marriage adorned by the procreation of children was a totally acceptable option available even to the clergy.

It was the cenobitical type of monasticism that came to dominate the Persian Church, and its beginnings go back, according to legend, to an Egyptian named Augen (Awgin, Eugene; *Chr de Séert*, PO 4, vii, pp 234-36). This individual from a village near modern Suez was a pearl fisher, and later he joined the monastery of Pachomius (d 346), where he served as baker. He subsequently felt called to go to northern Mesopotamia as a

---

[25] Three works by A. Vööbus are of prime importance:
The History of Asceticism in the Syrian Orient,
I. *The Origin of Asceticism: Early Monasticism in Persia*, CSCO 184, Subsidia 14, Louvain, 1958;
II. *Early Monasticism in Mesopotamia and Syria*, CSCO 197, Subsidia 17, Louvain, 1960;
III. *Syriac and Arabic Documents* (regarding Legislation relative to Syrian Asceticism), PETSE 11, Stockholm, 1960.

Christian missionary, taking with him 28 (or 66, or 70 or 72) monks, and they settled in Mount Izla, south of Nisibis, and from this point the associates of Augen fanned out to found monasteries and convents in different parts of the Persian kingdom. Augen himself, the story goes, had friendly relations both with the Roman emperor Constantine and with the Persian king Shapur II. He is said to have died c 363. The Augen narrative taxes our credulity in so many ways that most historians are inclined to ignore it completely. This is what A. Vööbus does in his *History of Asceticism in the Syrian Orient*, Vol 1, pp 217–20, a position which receives some support from the fact that Thomas of Marga seems to be completely unaware of the Augen tradition in his *Book of Governors*. However, the editor of the *Book of Governors*, E. A. W. Budge, appears to accept the Augen story at its face value (1, pp cxxv–cxxxi). For a more recent discussion of Mar Augen, see J. M. Fiey, *Jalons*, pp 100–12.

Between the strictly eremetical type of asceticism and the cenobitical, we should probably place the hermitage type, which designates a group of men, essentially hermits, who lived in solitary cells where they ate their food, and who came together only for worship in the chapel. This was the type of asceticism favoured by Antony of Egypt (d 356). The residuum of this variety of asceticism is found in the practice of some later monasteries in which one or more cells were set aside for recluses whose participation in the life of the institution was minimal.

Thomas of Marga speaks of Greek monks exiled by the emperor Valens (364–78) who settled near Mosul and remained there until permitted to return to the Byzantine world in 379 by the emperor Theodosius. We can only speculate on the effect of these monks on Persian monasticism (cf *Bk of Gov*, 2, VI. 1, pp 577–78).

Among the early founders of monasteries in the Persian Church we shall cite only Mar 'Abda and his pupil Mar 'Abdjesus.[26] Mar 'Abda, who belongs to the second half of the fourth century, was abandoned as a child, but was rescued and raised by a Christian family and eventually he became an ascetic and also a priest. He combined his performance as an ascetic with a zeal for missionary work, his activities in the latter regard apparently being confined to Beth Aramaye. He added to his fame by founding a monastery, which also contained a school, at Dair Qoni near later Baghdad, where he served as abbot and where he eventually gathered around him about sixty disciples. One of his pupils was Aḥai who became his successor as abbot and who c 410 was elected as the Nestorian Catholicos. Mar 'Abdjesus, mentioned above, came from Maishan and studied at the monastery and school of Mar 'Abda. He subsequently returned to Maishan where he did considerable missionary work. He was also active as the founder of monastic communities mostly in south-west Persia, in Maishan, on the island of Baḥrain and at Ḥira.

[26] A. Vööbus, HASO I, pp 266–70.

The growth of monasteries and the bringing of them into the fold of the Church, increased the repute of monks vis à vis the ecclesiastical hierarchy and made it possible for monks to fill responsible offices in the institutional Church. Thus in the early fifth century, two of the Nestorian Patriarchs were in fact monks, viz Mar Aḥai and Mar Yahbalaha I. Two centuries later, when the new Sasanian king Kavad II in 628 allowed the Nestorians once more to elect a Catholicos, the bishops' first choice was Mar Babai the abbot of the Mount Izla monastery. When the latter declined the honour, the bishop of Balad, Jesusyahb II, was chosen instead.

As the trend towards cenobitical asceticism increased, monasteries became the recipients of gifts from pious laymen or from monks who had inherited property, and as a result some of these institutions became comparatively wealthy. We learn, for instance, that one, Rabban bar Had Be-Shabba of the village of Hadod, who had earlier been in the Great Monastery at Izla, built in the last sixth century a monastery near his village and he gave to it large gifts and bequeathed to it all his family inheritance (*Bk of Gov*, 2, I. xv, pp 68–69). In the next century when Jesusyahb III, who had become Catholicos c 647–50, wished to establish a school in the monastery of Beth 'Abe (against the wishes of the monks), he said in defending his proposal, "I have adorned and endowed this monastery with property and earthly possessions" (*Bk of Gov*, 2, II, viii, p 149). When the Muslim era arrived, the property owned by some of the monasteries made the latter a tempting prey for lawless or fanatical individuals (*Bk of Gov*, 1, p lxvi; 2, IV, xxi, pp 450–54).

The so-called Canons of Marutha.

Marutha, the bishop of Maiperqaṭ, who was active in the Nestorian Synod of 410, is said to have given the Church some canons other than the twenty-one included in the record of the Synod in SO, pp 263–73. A. Vööbus believes that the canons he presents in his *Syriac and Arabic Documents* (pp 115–49) are basically those of Marutha, who was himself a monk and presumably interested in the spread of a disciplined asceticism. While these canons may contain material that is later than Marutha, they are being summarized below as evidence of the existence of monasticism in the Persian Church in the early fifth century and as illustrative of the ethos of Nestorian monasticism at this stage of its development. Each of the canons except number 59 is prefaced by "It is the will of the general synod." The first canon is numbered 25.

25. On the chorepiscopus. The bishop shall select the chorepiscopus from the order of the monks. The chorepiscopus shall select overseers (Syr s'wr') for the churches and monasteries. The bishop shall visit both the churches and monasteries of his diocese, and shall see that ever church and monastery has a priest.

26. On further duties of the chorepiscopus.

27. Monks shall gather once a year to honour the bishop and to share communion with him. Those who have recently become abbots of monasteries shall visit the bishop three times a year.

28–35 are missing.

36. On hospitals, which shall be in towns and each of which is to have a monk as its curator.

37–39 are missing.

40. On the election of an abbot.

42–46 are missing.

47. A monk is to be chosen as the overseer of prisoners. He is to dwell in the church or in the hospital, and he shall be the agent of the local prison, and shall act on behalf of the prisoners when necessary, e.g., he shall receive money to ransom a believer who has come to ruin through no fault of his own.

48. On the qualifications of an abbot. He shall have been educated in a monastery and shall be literate. He is to be subordinate to the bishop, the archdeacon and the chorepiscopus.

49. The steward, the door-keeper and the other servants of a monastery are to be chosen by the abbot.

50. On the qualifications and duties of a steward.

51. On the qualifications, duties, and behaviour of the door-keeper.

52. On the qualifications, duties, and behaviour of the overseer.

53. On the qualifications and duties of the young assistant to the abbot (the service of Elisha to Elijah is cited as an example).

54. On the internal discipline of a monastery:

All shall participate in the service, in prayer, in reading and in fasting;

item 2 suggests that the work of the monastery is allotted to each on a weekly basis (cf items 17, 18, 21, 24);

the seating of a stranger at the table;

complaints regarding food served at the table;

altercations between monks or physical violence against the abbot;

items 7–17 indicate how to cope with slander, intemperate drinking, laziness, quarrelsomeness, insubordination, rebelliousness, fornication, stealing, absence from the monastery, trouble-making, somnolence during the service;

working monks eat twice a day (sixth hour and evening), non-working monks once a day;

monks sleep on the floor in one house, or on the ground; the abbot and the sick may sleep in beds; there is to be no disrobing or loosening of the girdle when retiring;

there shall be seven services a day (morning, third, sixth and ninth hours, evening meal, evening, night);

all sound in health shall work;

there shall be two kinds of garments, one for the winter and one for the summer, and each is to have its wearer's name on it;

when it is too hot to work, reading must be done;

the time available each day shall be devoted to the service and reading, work (not specified), and meals and rest;

monks may drink a stated amount of wine;

items 26–33 deal with applicants for membership in the monastery; an applicant shall be interrogated by the abbot; a slave is permitted only if his master approves; if the applicant has been living with his parents, parental approval is required; if he is married, his wife must approve; if he is a parent, he is not to be received; a man fleeing from his wife may be received; a murderer may be received if he did not kill wilfully.

55 is missing.

56. Churches, martyria and monasteries are to be consecrated by either a bishop or a chorepiscopus.

57. The abbot of a monastery or the priest of a church cannot change the altar in the chapel of the monastery or in the church without the consent of the chorepiscopus.

58. The canons that pertain to the monks shall be read before them twice a year.

59. Various injunctions: monks are not to be married even spiritually (the pure union) to women (this is possible for clerics and laity); no meat shall be eaten in monasteries; regulations about garments, foot-wear, and tonsure; monastic garb is not to be worn outside the monastery.

60–65 are missing.

66. A monastery whose abbot has been made a chorepiscopus is to be honoured.

We should note that in the above canons, the institution of the sons and daughters of the Covenant is taken for granted (see ch 5, sect 9), and various rules for them are included in Marutha's canons (25.7; 26.2-4; 27.1; 41.1-3; 54.3; 58. 1; 59. 8).

The Rules of Abraham of Kashkar.[27]

Abraham of Kashkar,[28] born c 491-2, studied at Nisibis, and after serving as a missionary in Ḥira, he journeyed to Egypt and familiarized himself with the monastic traditions of that region. When he returned to the East, he retired to a cave on Mount Izla near Nisibis, and presently he founded a monastery at this spot (before 571), which came to be known as the Great Monastery and which he governed until his death in 588. Abraham gathered around him a group of eminent men who before and after his death propagated his ascetic ideals and practices in all regions of

---

[27] A. Vööbus, *Documents*, pp 150-62.
[28] *Bk of Gov*, 2, I. iv, pp 37-42.

Persia. The Great Monastery thus became a very influential institution, one reason being that its founder wished to associate the monasticism of his day more closely with the Church. Thomas of Marga goes so far as to say that the monastery of Mar Abraham served Persian monasticism in a similar way that Athens served Greek philosophy (*Bk of Gov*, 2, I, iv, p. 42)

What follows is a summary of Abraham's rules, which are dated 571:

1. On the need for tranquility and for avoiding idleness.
2, 5, 9. On fasting.
3. On prayer, the reading of the Scriptures, and the seven daily services.
4. On silence, serenity, loneliness, and quietness of speech.
5. In the Lenten fast, no one shall go out of his cell, except in an emergency.
6. On avoiding contact with other monasteries or with the houses of believers.
7. On avoiding the calumniation of a brother.
8. If one is early for the Sunday service, he should improve the time by reading the Scriptures.
9. Fasting shall be terminated only for special reasons.
10. New brothers are to be on probation (for how long is not indicated).
11. A sick brother shall not be brought to the house of a believer, but to the town hospice.
12. On a monk who is indifferent to the rules.

The Rules of Dadjesus.[29]

Dadjesus came from Beth Aramaye, and after studying at Nisibis he came to mount Izla, being, so Thomas of Marga claims, Mar Abraham's first disciple.[30] He became Abraham's successor and served as abbot of the Great Monastery 588–604. Selections from his twenty-eight canons, which are dated 588, are given below. It is clear, particularly from canons 1 and 2, that the times were marked by theological disputes, and that it was more necessary than ever for the monks to be loyal to the orthodox faith of the Nestorian Church.

1. The brothers are expected to adhere to the orthodox faith and to the teaching of Diodorus, Theodore, and Nestorius.
2. There are to be no dealings with heretics, soothsayers or charmers.
3. The steward, not the abbot, is to manage gifts for the monastery.
4, 16. The services on Sundays and fast-days are not to be neglected, nor the reading of the Scriptures interrupted.
5. On the treatment of a brother who leaves the monastery and wanders around the country.

---

[29] A. Vööbus, *Documents*, pp 163–75.
[30] *Bk of Gov* 2, I. v, pp 42–44.

6. Visits to town and all travelling must receive the permission of the abbot.

7. A new brother must be able to read.

10. All the brothers shall share in the work of the community (no details of the work are given).

12. A visiting brother with personal problems ("being vexed by an evil spirit") shall be accepted only for a few days of prayer.

13. A new brother must live for three years in the community (Syr *qnwbyn*). If his conduct prove satisfactory, he may then be given an empty cell, or build a cell for himself with the help of the other monks.

15. Bread is not to be baked in the monastery except under special circumstances.

17. Boys (Syr *ṭly'*) shall not be accepted into the community.

18. Deposits from laymen shall not be accepted.

19. A brother is subject to the commands of the fraternity.

20. This appears to mean that if some of the brothers have to go outside on business, there must always remain five brothers in the monastery.

21. The steward is under the supervision of the abbot.

22. The steward shall visit the brothers in their cells once a month.

23, 25. The abbot, in counsel with the brothers, shall distribute daily the available food to all equally.

24. If the abbot does not rebuke a brother who violates the rules, he shall have to give an account before the judgment seat of Christ.

26. On correcting a brother who disturbs the community or who slanders a fellow monk or who is generally difficult and contentious.

27. If a brother takes sick and he does not wish to go to the hospice in town, a brother shall be appointed each week to take care of him.

The Monastery of Beth 'Abe.

A concrete example of a Nestorian monastery is described in *The Book of Governors* by Thomas, bishop of Marga.[31] This is the history of the abbots and monks connected with the monastery of Beth 'Abe ("house of the forest") from its foundation until the time of Thomas. Thomas had entered the monastery as a young man about 832. In 837 he became secretary to the Patriarch Abraham by whom he was made bishop of Marga (north-east of Mosul), and afterwards metropolitan of Beth Garmai.

The location of Beth 'Abe is not known precisely, but it seems to have been not far from the Great Zab river, and c 60–70 miles north-east of Mosul. Thomas's chronicle commences with an account of Abraham of Kashkar, who was baptized by the Catholicos Babai and who as we have earlier seen was the founder of the Great Monastery on Mount Izla. Eventually there were three

---

[31] *The Book of Governors*, 2 vols, London, 1893, ed by E. A. W. Budge. Vol 1 is the Syriac text, with an English introduction, and vol 2 is the ET.

other monasteries on this mountain. Abraham is said to have instituted a distinctive Nestorian tonsure (like a wheel and a crown), which a monk received after three years and three months in the monastery.

It is difficult to visualize the physical structure of the Great Monastery so that some monks could use their cells to house the women with whom they were living (as well as children), and this not be known to the abbot. But this in fact was the case, and it was only brought to light when one of the monks, Elijah, discovered the situation accidentally. The erring monks and their families were then expelled from the monastery and their cells were burned. This was not the end of the matter however. Mar Jacob, one of the monks, whose cell was near those of the men who had been expelled, was now accused by Elijah of sheltering the monks who had sinned, and the abbot, Mar Babai, who was "somewhat hasty of speech and harsh in command," determined that he too should leave the community. So Mar Jacob and a disciple "went forth to the mountains of Qardo to lead the life of anchorites." We read that Mar Jacob took with him "the book of the Gospels." The expulsion of Mar Jacob led to disagreement among the brothers, and many of them left Izla and eventually founded monasteries elsewhere. Thomas reports, "they filled the country of the East with monasteries and convents and habitations of monks" (*Bk of Gov*, 2, I, xiv, p 68).

After a period of unstated length Mar Jacob returned to the monastery of Mount Izla, where the abbot Mar Babai received him. But he remained in his old haunt only a short time, for he was moved, with the benediction of Mar Babai, to leave the monastery once more, this time taking nine brothers with him, and he headed for Beth 'Abe. Evidently there was an older monastic foundation at Beth 'Abe, but the date of its founding is a matter of speculation. There is some evidence that it was consecrated by the Catholicos Tomarsa (364–65 to 372–73), but if so, by Mar Jacob's time it had fallen into disuse (*Bk of Gov*, 1, p xliv). When Mar Jacob reached the site, c 595–96, the monastery apparently had to be completely rebuilt, and in that sense he was its founder. When Mar Babai inspected the Nestorian monasteries in the early seventh century, Beth 'Abe was one of the institutions he visited (*Bk of Gov*, 2, I xxix, pp 97–100).

The monastery of Beth 'Abe was a comparatively modest establishment. Its central and most important structure was of course the chapel or church (where there were seven daily services), and close to it were a number of other buildings housing the cells of the monks. The latter numbered in the early days about eighty men, but in the mid-seventh century this figure had risen to three hundred (*Bk of Gov*, 1, pp lxxiii, xlvii). Quarters were set aside for the kitchen, the refectory, sleeping accommodation for the novices, the entertainment of strangers, and the library. The library was gradually built up, thanks to donors and benefactors, and it is estimated that by the early ninth century it contained 700–1000 volumes (*Bk of Gov* 1, pp lix–lxiv, cvii; 2, pp 174, 179, 239, 282, 299).

The library of Beth 'Abe was only one of the many libraries housed in the Nestorian monasteries. While the subject matter of the books appears to have been restricted to biblical and theological themes, the fact that monks were required to spend part of their time reading manuscripts and/or recopying them meant that an intellectual tradition, even though limited in scope, was maintained in the Church.

On a somewhat lower level academically we should note that the Nestorian monasteries, like those in the Byzantine world, were involved in the education of the young, doubtless with a view to recruiting from their ranks suitable persons as "sons of the Covenant," as well as priests and monks. The *Chronicle of Arbela* tells us that in the time of bishop Ḥenana (early sixth century), Abraham of the School of Nisibis had sent one, Paul, to Mar Ḥenana to establish a school for the children of Adiabene. Paul is reported to have been engaged in this work for more than thirty years.[32] The *Histoire de Marouta* by F. Nau records that the Jacobite Patriarch paid tribute *en passant* to the schools established in the towns by the Nestorians (PO 3, p 65). We have to move on a century to pick up further data on education. Thomas of Marga relates that Babai the musician, who flourished in the mid eighth century, did much in the country of Marga for its schools, founding or restoring sixty of them and providing a teacher for each one (*Bk of Gov*, 2, III, i–ii, pp 296–97; iii, pp 306–7). At least five of these schools were located in monasteries. Not all monasteries welcomed a school either in their midst or even near them. When the Catholicos, Mar Jesusyahb III, in the seventh century proposed to establish a school in the monastery of Beth 'Abe, he was opposed by the abbot and the monks. "It is not good for us monks . . . to be disturbed . . . by the noise of the voices of the school boys." (*Bk of Gov*, 2, II, vii, pp 131–32; viii–x, pp 147–53). The result was that the Catholicos gave up his project for Beth 'Abe, and built instead a school in his native village, Kuphlana.

Monophysite Monasticism.

Monasticism was as much a feature of the Monophysite Church as it was of the Nestorian. The leading monastery of the Monophysites was that of Mar Mattai in Jebel Maklub, near Mosul, whose founder, Mattai (Matthew), was martyred by Shapur II. For a description of the monastery as it was in 1843, see G. P. Badger, *The Nestorians and their Rituals*, 1, pp 96–97.

A. Vööbus claims that a group of canons of anonymous origin, twenty-six in number, preserved by Bar Hebraeus, and which the latter calls the canons of the Persians, are in fact rules for Monophysite monks.[33] Despite differences related to the tonsure, these rules are essentially the same as those for Nestorian monasteries. We draw attention only to the following:

---

[32] *Chronicle of Arbela*, p 75 of the Syriac text, 11 48–54.
[33] *Documents*, pp 87–92.

3,4,5. On the steward, the door-keeper and the overseer.

9. A monk assisting a priest in a church in town or in a village, shall put a white garment over his monastic robe.

11. When a monk finishes his manual work, he shall meditate in the divine books.

13. A homily shall be read while the brothers dine.

14. The monastic garb is put on only after three years in the monastery.

15. A monk shall take care of the correction of himself only, and not that of his brothers.

18. "A monk shall not pass the night in the cell of his fellow-monk."

19. On a monk inheriting property from his family.

20. The tonsure is to be given by the abbot only after a year's probation.

22. "A monk who knows only one psalm, shall repeat the same in all the prayers."

23. "A monk who eats meat shall be punished as one who fornicates."

24. "If a monk wants to pray in his cell, this shall be allowed to him only on ordinary days, and not on the feasts or on Sundays."

Conclusion

As the Syriac-using Christians in Roman Syria were in fact part of the Church in the Byzantine world, we shall not attempt here to include them in this retrospective view of our subject. Such virtues and deficiencies as they had were shared by their Greek-speaking brethren, and their future in a considerable measure was bound up with them. Even the Syrian Monophysites (or Jacobites) were but one segment of the Monophysitism we meet with both in Egypt and in Armenia. All of them, whether orthodox or Monophysite, with the exception of those whose good fortune it was to live in Asia Minor west of the Taurus mountains, were destined to be involved in the Arab maelstrom of the seventh century, and while most of them survived under Arab rule, life for them was never to be quite the same again.

Our principal concern here is therefore with the Church in Sasanian Persia. Its beginnings in the Parthian era are obscure, but to the best of our knowledge, relatively peaceful. It was the advent of the Sasanians which changed this picture. Christians in Persia now found themselves under a regime which was only occasionally benevolent, was sometimes indifferent, and frequently was opposed to their very existence. The goodwill which some of the Sasanian rulers displayed towards their Christian subjects was often offset by the antagonism of others. On occasion the election of a Catholicos or the holding of a Synod were interfered with either by the king himself or by the machinations of his advisers. The one constant factor in this situation was the hostility of the Zoroastrian hierarchy. When the influence of the Magi was strong, then Christians, particularly Persians who had abandoned their traditional religion, were in for an unpleasant time, and for some this meant eventual death. At such times anti-Christian feelings, possibly whipped up by local government officials, frequently involved the pillage and even the destruction of Church property. In short, the Persian Church, in the four centuries we are considering, led a somewhat precarious existence.

In the light of the circumstances under which it operated, we cannot but admire the Persian Church's faithful and stubborn witness to the Christian faith, and we here include both the Nestorians and the Monophysites. It is true that while it has given us competent Church historians (who flourished mostly in the Islamic era), it never produced theologians or polemicists such as were found in the Byzantine West, nor did it ever exert any real influence upon the main stream of Greek and Latin Christianity. Its theology, basically that of the Nicene Creed, was derived from the Greek Church, as were its

Scriptures and much of its canon law. Nevertheless its devotion to the Scriptures, and its relatively simple institutions—the priesthood, the episcopate, the monasteries, the schools, the liturgy—seem to have given the Persian Church a vitality which assured its survival in the trying conditions under which it often had to carry on its work. This valiant Christian effort in the Sasanian period on behalf of the City of God must be viewed as part of the total history of the Christian Church, and it is then seen as another exemplification of that deep Christian faith which finds its classical literary expression in the NT in Hebrews 11:1-12:2.

Appendices

The dates cited here frequently go beyond the chronological limits of the main text.

1. The Early Missionary Efforts of Syriac Christians.

In Arabia.

The vast peninsula of Arabia lay just to the south of Roman Syria and Palestine and Sasanian Persia, but it never seems to have presented itself to Syriac Christians as a field for serious Christian evangelism. This may have been partly due to the tribal organization of Arab society and to the nomadic or semi-nomadic character of most of the population, features of Arab life which made traditional methods of Christian proselytization difficult to apply. The Ghassanid Arabs of north-west Arabia, to whom reference was made earlier in this study (ch 3, sect 6), became Christians of the Monophysite variety, and they were undoubtedly responsible for some Christianity percolating into the Ḥijaz and as far south as Yaman. We know from various sources (e.g., A. Moberg, *The Book of the Ḥimyarites*, Lund, 1924) that about 500 A.D. there were substantial numbers of Christians, as well as Jews, in south-west Arabia, mostly in Yaman. We must also remember that the Lakhmid Arabs were in the north-east of the peninsula, and that their king (as it happened, their last king), al-Nu'man III (c 580–602), adopted the Nestorian version of Christianity prevalent in Persia. But long before the king's conversion, the Lakhmid capital Ḥira (Ḥirta) was the location of a Christian bishopric (SO, the Synods of 410, 424, 486, 497, 585). It is therefore likely, with the existing economic ties between the Lakhmids and south-west Arabia, that zealous Christians from Ḥira were another source of the Christianity in the south-west of the peninsula. Even after the rise of Islam, and despite the dictum of the Caliph 'Umar (634–44) that only Muslims should be found within Arabia, it is curious that the small Nestorian Synod of 676, called by the Catholicos Mar George I, was attended by one metropolitan and five bishops, all of whose sees were located in or near the Persian Gulf; one bishop was from Beth Qatraye, on the Arabian mainland opposite the Baḥrain islands, and another was the bishop of the Mazonaye (the inhabitants of 'Uman). About a hundred years later, when Thomas of Marga was recording the bishops consecrated by the Catholicos Timothy I (780–820), he refers to the bishop of Yaman and of San'a (*Bk of Gov*, 2, IV. 20, p 448). This was now the era of the somewhat more tolerant 'Abbasid line of Caliphs, and the older prescription against infidels within Arabia was evidently not always enforced.

In India and China.

We do not know what part Nestorian Christians from Persia played in establishing the Christian cause in India. As is well known, the Malabar Christians of south-west India trace their origin to the legend of St. Thomas who brought the Gospel to India and was martyred there. It is Eusebius who records a variant of this tradition, viz. that Pantaenus (d c 190), the first known head of the Catechetical School of Alexandria, visited India and found there Christians whose forbears had been evangelized by Bartholomew, one of the Apostles (*Eccl Hist* V. x. 1-4). The fact, however, that these Indian Christians for many centuries have used Syriac in their liturgy favours the view that Christianity was introduced among them by Nestorian (or Monophysite) missionaries from Persia. If this is so, it is odd that the Synods of the Nestorian Church, down to 775 (as recorded in the *Synodicon Orientale*), have no references to Christians or Christian bishops in India.

The Nestorian Church appears to have been more interested in the areas served by the old trade route which led from Persia to Merv and thence to China.[1] It was along this route that most of the silk merchandise was brought from China to Persia and the Byzantine world. It was in Justinian's time that Constantinople began to be less dependent on this source for its silk, after some monks (not further identified), who had been in China, had brought silk worm eggs and the basic technology of silk production to the Byzantine capital (Procopius, *Wars* VIII. xvii. 1-8). Just how early Persian Christians went into these more easterly regions we do not know. The Nestorian Synod of 424 had under its jurisdiction bishops from Ḥerat and Abrashahr (both in Khurasan) and Merv (north of Khurasan)(SO, pp 285-98), and Merv continues to appear in the records of Synods held in 486, 497, 554 and 585.[2] To push eastwards from Merv into China would not be all that difficult for intrepid and dedicated missionaries, especially if they had the guidance of knowledgeable merchants. On Christian bishops travelling with merchants, see *Bk of Gov*, vol 2, V. x, pp 506-7. A Nestorian family bearing the name of Mar Sargis, is said to have come to Lin-t'ao, Kan-su, as early as 578, and Nestorian Christians are reported to have appeared at the court of the emperor of China in 635, in the Chen-kuan period (L. M. Outerbridge, *The Lost Churches of China*, Philadelphia, 1952, pp 35-36). It is Thomas of Marga who tells us, apropos of the times of Timothy I (780-820), that the Catholicos had consecrated one, David, as metropolitan of China (Syr *byt ṣyny*'; *Bk of Gov*, vol 2, IV. 20, p 448). Later

---

[1] For a popular account, with bibliography, of early Nestorianism in China, see L. M. Outerbridge, *The Lost Churches of China*, Philadelphia, 1952, pp 30-48.

[2] A. Vööbus (HASO I, pp 263-65) notes the reference in the *Chronique de Séert* (PO 5, p 256) to a monk named Barshabba who did missionary work in and around Merv between 355 and 385.

in his chronicle Thomas refers to bishops appointed to the countries beyond Gilan and Dailom or Delum (territories south-west of the Caspian Sea); "And they lightened all the ends of the east . . . and moreover the bread in those countries is made of rice" (*Bk of Gov*, 2, V. 7. pp 490–91, 493).

The most important single piece of evidence concerning Nestorian activity in China comes from the period of the T'ang dynasty (618–907), a dynasty which was one of China's most liberally minded, and which in particular was quite tolerant of Christian missionary efforts. About 1623 in Sian-fu a massive slab of stone, nine feet high, was found, inscribed in both Chinese and Syriac characters. This monument, whose authenticity was questioned for over two hundred years, is now generally regarded as genuine. It bears an imperial edict, and appears to have been first erected in 781; in its Syriac portion it records the names of sixty-seven Nestorian missionaries who have been active in Sian-fu. In modern times various other bits of evidence of Nestorian activity in Shan-si and Shen-si have come to light. Towards the close of the T'ang dynasty a Confucian revival occurred in China, which, among other things, polemized against both Buddhism and Christianity as being foreign religions. The result was that Nestorianism in China, after a period of toleration which lasted nearly three hundred years, was almost completely obliterated, leaving mostly stone records of its existence, records which were to be properly evaluated only in the modern period.

2. The Transmission of Western Science and Learning to the Arabs.[3]

It is a fact that within three centuries of the rise of Islam, the Arab world had appropriated through individual scholars and through translations a good deal of the science and learning which it found in Persia and in the conquered Byzantine territories. While this appropriation by the Arabs is incontestable, it is almost impossible, because of the lack of supporting data, to trace this process in detail, and we have to content ourselves with broad generalizations backed by the few certainties that can be discovered. Furthermore, the nature and chronological limits of the present study warrant us in giving this topic only a minimum amount of attention.

The Monophysite and Nestorian Churches as such had little or no interest in enriching the cultural life of the Moslem world. Their academies, such as the Nestorian foundations in Nisibis and Seleucia, were primarily theological institutions, with a strong emphasis on biblical studies, and such libraries as they had would reflect these interests. While, therefore, the organized Churches played no real part in the cultural transmission we are dealing with, individual Christians, and to a lesser extent individual Jews, were very active in this enterprise and deserve at least a passing notice.

---

[3] See P. K. Hitti, *History of the Arabs*, London, 1937, ch 24, pp 297–316; A. O. Whipple, *The Role of the Nestorians and Muslims in the History of Medicine*, New York and Princeton, 1967.

It was in the sixth century that Khusro I (531–79) either founded a medical school, or strengthened an existing one, at Gundeshapur (Beth Lapaṭ was the Christian name for the city). The school must have utilized Persian medical lore, but it also seems to have been familiar with the Greek tradition as represented by Hippocrates and Galen, and from the sixth century on it was the most famous of Persia's medical schools. In the Islamic world it was known as Jundi-Shapur. Some of its teachers were undoubtedly Persians, but others were Christians, mostly Nestorians. We know, for instance, that when the Muslim era opened the family of Bukht-Jesus, a Christian physician, was active in the school, and for six generations members of this family continued to be conspicuous in the school's life. It is thought that the Christian, al-Ḥarith ibn-Kalada, of al Ta'if, who was well known in Arabia in the seventh century, had been trained at Jundi-Shapur. In the eighth century, the Caliph al-Manṣur (754–75), ill with stomach trouble, summoned from Jundi-Shapur the prominent Nestorian physician, Jurjis (George) ibn-Bakhtishu. Jurjis apparently improved the Caliph's health, and remained in Baghdad to become the founder of a line of physicians to the Caliphs.

It is self evident that if scientific and scholarly material was to have its maximum usefulness in the Muslim community, it would have to be translated from whatever language it was in (Greek, Syriac, Pahlavi, Sanskrit) into Arabic. Thus the role of translators was paramount in the transmission of foreign learning into the language of Islam. Even in the days of Khusro I, the need for translation was recognized, as we learn from the career of Burzoe, the king's physician, who on his return to Persia from a visit to India, brought with him Indian works, presumably in Sanskrit, and these had to be translated into Pahlavi.[4] It was a Nestorian physician, Yuḥanna ibn Masawayh, who was trained at Jundi-Shapur, to whom the Caliph Harun al-Rashid (786–809) entrusted the translation into Arabic of the many Greek manuscripts which were now coming into Muslim hands. He served as court physician to four Caliphs, and was also a distinguished medical teacher, his most famous pupil being Ḥunayn ibn Isḥaq (809–74). Ḥunayn became the best known, as well as the most prolific of the translators from Greek into Arabic, and he tells us a great deal about his predecessors in this field. Ḥunayn was appointed head of the Caliph's academy in Baghdad, and had charge of all scientific translation work. He was assisted in these endeavours by his son and nephew. In some cases Ḥunayn did the basic translation from Greek into Syriac, and his collaborators then turned the Syriac into Arabic.

3. Observations on the Syriac Liturgies.

The Syriac Churches both Nestorian and Monophysite, like the Greek and Latin Churches, developed their own forms of worship or liturgies, but

[4] Christensen, p 429.

the history of these formularies is obscure. The earliest stages in this liturgical tradition can be readily identified, but once we are beyond these beginnings the path of the tradition is difficult to trace. To start with, there is the pattern of the Jewish synagogue service with its three basic elements of prayer, Scripture reading and homily. At what time the chanting or singing of Psalms became part of the service is uncertain. In any case Christians with a Jewish background would be partial to a form of Christian worship modelled on that of the synagogue. Second, there is the Last Supper described in the Synoptic Gospels and in I Cor 11:23-26. Since the identification of this Supper with the Passover cannot be maintained, it seems to follow that the Supper was remembered because it was the last meal that Jesus had with the Twelve. This occasion may have been formally a *ḥaburah* gathering (a *ḥaburah* was a company of like-minded friends), but what was said and done by Jesus on this occasion was never forgotten. Whether or not the words in Paul's account of the Supper, "Do this in remembrance of me" are an accurate translation of whatever Jesus said in Aramaic, the Greek text did ensure, as it turned out, that the memorial aspect of the Supper would never be lost. By the time of the *Didache* (second century), the Lord's Supper had become the Eucharist; it was observed on Sundays and it was available only to baptized persons (IX. 1-5; cf X. 1-7). It should be noted, however, that some scholars take these references in the Didache to be prayers for the *agape* and not for the Lord's Supper. Third, there is the *agape* or "love-feast" of the early Church (*Acts* 2:42, 46, 6:1-2; I Cor 11:20-21; Jude 12; Ignatius *Smyr* VIII. 2; Pliny, *Letters* X. 96). This was an occasion for religious fellowship among Christians, and apparently also for assistance to the needy brethren. If there was at one time a close connection between the *agape* and the Lord's Supper (cf "as they were eating" in Matt 26:21, 26; "after supper" in I Cor 11:25), it seems that by the second century the two observances had become separated. What is somewhat puzzling to many students of Church history is that out of these rather simple beginnings, the Churches should have fashioned their elaborate liturgies, and our perplexity is not lessened when we consider those used by the Syriac Churches. In actual fact there is an hiatus between the earliest practices of the Church and the later fully developed liturgies centering in the celebration of the Lord's Supper or Eucharist, and in our present state of knowledge this gap cannot be satisfactorily bridged.

It is in Edessa, in north-east Syria, that we find an ancient liturgy known as the *Liturgy of Saints Addai and Mari* (who supposedly had evangelized this region), the text of which is found in G. Dix, *The Shape of the Liturgy*, pp 177-87. Because of its brevity, simplicity and basically Semitic character, this may very well be one of the earliest of the Christian liturgies. Dix observes (i) that most of it appears to be addressed to the Son, not the Father; (ii) that it does not seem to have used the Pauline narrative

(I Cor 11:23-25) about the institution of the rite; (iii) that it includes a prayer that the Holy Spirit may come and "rest upon this oblation"; and (iv) that the oblation is described as "the likeness of the passion and death and burial and resurrection of our Lord." It is also to be noted that the oblation is "for the pardon of offences and the remission of sins, and for the great hope of resurrection from the dead and for new life in the kingdom of heaven."

A much more developed form of worship is seen in the *Liturgy of St. James*, known and used in Antioch in the early fifth century, the text of which appears in F. E. Brightman, *Liturgies Eastern and Western* I, pp 31-68; for comments on it, see Dix, pp 187-96. This liturgy is evidently an adoption and/or expansion of the rite celebrated in Jerusalem by Bishop Cyril of that city in 348. It is presumed that there was an old rite used in Antioch in the fourth century and that it was modified by the St. James material (cf Dix, *op cit*, pp 175-77, 187-207). When we turn to look at the two main Syriac liturgies, that of the Syrian Jacobites or Monophysites and the Persian Nestorians (an ET of the text of these liturgies is found in Brightman, pp 69-110 and 247-305), it is clear that both of them must go back to a common ancestor, either to the *Liturgy of St. James* or to something closely resembling it. This indebtedness can be taken for granted in the case of the Jacobites of Persia, who had associations with Antioch as late as the early seventh century. The Jacobite use of *Kurillison* (Syr *qwry' 'lyswn*) is but one example of a direct borrowing by them, in this case, of the Greek *kurie eleeson* ("Lord, have mercy"). The Nestorians, in their early days, were also debtors to the West, as canon 13 of the Synod of 410 acknowledges (SO, p 266).

It is evident that as early as 410, the Nestorians were concerned with correct liturgical practice (SO, pp 263-73). In canon 9 of this Synod we read, "Each Sunday the Gospel should be read along with the other books; the Word of God should be preached until the third or fourth hour; and that the sacrifice should be offered." These injunctions are repeated in the next century in canon 25 of the canons of Mar Aba, 544 (SO, p 559). Canon 13 of the Synod of 410 reads, "In each city the deacons shall make the 'proclamation' (a kind of bidding prayer at the beginning of 'the mass of the faithful'); the Scriptures shall be read; the pure and holy oblation shall be offered in all the churches on an altar." The ancient custom of offering the sacrifice in the homes of the faithful is no longer to be practised. The same canon enjoins that the festivals of the Church are to be observed at the same times as in the Western Church. Canon 15 reads, "In the bishop's city, the archdeacon on Sundays shall make the 'proclamation' in the presence of the bishop, and he shall read the Gospel." From canon 9 quoted above, we see that allowance is made for a sermon or homily to be preached after the readings from the Scriptures. Brightman notes (*op cit*, under "Sermon," p 588) that the sermon "is not generally provided for in the rubrics" of the liturgies, and that "it is commonly misplaced in practice."

As evidence of the way in which the Nestorian liturgy expanded or was altered, we draw attention to the following. Narseh, the first director of the School at Nisibis (d c 503), is said to have produced a liturgy, which must mean a revision of the one hitherto in use.[5] Mar Aba, Catholicos 540–52, who in his younger days had learned Greek at Edessa, is credited with translating the liturgy of Nestorius, and possibly that of Theodore of Mopsuestia, from Greek into Syriac.[6] Canons 3, 4, and 5 of his Synod of 544 deal with liturgical proprieties involving priests, deacons and sub-deacons (SO, p 556). The works of Henana of Adiabene, who became director of the School of Nisibis c 570–71, include expositions of the creed and the liturgy.[7] It was evidently not until the time of the Catholicos Ezekiel that the name of the Catholicos was formally proclaimed in the liturgy (canon 14 of the Synod of 576; SO p 380). While the liturgy was in the process of taking on its definitive form clerics must frequently have been uncertain about correct procedures. This is illustrated by the fact that the Catholicos Jesusyahb I (582–96) has given us his twenty canons. The term "canon" here is anomalous, for these rescripts did not emanate from the Synod of 585. They are the opinions of the Catholicos, written for the guidance of James, bishop of Darai, and they cover, among a variety of subjects, various points connected with the liturgy, such as, How should a priest commence his duties at the altar? When should a priest who celebrates take communion? And so on (SO, pp 424–51). We may note also that unwarranted changes in liturgical practice were frowned upon, as we may infer from the opinion on this subject voiced at the Synod of Sabarjesus held in 596 (SO, pp 459–60).

The Persian Jacobites, like the Nestorians, were not exempt from the need to elucidate their liturgy or even to amend it. Thus we learn that Marutha, the Monophysite patriarch in Persia (628–49), compiled a liturgy (improved an existing one?),[8] and we have from the pen of the distinguished Jacobite bishop, Moses bar Kepha (d 903), a commentary on the liturgy (R. H. Connolly and W. W. Codrington, *Two Commentaries on the Jacobite Liturgy*, London, 1913, pp 24–90).[9]

No attempt will be made here to analyse the Nestorian and Jacobite texts or to demonstrate in detail their relationship to one another or to other liturgical traditions, particularly to that of St. James. We shall, however, draw attention to some minor features of the Nestorian liturgy that may be of interest to western readers. At the outset this liturgy gives the procedure for the making and baking of the loaves of the oblation, this being done in

[5] Wright, p 59; Chabot, p 50.
[6] Wright, p 117; Chabot, p 54.
[7] Wright, p 127; Chabot, p 58.
[8] Wright, p 137. Chabot (p 82) doubts whether the liturgy in question belongs to him.
[9] A study which I have not been able to examine carefully is W. C. Macomber, *Six Explanations of the Liturgical Feasts*, CSCO 355, 356, Scriptores Syri 155, 156, 1974. This work is credited to one, Cyrus of Edessa, of the sixth century.

an area adjacent to the altar which is furnished with a small oven (Brightman, pp 247-49). The first part of the service, after the Prothesis and the Enarxis (see Brightman, pp 576, 586), constitutes the "Mass of the Catechumens," and here we have provision, in "the Lections," for Scripture readings, from the OT, St. Paul and the Gospel. The catechumens, not being baptized, cannot receive communion, and at an appropriate point in the proceedings (after the offertory), they have an opportunity to leave. The "Mass of the Faithful," which includes the recitation of the Creed by the priest, makes up the remainder of the service (Brightman, pp 262-305). Some of the rubrics are very precise, as for instance, "And his (the priest's) position shall be about a cubit distant from the altar, and the space between his hands of like measure" (p 274). It is in this "Mass of the Faithful" that we have the reading of the Diptychs (in Syr, "the book of life" or "the book of the living"). This recital is a prayer for the saintly dead, both biblical (commencing with Adam) and (mostly) post-biblical, most of whom are named; in Brightman's presentation this takes up pp 275-81 (cf the Jacobite counterpart, pp 91-96). It concludes with, "Also for presbyters and deacons and scholars who have departed from this church." We suspect that this last petition may give a hint about how the reading of the Diptychs originated: it probably arose out of the commemoration of the dead in a local parish. At the conclusion of the liturgy we have the "Eulogia," the distribution of the surplus bread to the worshippers.

Whatever may have been used by the Nestorians before the mid-seventh century, it was Jesusyahb III, metropolitan of Ḥazza and Mosul (and later, Catholicos c 647 to 657-60), who drew up with the invaluable assistance of 'Ananjesus of the monastery of Beth 'Abe a service book (Syr *ḥwdr*') for the Sundays of the whole year, for the Rogation of the Ninevites, for Lent, and for other special occasions such as baptism. This book in the words of Budge "has remained in use with comparatively little alteration until the present day" (*Bk of Gov*, 1, p lvi; cf 2, II, xi).

There was a musical element in the liturgical services, hymns, anthems and responsories being sung or chanted in appropriate places in the worship. Some of the hymns used were ascribed to Ephraim of the fourth century, to Narseh of the fifth century, to Jesusyahb II (Catholicos 628-43), and to others. But the successful use of music in the churches was dependent on the choice of suitable items to be sung or chanted, the availability of basic musical talent, and the training the voices had received. Since, however, these conditions could not always be met, the result was that the services in churches were frequently anything but edifying. Jesusyahb III tried to cope with this situation, in part, through his service book. It was not until the early eighth century that Babai "the musician" appeared, at a time as Budge puts it when "the condition of the musical portions of the services was deplorable" (*Bk of Gov* 1, p lvii). Babai, from the region of Samarra, had great musical gifts which he used in the service of the Church. He not only founded his own school in Kephar 'Uzzel (on the east side of the Great Zab river), but in the country of Marga he founded or re-established with the help of the local nobles no fewer than twenty-four schools,[10] where the pupils were taught among other things "to perform the musical portions of the services in a careful and accurate manner" (Bk of Gov, 1, pp lv–lix; 2, III. 1–2, pp 289–97). Budge notes that the maintenance for any length of time of a high standard of liturgical performance was difficult, and that many of the results of Babai's work had disappeared after some years. This decline in musical performance, apparent in the churches as a whole, was also seen in the monasteries, which often suffered from a dearth of good male voices and whose ascetic habits did not promote the culture of the human voice. Even the monks of Beth 'Abe had, at one time, to have an outside person, one Solomon of Beth Garmai, to teach them how to read the service book and how to sing the hymns and responses (Bk of Gov, 1, p lviii).

With regard to the actual church buildings in which worship was conducted, we may assume that Persian Christians followed the structural patterns used in north and north-east Syria, where all the identifiable ecclesiastical ruins are thought to date from the fourth century and later. These have been studied, mostly on the basis of surface inspection, and the findings published, by H. C. Butler (ed by E. B. Smith) in *Early Churches in Syria* (1929). The typical church in this area was the basilica, oriented to the east, and basically it consisted of two parts, the nave and the sanctuary. But this primary plan was subject to endless variations, as the ruins testify. For the ground plan of what might be called the average Nestorian church, see the diagram on p l iii in Bk of Gov, vol 1. For a good description of the ruins of the Church of St. Sergius (*Qasr Serij*), sixty km north-west of Mosul, see D. Oates, *Studies in the Ancient History of Northern Iraq* (Oxford 1968), pp 106–17. This was a Monophysite structure, and dates probably from the sixth century.

4. Canon Law of the Western Syrian Church.

A comment on two recent studies by A. Vööbus, *Die syrische Kanonessammlungen* I–II (1970), and *The Synodicon in the West Syrian Tradition* I–IV (1975–76).

Each of these works is in fact a *mélange*, and each ranges over a considerable span of time. Volume 1 of *Kanonessammlungen* (pp 1–262), for instance, furnishes us with the canons of general synods from 785 to 1174 (pp 5–88), and, in another section, the canons of local synods from 629 to 1153 (pp 89–121). There are the canons of Rabbula (pp 128–138), and of others, including John of Tella and Jacob of Edessa (pp 138–212); in the

---

[10] The location of these is given in Bk of Gov 2, III. ii, pp 296–97.

midst of these is a section on ordination (pp 146–156). The materials in pp 216–262 come from the Islamic period. Volume 2 (pp 263–561) records Question and Answer Sessions from the sixth to the ninth century (pp 263–303). It gives us canons for monks or for monasteries from Rabbula to the twelfth century (pp 307–398), and the canons of Dionysius bar Ṣalibi (d 1171) in pp 405–439. At this point the editor supplies a description of the manuscript resources for the subject (pp 440–498). The major topic near the end of the volume is the codification work of Bar Hebraeus (pp 499–552).

The *Synodicon* volumes are similarly varied in their content. Volume 1 gives us the Testament of the Lord, with canons (pp 27–64); a collection of all the canons of the holy apostles and synods (pp 65–83); the canons of the ecumenical synods from Nicaea to Chalcedon (pp 95–138); the canons of John, bishop of Tella (pp 142–151); the canons for monks established by Rabbula (pp 152–154); the teaching of Addai the Apostle (pp 187–197); etc. It concludes with the canons of Jacob of Edessa (pp 245–247). Volume 2 gives us the canons of the Patriarch George, 758–790 (pp 2–7); those of the Patriarch Qyriaqos, 793–819 (pp 7–18), and of other Patriarchs (pp 19–48, 53–68); the laws of the Christian kings, Constantinus, Theodosius, and Leo (pp 97–157); a record of the 154 episcopal sees under Antioch (pp 189–194); the canons of the monastery of Mar Mattai (pp 197–208). Pages 212–269 relate to the Islamic period, as does some of the earlier material.

Clearly, all the contents of the *Kanonessammlungen* and the *Synodicon* volumes are invaluable, although they would be more useful if their materials were arranged chronologically. In any case, they need to be critically evaluated, and their relationship, if any, to canons of the Greek Church established. We could then use them more freely to throw light on the internal life of the Syriac Church. This is a very demanding and important task, but in a survey such as this volume offers it cannot be attempted here.

Bibliography

Syriac Chronicles:

Acti Sancti Maris (Analecta Bollandiana 4), ed. J. B. Abbeloos, Paris, 1885, pp 43–138.
Ancient Syriac Documents, ed W. Cureton, London, 1864.
Book of Governors, The, by Thomas, Bishop of Marga, 2 vols, ed E. A. W. Budge, London, 1893.
Chronicle of Arbela (Histoire de l'Église d'Adiabene sous les Parthes et les Sassanides), by Mshiḥa-Zkha, ed A. Mingana, *Sources syriaque*, I, Leipzig, 1907, pp 1–75.
Chronicle of Edessa, CSCO, Scriptores Syri, 3rd series, tome 4, *Chronica Minora*, ed J. Guidi, 1893.
Chronicle of Joshua the Stylite, ed W. Wright, Cambridge, 1882.
Chronicum Ecclesiasticum by Bar Hebraeus (Gregory abu 'l Faraj), ed J. B. Abbeloos and T. J. Lamy, 3 vols, Louvain, 1872–77 (Syriac and Latin tr).
Chronique de Michel le Syrien, ed J. B. Chabot, 4 vols, Paris, 1899–1910.
Chronique de Séert (Histoire nestorienne), ed A. Scher, PO, 4, 5, 7, 13, Paris, 1908–19.
Opus Chronologicum, Eliae Metropolitae Nisibeni, ed E. W. Brooks, CSCO, Scriptores Syri, 3rd Series, tome 7, Rome, 1910.
Synodicon Orientale, ed J. B. Chabot, Paris, 1902.
Third Part of the Ecclesiastical History of John, Bishop of Ephesus, The, ed R. P. Smith, Oxford, 1860.

Greek Church Historians:

Eusebius—covers NT times to 323;
Theodoret—322 to 427/8;
Sozomen—323 to 425;
Socrates—305 to 439;
Evagrius—431 to 594.

Modern European writers on the history of Eastern Christianity:

Atiya, A. S.   *A History of Eastern Christianity*, London, 1968.
Chaumont, M.-L.   "Les Sassanides et la christianisation de le 'Empire iranien au IIIe siècle de notre ère," *Revue de l'Histoire des Religions*, 165 (1964), pp 165–202.

Fiey, J. M. — *Jalons pour une histoire de l'Église en Iraq*, CSCO 310, Subsidia 36, Louvain, 1970. *Nisibe*, CSCO 388, Subsidia 54, Louvain, 1977.

Haase, F. — *Altchristliche Kirkengeschichte nach orientalischen Quellen*, Leipzig, 1925.

Honigmann, E. — *Évêques et Évêchés Monophysites d'Asie Antérieure au VIe Siècle*, CSCO 127, Subsidia 2, Louvain, 1951.

Kidd, B. J. — *The Churches of Eastern Christendom from A.D. 451 to the Present Time*, London 1927.

Labourt, J. — *Le Christianisme dans l'Empire perse sous la dynastie sassanide (224-632)*, Paris, 1904.

Spuler, B. — *Die morgenländischen Kirchen* (Handbuch der Orientalistik, Erste Abteilung, Band VIII, Abschnitt 2), Leiden, 1961.

Wigram, W. A. — *An Introduction to the History of the Assyrian Church*, London, 1910.

General:

Ante-Nicene Fathers, 1-10, Buffalo, 1885-96.

Badger, G. P. — *The Nestorians and their Rituals*, 2 vols, London, 1852.

Bardaisan, — *The Book of the Laws of Countries*, ed H. J. W. Drijvers, Assen, 1965.

Barḥadbeshabba, — *Cause de la Foundation des Écoles*, ed A. Scher, PO 4, 1908, pp 317-404.

Baumstark, A. — *Geschichte der syrischen Literatur*, Bonn, 1922.

Brightman, F. E. — *Liturgies, Eastern and Western*, 1, Oxford, 1896.

Butler, H. C. — (ed E. B. Smith), *Early Churches in Syria*, Princeton, 1929 (Amsterdam, 1969).

Carrington, P. — *The Early Christian Church*, 2 vols, Cambridge, 1957.

Chabot, J.-B. — *Littérature syriaque*, Paris, 1934.

Christensen, A. — *L'Iran sous les Sassanides*, 2nd edit, Copenhagen, 1944

Colledge, M. A. R. — *The Parthians*, London, 1967.

Dix, G. — *The Shape of the Liturgy*, London, 1945

Doctrine of Addai the Apostle, The, ed E. Phillips, London, 1876.

Downey, G. — *A History of Antioch in Syria*, Princeton, 1961.

Drijvers, H. J. W. — *Bardaisan of Edessa*, Assen, 1966.

Dura-Europos, Excavations at, in various parts, with various editors and various dates, New Haven, 1929-52.

Fiey, J. M. — *Nisibe*, CSCO 388, Subsidia 54, Louvain, 1977.

Frend, W. H. C. — *The Rise of the Monophysite Movement*, Cambridge, 1972.

Frye, R. N. — *The Heritage of Persia*, London, 1962. (This volume supplies the Parthian and Persian dates used by the present author.)

Hitti, P. K.	*History of the Arabs*, London, 1937.
Josephus	*The Jewish Antiquities*, Loeb Classical Library, 6 vols, London, New York, and Cambridge (U.S.A.), 1930–65.
Josephus	*The Jewish War*, Loeb Classical Library, 2 vols, London, 1927–28.
Klijn, A. F. J.	*The Acts of Judas Thomas the Apostle* (Supplements to *Novum Testamentum*, V), Leiden, 1962.
Neusner, J.	*A History of the Jews in Babylonia*. I. *The Parthian Period* (Studia Post-biblica 9), 2nd edit, Leiden, 1969.
	II–V. *The Sasanian Period* (Studia Post-biblica 11–12, 14–15), Leiden, 1966–70.

Nicene and Post-Nicene Fathers, 1–13. Oxford and New York, 1890–98.

Rosenthal, F.	*Die Aramäistiche Forschung*, Leiden, 1939.
Segal, J. B.	*Edessa 'the Blessed City,'* Oxford, 1970.
Severus of Antioch,	*Lives of the Eastern Saints*, tr E. W. Brooks, PO 17.1 (1923); PO 18.4 (1924); PO 19.2 (1926).
Stratos, A. N.	*Byzantium in the Seventh Century*, tr M. Ogilvie-Grant, I, 602–34, Amsterdam, 1968; II, 634–641, Amsterdam, 1972.
Vööbus, A.	*Studies in the History of the Gospel Text in Syriac*, CSCO 128, Subsidia 3, Louvain, 1951.
	History of Asceticism in the Syrian Orient,
	I. *The Origin of Asceticism; Early Monasticism in Persia*, CSCO 184, Subsidia 14, Louvain, 1958.
	II. *Early Monasticism in Mesopotamia and Syria*, CSCO 197, Subsidia 17, Louvain, 1960.
	History of the School of Nisibis, CSCO 266, Subsidia 26, Louvain, 1965.
	Literary, Critical and Historical Studies in Ephrem the Syrian, PETSE 10, Stokholm, 1958.
	Syriac and Arabic Documents (regarding Legislation relative to Syrian Asceticism), PETSE 11, Stockholm 1960.
	The Statutes of the School of Nisibis, PETSE 12. Stockholm, 1961.
	Die syrische Kanonessammlungen I–II, CSCO 307, Subsidia 35; 317, Subsidia 38, Louvain, 1970
	The Synodicon in the West Syrian Tradition I–IV, CSCO 367–68, Scriptores Syri 161–62, Louvain 1975; CSCO 375–76, Scriptores Syri 163–64, Louvain 1976.
Wright, W.	*A Short History of Syriac Literature*, London, 1894, reprinted Amsterdam, 1966.
Zaehner, R. C.	*The Dawn and Twilight of Zoroastrianism*, London, 1961.

Index

A

Abercius Marcellus, 22
Abgar vii of Edessa, 4
Abgar viii of Edessa, 6
Abraham of Kashkar, 170
Acacius, bishop of Amid, 63–64
Addai, 98
Adiabene, 4, 8
Ahudemmeh (Monophysite bishop), 153
Antony, 4
Aphraates (Aphrahat), 114–16
Ardashir I, 38
Arius, Arianism, 47, 57
Artabanus V, 38
Asceticism and Monasticism, the early history of, 68–78
Asceticism and Monasticism, in Parthia and Persia, 166–68
Assyria, Roman province of, 4

B

Barbarian invasions of the Roman world, 41
Bardaisan, 22, 28–31
Barsauma of Nisibis, 131
Batnae (in Serug), 8
Beth'Abe, monastery of, 172–74
Bithynia, Christians of, 18
Boran, Queen, 46

C

canon law of the Western Syrian Church, 89
canons of the Oriental Church, 122–23
Carrhae, 4
Christianity, early, in Syria, 15
Christians and the Roman Government, 18
Chronicle of Edessa, 33
Commagene, 3
Constantine the Great, 40
Crassus, 4

D

Dadjesus, rules of for monks, 171–72
Dara, 42
Decius, 38
Denkart, 95
Diatessaron of Tatian, 31–32, 86
Diocletian, 37
Doctrine of Addai, 25
Dura Europus, 11, 54

E

Easter, controversy over, 23
Edessa (Urfa), 4, 23, 34, 42
Edessa, religion at, 14
Edessa, School of, 61–62, 67–68
Ephraim of Nisibis and Edessa, 57–61

G

Gathas, 94
Ghassanid Arabs, 42–43

H

Helena, Queen of Abiabene, 8
Heraclius, 44–45, 51
Ḥira, al- (Ḥirta), 163

I

Ibas (Hiba), bishop of Edessa, 65
Ignatius, bishop of Antioch, 16–17
Imperial cult (of the Romans) in Syria, 10
Isaac of Antioch, 66
Isidore of Charax, 7, 95

J

Jacob Baradaeus, 83
Jacob of Serug, 79
Jesusyahb II, Catholicos, 628–43, 162–64
Jesusyahb III, letters of, 160–62
John, bishop of Ephesus, 50
John, bishop of Tella, 82–83
Joshua the Stylite, Chronicle of, 68

Judaism, 15, 105–8
Julius Africanus, 32
Jewish uprisings against Rome, 115–17, 5
Jews in Parthia, 95–97

K

Kavad I, 42
Khusro II, 44, 157

L

Lakhmid Arabs, 43–44
languages of Syria, 9
liturgies, Syriac, 182–87
Lucian of Samosata, 17

M

Mabbog, gods of, 12
Magi, 94–95
Mani, Manichaeism, 102–5
Ma'nu of Edessa, 5
Marcion, Marcionism, 26–28
Mari, 98
Marutha of Maiperqaṭ, 63, 168–70
Maurice, 44
Mazdak, Mazdakism, 108–9
Mishnah, 97
Missionary efforts of the Syriac Christians, 179–81
Monasteries, growth of, 73
Monasticism and Literary Culture, 75
monasticism, Monophysite, 174
Monophysitism, beginnings of, 48–50
Monophysitism in the Persian Church, 130–31, 151–54, 174–75
Monophysitism, reaction to, in Syria, 78
Muslim Arabs, early expansion of, 46

N

Native cults in Syria, 11
Nestorius, Nestorianism, 47, 127
Nicene Creed, 122
Nicene Creed adopted by the Persian Church, 122
Nisibis, 6, 58
Nisibis, School of, 128–30, 155–57

O

Odes of Solomon, 33
Oroses, 4

P

Palmyra, 12, 37
Parthia and Rome, 3
persecution of Christians in Persia, 126
persecution of Christians in the Roman world, 55
Peshitta, 85
Philoxenus, bishop of Mabbog, 80–81
plague in Mesopotamia, 5
Pliny, 21

R

Rabbula, bishop of Edessa, 64
Rabbula, monastic rules of, 73–74

S

Samosata, 3
Science, western, reaches the Arabs, 181
Scriptures, the Syriac, 85
    Old Testament, 85
    New Testament, 86
Synod of Isaac, 410, 121
Synod of Yahbalaha, 420, 124
Synod of Dadjesus, 424, 125
Synod of Acacius, 486, 132
Synod of Babai, 497, 133
Synod of Aba I, 544, 136
Synod of Joseph, 554, 139
Synod of Ezekiel, 576, 142
Synod of Jesusyahb I, 585, 145
Synod of Sabarjesus I, 596, 148
Synod of Gregory I, 605, 150
Synodicon Orientale, 121
Syriac, the language of the eastern Churches, 9–10

T

Talmud, Babylonian, 107
Tatian, 31

trade, Roman, with the Orient, 7
Trajan, 4, 21–22

U

Urfa (Edessa), 13

V

Valerian, 39
Varahran I, 41
Varahran Chobin, 44
Vologeses III, 5

Y

Yazdagird I, 63
Yazdagird III, 46

Z

Zeno, 50
Zoroaster, Zoroastrianism, 94, 101–2